101 HIKES IN THE NORTH CASCADES

Text: Ira Spring and Harvey Manning
Photos: Bob and Ira Spring
Maps: Helen Sherman

THE MOUNTAINEERS • SEATTLE

THE MOUNTAINEERS

Organized 1906

To explore and study the mountains, forests, and watercourses of the Northwest;

To gather into permanent form the history and traditions of this region;

To preserve by the encouragement of protective legislation or otherwise the natural beauty of Northwest America;

To make explorations into these regions in fulfillment of the above purposes;

To encourage a spirit of good fellowship among all lovers of outdoor life.

First edition, July 1970

Second edition, January 1973

Third Printing, October 1974

Copyright© 1970, 1972

The Mountaineers, Seattle, Washington 98111
P.O. Box 122

Manufactured in the United States of America

Book design by Marge Mueller

Library of Congress Catalog Card No. 77-133504

Cover photo: Sloan Peak and Lost Creek Ridge trail—Hike 49

Title photo: Glacier Peak from ridge above Cub Lake—Hike 39

AGENDA FOR PROTECTING THE NORTH CASCADES OF WASHINGTON

The North Cascades Act of 1968 established the two-unit North Cascades National Park of 504,500 acres; the 105,000-acre Ross Lake National Recreation Area and the 62,000-acre Lake Chelan National Recreation Area, both administered by the National Park Service; the 520,000-acre Pasayten Wilderness Area, administered by the U.S. Forest Service; and a 10,000-acre addition to the 458,500-acre Glacier Peak Wilderness Area set aside by the Forest Service in 1960 and given statutory protection by the Wilderness Act of 1964.

With the magnificient achievement of 1968, climaxing a 60-year effort by citizen-preservationists, a total of 1,660,000 acres, or 2594 square miles, of the Washington Cascades between Stevens Pass and the Canadian boundary now have a dedicated status and certain guarantees.

Measured against the opportunity, though, the achievement leaves much to be desired. The 1968 legislation was a compromise, and in each instance of controversy the exploiters were given a mile and preservationists an inch. An area of the North Cascades of Washington at least as large as the dedicated lands is equally deserving of protection from multiple-abuse exploitation and doesn't have it. Moreover, the "protection" given some of the 1,660,000 acres is a delusion, as will be discussed below.

Hikers who follow the 101 routes described here, a selection representing all the varied geographical provinces from Puget Sound to the Okanogan, will find over and over again in the Mt. Baker, Snoqualmie, Wenatchee, and Okanogan National Forests they are traveling beautiful, endangered lands.

1968 was not the end of efforts to preserve the North Cascades, but a fresh beginning. The purpose of this book is to make more friends for the land, to gain the new recruits needed for the hard fights in progress and ahead.

Immediate Crises

At this writing the fiercest conservation battle in the history of the Cascades is underway. Seattle City Light proposes to increase the height of Ross Dam and raise the level of Ross Lake by 122½ feet. The project would drown 6 miles of the Big Beaver valley, destroying a wildlife wonderland of marshes and meanders containing among many other delights the largest stands of river-terrace western red cedars (some more than 1000 years old) left in the United States. It would drown 9 miles of the Skagit River in Canada, flooding 10 square miles of prime valley recreation lands, including the best natural trout fishery in the Northwest and the winter range of hundreds of game animals. It would drown all of Ruby Creek and the lower portions of still other streams. It would obliterate the spawning grounds which sustain the famous trout population of Ross Lake. And for what? To squeeze a few more kilowatts from the Skagit River—kilowatts that can be obtained by other means at less cost and without such tragic damage to the ecology and scenery. Seattle City Light is guided by principles that were considered idealistic and progressive in the 1930s but it is blind to environmental concerns of the 1970s; the bureaucrats must be roughly shaken out of the past into the future.

Miners Ridge is the scene of another confrontation which could well attain epic proportions. Kennecott Copper Corporation holds patented mining claims within the Glacier Peak Wilderness Area and declares, with 19th-century brutality, its intention to dig an open pit copper mine (literally visible from the Moon) between Image Lake and Suiattle Pass and to build a concentrator plant and town in Miners Creek and a road up the Suiattle River. The mine would produce an amount of metal insignificant when measured against the nation's annual consumption. At what cost? Hike to Image Lake and see. The nation-wide uproar that greeted announcement of its plans caused Kennecott to back off temporarily, but the firm doggedly affirms an intent to mine when it pleases. Preservationists must stand ready to fight Kennecott's wilderness-wrecking pit, plant, town, and road with every available administrative, legislative, and legal action.

Throughout the North Cascades and the nation there are de facto wildlands which do not have, but are being considered for, statutory protection.

However, the timber industry seeks an abrupt cut-off to debate by forcing the U.S. Forest Service to open to intensive logging—immediately— all lands outside the existing National Wilderness Preservation System.

These are three of the current major threats to the North Cascades. There are others, no end of others.

Continuing and Impending Crises

Wildlands lacking statutory protection are plagued by an infestation of roads—more roads every year, more roads planned. Road-boomers are promoting gasoline alleys from the North Cascades Highway up Canyon Creek to Harts Pass and across the ridge from Ruby Creek to the shores of Ross Lake. As Ira Spring discusses in following pages, the time has come in the Cascades to say—"no more roads!"

With ears gone dead from the racket of the chainsaw, many Forest Service officers (but not all) have gleefully welcomed trailbikes to once-peaceful valleys and lakes and ridges. Compounding the crime against quiet, certain National Forests are actually constructing trails specifically designed for motorcycles. Again as Ira Spring emphasizes, every trail, everywhere, must be firmly and finally barred to mechanized travel of every variety.

The frontier is a fading memory, but the frontier-style 1872 Mining Law (only a few of the most flagrant abuses eliminated by Congress in 1955) still permits prospectors to appropriate the public domain for private gain and willfully desecrate scenic resources, whether or not significant mineral resources exist. Moreover, the 1964 Wilderness Act contains a provision—insisted upon by mining state congressmen as the blackmail price of passage—that allows claims to be staked in dedicated Wilderness Areas until 1984 and development of such claims indefinitely thereafter. Further, mining claims within the North Cascades National Park, notably near Cascade Pass and Thunder Creek and Baker River, are time bombs ticking away in the very heart of the Park. The mining laws must be fundamentally revised to preserve our national heritage from Kennecott-style blasphemy.

Because of another loophole in the Wilderness Act, many hikes in dedicated wilderness areas are flawed by "hoofed locusts," as John Muir called sheep—as at White Pass and Buck Creek Pass— and by cattle—as in Horseshoe Basin. Cattle and sheep also graze high gardens, such as those of the Chelan Crest, that are outside but should be inside Wilderness Areas. The grazing fees received by federal and state agencies are ridiculously small. The damage to fragile highlands is intolerable.

Many free-flowing streams in the North Cascades are being eyed by dam-builders, a species of human that is affronted by the sight of wild water and can always find a reason to tame it, whether for electricity, irrigation, flood control, or navigation. Seattle City Light wants not only to raise Ross Dam but to drown Thunder Creek and Copper Creek. There is a plot afoot to reservoir-ize Lake Wenatchee and flood much of the Chiwawa River. The dam industry (like the highway industry) must be bluntly told and forever convinced it has outlived its usefulness in the North Cascades.

Once the only threats to the North Cascades were from traditional commodity exploitation. But now recreation has become a commodity. The tramway-and-restaurant industry is shuffling impatiently, waiting for the opportunity to "Alpinize" wildlands with cable-cars and chalets. Helicopter entrepreneurs would do to the skies and remote ridges what motorcycles are doing to the trails.

Plan for the Future

While stomping out brushfires and staying alert for others that may explode anywhere at any minute, preservationists must get off the defensive and resume the offensive, building on the foundation provided by the 1968 North Cascades Act. All around the boundaries of the National Park, the two National Recreation Areas, and the two Wilderness Areas are valleys and peaks of scenic, recreational, and ecologic value which need statutory protection of one kind or another. Without going into details of boundaries or the specific protection required (National Park, National Recreation Area, Wilderness Area, or other) the following provinces (and surely others to be identified as time passes) are the concern of Phase Two of the North Cascades campaign:

The Mount Baker region, including the entire volcano and all its drainage valleys, lands north of the Nooksack River at least as far west as Church Mountain, and the country between Baker River and the Skagit River.

The Cascade River at least as far downstream as Marble Creek and the ridges north and south of the valley.

All the west-side drainages of the Glacier Peak area, including the valleys of Illabot Creek, the Suiattle River with its tributary Sulphur, Downey, and Buck Creeks, the White Chuck River and North Fork Sauk River.

The surroundings of Mt. Whitehorse and Three Fingers Peak, including Squire Creek and Clear Creek and Boulder River.

The Monte Cristo region and the entirety of the Mountain Loop Highway.

All the lands adjoining the Stevens Pass Highway to the north. (Those to the south are the subject of a related and equally critical campaign for an Alpine Lakes Wilderness and National Recreation Area.)

The Cascade Crest and environs south from the Glacier Peak Wilderness Area to Stevens Pass.

All the east-side drainages of the Glacier Peak area, including the valleys of Lake Wenatchee, the Little Wenatchee River, White River, Chiwawa River, and Entiat River.

Lake Chelan, with its west shore and all westside tributaries up-lake from Twenty Five Mile Creek.

The Chelan Crest and all drainages which empty along the eastern shores of the lake, from Safety Harbor Creek northward, and also including headwaters of the valleys that drain from the crest to the Methow River and Twisp River.

The entire valley of Granite Creek, Rainy Pass, Washington Pass, and the upper Early Winters Creek country, including Silver Star and Gardner Mountain—the route of the North Cascades Highway.

All the Cascade Crest north from Rainy Pass to Harts Pass and Windy Pass, including the valleys of Slate Creek and Canyon Creek and the upper portions of the West Fork Methow River and Rattlesnake Creek and Trout Creek and adjacent highlands.

The upper drainages of Eightmile Creek, the Chewack River, Toats Coulee Creek, and all the region bordering the Pasayten Wilderness Area on the south.

East of the Pasayten Wilderness Area, at the very edge of the North Cascades, Chopaka Mountain and vicinity.

And across the international boundary in Canada, the upper valleys of Tomyhoi Creek and Silesia Creek, Chilliwack Lake, the Skagit River and environs north of Ross Lake, and the wildlands bordering the Pasayten Wilderness Area—some of which but not enough are within E. C. Manning and Cathedral and Sapper Parks.

What Can a Citizen Do?

The above agenda for the North Cascades of Washington is large—as large as the land. And so brief an outline cannot give any adequate notion of the innumerable individual issues and controversies—and dangers.

Many as are the threats to these North Cascades, and powerful and wealthy and single-minded as the exploiters are, a citizen effort gained passage of the 1968 North Cascades Act against what seemed impossible odds. With the knowledge that victories can be won, and with growing reinforcements of citizen-preservationists, Phase Two is now underway.

A concerned individual can join the campaign by writing letters to senators and congressmen and governors and legislators and newspapers, by informing friends of the issues and soliciting their support. He can also write letters to administrative officials—the Superintendent of the North Cascades National Park and the Supervisors of Mount Baker, Snoqualmie, Wenatchee, and Okanogan National Forests—offering comments, suggestions, criticisms, and protests about current or proposed management practices. To give his voice maximum impact, however, a citizen should also join a conservation organization, The Mountaineers or any of its allies, to be well-informed about impending dangers and to contribute personal time and knowledge—and money, of which exploiters always have plenty and preservationists never enough—to the effort which must go on and on until every human everywhere has learned to respect and honor our only home, this space-ship Earth, and to reverence as holy temples of nature, as places of worship, the rivers and forests and meadows and glaciers of the North Cascades.

The Mountaineers: An Invitation

The Mountaineers, with groups based in Seattle, Everett, Tacoma, and Olympia (and groups elsewhere in the planning stage), invite the membership of all lovers of outdoor life who sympathize with the purposes of the organization and wish to share in its activities.

Preservation of the natural beauty of Northwest America is one side of the coin; the other is using and enjoying the country.

The Mountaineers sponsor a year-around program of climbing, hiking, camping, ski-touring, snowshoeing, kayaking, and canoeing. Hundreds of outings are scheduled each year, ranging from single-day walks to trips lasting 2 weeks or more.

On a typical weekend as many as 30 or 40 excursions may be offered from ocean beaches to the summit of Mount Rainier. In addition, members engage in countless privately-organized trips of all kinds; perhaps a major value in belonging to The Mountaineers is the opportunity to meet people with similar interests, to make new friends.

For information on club activities and for a membership application, write or visit The Mountaineers clubroom and office, 719 Pike Street, Seattle, Wa. 98111.

HARVEY MANNING

December 1972

A PLEA FOR FREEDOM FROM MACHINES

The Forest Service has no uniform, positive policy for administration of roadless areas, no clear notion of their highest and best uses. Guidelines ultimately must come from Congress, but until such time, we forest travelers must help shape Forest Service plans.

The Forest Service contains many dedicated men, some even ardent preservationists. However, most of them are more oriented to growing and cutting trees, and fitting in any and all other exploitations of commodity and recreational resources, than they are to protecting unique environments. The Supervisor of a National Forest walks a delicate line, trying to balance user demands from all sides. He really should not be in this position, or have such wide latitude to make major land-use decisions on a "political" basis, but should operate under very tight reins held by Congress. Under present circumstances, though, we forest citizens must make the best of a bad situation by letting the Forest Supervisors hear our individual voices loud and often. If every person who uses this book writes at least one letter a year, the trails can be saved from the invasion of machines and returned to the hikers.

Roadless areas are an increasingly rare and precious resource. Unfortunately, they are also a constant challenge to exploiters brought up in traditions of the frontier. But what challenge is there in building roads to the tops of high peaks or bridging canyons with cable cars? Such feats aren't even unusual anymore. The challenge of today is to value and preserve roadless areas. But the Forest Service continues in the old ways. Trails are obliterated by logging roads, some of them unnecessary even for the purpose of taking out timber, and hundreds of miles of foot trails are turned into motorcycle "roads." All this without consulting those who use and appreciate roadless country.

Three important reasons for hiking can be given. One is obvious—to enjoy scenery that can't be viewed from a car. Another is the physical challenge of doing something on your own that demands hard work. A third is to get away from the civilized world, away from the noise and stink of modern contraptions, and to gain a feeling of self-sufficiency. By mounting a machine, a forest traveler loses two of these three reasons not only for himself but for everyone else on the trail.

Motorbikers, of course, have their own reasons. They may enjoy the scenery, the same as a hiker. They like the challenge of wrestling a mechanical beast through tough terrain. Finally, they just have a lot of fun riding.

However, two of these three reasons for riding machines can be satisfied in non-hiking areas, such as abandoned gravel pits. As for the third goal of bikeriders, the scenery, they can get this the way the rest of us do, by **hiking** to beauty spots. The machine riders who claim they aren't able to hike because of some physical disability **are** not telling the truth. Except on a few raceways, more strength is required to get a bike up a trail than to walk.

Motorbikes are so cheap just about anybody can afford one. Sales figures show the craze is spreading like wildfire. In the Twisp River area, on the first 4 miles of the Entiat River trail, and elsewhere in the Cascades there are already so many machines as to make hiking miserable. The worst is yet to come. The motorbike industry, with a million dollars to spend on advertising, is using TV, newspapers, magazines, and billboards to promote machines as the family way to the wilderness.

Except for Forest Service maintenance work there is utterly no reason any machine should be allowed on any established hiking trails, which includes all the trails in this guide book. But while hikers were busy battling for the North Cascades National Park, motorbikers were multiplying and uniting in powerful clubs that are now demanding—and getting—better trails for their vehicles. Something got way out of proportion because the Forest Service, without any public hearings, arbitrarily allowed motor use of miles and miles of trails. Now that the use is established, public notices and hearings are required to **close** a trail to machines. Is this fair? Why not reverse? Why didn't hikers get this consideration, so that no trail would be **opened** to machines without public notice and hearings?

It is now necessary for hikers to reclaim their trails one at a time. To do this, every hiker must write often—at least once a year—complaining to Supervisors of National Forests. In the North Cascades, the Supervisor of Wenatchee National Forest is going to be the hardest to convince, because unlike other Supervisors who detest machines on trails, the man currently in charge of Wenatchee likes machines and is providing them with a system of raceways.

Hikers stay away from trails they've found converted into motorcycle "roads." Rangers decide what to do with a trail on the basis of the kind of use it gets; they interpret a hikers' boycott of a trail as evidence it should be devoted entirely to machines.

Don't let machines drive you off your favorite trails. Keep hiking them. When you meet machines, make them obey the Forest Service trail courtesy rule, which is that **pedestrians have the right of way.** Stay in the trail and make the riders give you safe passage, but don't play "chicken" with a racing machine; you could get hurt. But if the rider doesn't obey the rules, be sure the Forest Supervisor hears about it in writing.

Wenatchee National Forest as a whole, and some ranger districts of Okanogan National Forest, have been the worst offenders in handing over trails to motorcycles. Mt. Baker Forest, by contrast, has closed nearly all trails to machines, and instead marks for their use the hundreds of miles of low-standard logging roads.

Snoqualmie and Gifford Pinchot National Forests are the prime examples of another Forest Service fault—relentless road-building with very little thought to maintenance of roadless areas.

Certainly we need lumber as much as we need dedicated wilderness museums of virgin forest. And certainly there are spots that are well-suited to tree-farming and have lesser recreational values. But there are also large portions of National Forests where proper planning could make hiking and logging perfectly compatible. However, no such genuine "multiple-use" is possible within Forest Service networks of high-standard, permanent logging roads. If the Forest Service was oriented to real multiple use, they would build a certain number of heavy-use trunk roads and do the actual logging from low-standard spurs that are "put to bed" when the harvest is complete. The trunk roads could be located away from the prime hiking routes; the trails would thus be out of use only during the several years of logging, a small part of the 50-80-year tree-growing cycle.

But Snoqualmie National Forest, with total blindness to the environment, built a permanent road next to the north boundary of Mount Rainier National Park, turning 3-day hikes into afternoon walks, and in one swoop ruined the only true wilderness within the Park. The trunk road could have been kept several miles from the Park and the boundary logging done on cat roads. This way the wilderness would have remained remote and truly wild. Another example of Snoqualmie Forest insensitivity is the East Fork Miller River road, a completely unnecessary desecration of a roadless area.

Gifford Pinchot National Forest is so thoroughly crisscrossed with roads that except for relatively small dedicated areas, all that remains of the vast and glorious trail country that existed 20 years ago are a few 1-2-mile hikes. This is an efficient method of "tree farming" but a poor way to sustain the recreation resource. A far cry from genuine multiple use. Since the first printing of this book in 1970, we have lost two of the original hikes to logging roads, Evergreen Mountain near Skykomish and Lookout Mountain near Twisp.

No National Forest ever should be given up as a lost cause. Pinchot seems a desperate case where roading is concerned and Snoqualmie not much better. At present Okanogan and Wenatchee seem to be managed less for hikers and more for trailbikers and every other variety of off-road machinery.

However, letters to supervisors of Mt. Baker, Snoqualmie, Gifford Pinchot, Wenatchee, and Okanogan National Forests are read (and answered), and enough letters (and the need to write answers to specific complaints) can make the Supervisors change their minds about building high-standard roads up valleys which could be logged on temporary roads, and about leaving trails open to mechanized travel and improving them to make such travel easier.

The rule is: each hiker must write at least one letter a year to a Forest Supervisor pleading for the preservation of roadless areas.

However, the only long-range security, the only final freedom from machines, lies in the continuing fight for more and larger wilderness areas dedicated by Congress and thus removed from the personal whims of transient Forest Supervisors. There are Supervisors (and other Forest Service personnel) who have an unsurpassed knowledge and appreciation of the land, and carefully and respectfully look after every quality of their beloved home terrain. These men we admire and trust as custodians of our natural heritage. But the next Supervisor may be in office only a few years and raise havoc with hundreds of square miles of the American Earth.

If you, the readers of this book, agree with me, please start writing those letters. Only together, by a concerted effort, can we save our trail country from the machines.

December 1972   IRA SPRING

INTRODUCTION

In decades past, when the North Cascades of Washington were little-known beyond the immediate vicinity, visitors often capsulized impressions of the sharp peaks and bright glaciers by describing the range as "America's Alps." However, the North Cascades have no need of fame borrowed from other mountains, not with their own richness and variety of scenic glories. Indeed, local partisans object to the comparison, which focuses on rock and ice and ignores the very un-Alpine characteristic of the North Cascades, which is that the rough and icy peaks are set amid a wilderness of flowery meadows and virgin forests and wild rivers.

The area covered by his book extends 100 miles from slopes of Mount Baker on the west to the scarp of Chopaka Mountain on the east, and some 90 miles from the Stevens Pass Highway to the Canadian border. The limits south and north are artificial, set merely to split the region between several books. A companion volume, **102 Hikes in the Alpine Lakes, South Cascades, and Olympics**, reaches southward from the Stevens Pass Highway. Another, **100 Hikes in Southwestern British Columbia**, treats that portion of the North Cascades which spills over into Canada—there to merge with other ranges continuing without a break north to the Yukon and Alaska.

This is a large mountain province, too complex to summarize in a few simple sentences. The hike descriptions and photographs and maps describe the land in some detail, at least along the 101 suggested hiking routes (and the hundreds of variations). But general prefatory comments can be made.

The west edge of the North Cascades is battered and drenched by ocean storms; precipitation is heavy, winter is long, snows pile deep, glaciers are large, peaks are sharply sculptured, vegetation is lush. The east edge of the range is sheltered from the ocean; the climate is drier, summer is longer, vegetation sparser, ridges rounder and gentler.

On the far west, high-country hiking doesn't get well underway until mid-July or later and the weather can be terrible any day of summer. On the far east, the meadows melt free from snow as early as late May and the major weather problem is the possibility of too much hot sun.

On west and east, there are short and easy hikes that can be done by little kids and elderly folks with no training or equipment for mountain travel. And also there are long hikes, difficult hikes, and long-and-difficult hikes, which should be attempted only by experienced wilderness roamers.

Some trails are broad, well-graded, and clearly marked. Others are sketchy, ill-defined tracks built and maintained solely by hooves and boots.

There are hikes that can be done by any person capable of putting one foot in front of another for a morning or afternoon. And there are adventures that can take a party back through time to the frontier, into wildlands where the walker is utterly on his own, with no help from anyone if things go wrong.

Administration

Except for a large block of state land around Chopaka Mountain, scattered enclaves of private lands mostly dating from mining and homestead days, and miscellaneous bits and pieces such as the Seattle City Light holdings on the Skagit River, the entirety of the North Cascades is federally owned, the property of all the people of America. The U.S. Forest Service is the principal trustee of the land, the responsibility shared by Snoqualmie, Mt. Baker, Wenatchee, and Okanogan National Forests. Since 1968 the National Park Service is in the middle of the scene, with the North Cascades National Park and the Ross Lake and Lake Chelan National Recreation Areas.

Because regulations on use vary, hikers should be aware of which administrative units they are traveling—not always easy to know, what with the illogical lines of many boundaries.

Under U.S. Forest Service jurisdiction are the Glacier Peak and Pasayten Wilderness Areas, where "the earth and its community of life are untrammeled by man, where man himself is a visitor who does not remain." Motorized travel is forbidden absolutely and horse travel is beginning to be regulated or even eliminated at some points; some restrictions now are placed on foot travel and camping and the back-country population explosion ultimately will require more controls to protect the fragile terrain. Starting in 1972, travelers are required to obtain wilderness permits, available at any Forest Service office or ranger station, before entering a dedicated Wilderness Area. By this means the Forest Service can keep track of wilderness usage and accordingly determine future administrative needs.

Other portions of the National Forests are designated now, or may be in future, as recreation areas, scenic areas, or roadless areas, each of which has certain limitations on commodity exploitation and some sorts of recreation. Multiple-use areas are devoted mainly to logging, though with some consideration of other uses; here things often change violently from one year to the next and the hiker may find roads and trails radically different from descriptions in this book.

The North Cascades National Park has been set aside, to use the words of the National Park Act of 1916, "to conserve the scenery and the natural and historic objects and the wildlife. . . ." Each visitor must therefore enjoy the Park "in such manner and by such means as will leave it unimpaired for the enjoyment of future generations." A good motto for Park users is: "Take only a picture, leave only a footprint."

Most of the Park soon will be dedicated as wilderness, so that not only the National Park Act of 1916 but the Wilderness Act of 1964 will apply, giving the highest degree of protection of any lands in the North Cascades. Motorized travel on Park trails is forbidden and horse travel closely regulated. Hunting is banned—but not fishing. Pets are not allowed on trails, since their presence disturbs the wildlife.

The Ross Lake and Lake Chelan National Recreation Areas may be described as "National Parks with hunting allowed." Portions of these areas will be placed in wilderness, though mostly they will be administered to allow a certain degree of development, including the possibility of one or more tramways to high overlooks—though this proposal remains controversial, as does the current permission to use motorcycles on several trails.

Camping permits are required for all overnight hikers on National Park Service lands. These may be obtained at Park headquarters in Sedro Woolley and ranger stations at Marblemount, Chelan and Stehekin. The Park Service requests hikers who may not be passing an office when open to write for a permit in advance whenever possible, address: North Cascades National Park, Sedro Woolley.

Maps

Each hike description in this book lists the appropriate topographic maps (if such are available for the area in question) published by the U.S. Geological Survey. These can be purchased at map stores or mountaineering equipment shops or by writing the U.S. Geological Survey, Federal Center, Denver, Colorado 80225. The USGS maps are the hiker's best friend.

The National Forests and the National Parks publish recreation maps which are quite accurate and up-to-date. Forest Service maps may be obtained free of charge at ranger stations or by writing the Forest Supervisors at:

Mt. Baker National Forest
Federal Office Building
Bellingham, Washington 98225

Snoqualmie National Forest
919 2nd Avenue
Seattle, Washington 98104

Wenatchee National Forest
P.O. Box 811
Wenatchee, Washington 98801

Okanogan National Forest
P.O. Box 432
Okanogan, Washington 98840.

National Park maps, also free, may be obtained from the headquarters and ranger stations noted above.

Clothing and Equipment

Many trails described in this book can be walked easily and safely, at least along the lower portions, by any person capable of getting out of a car and onto his feet, and without any special equipment whatsoever.

To such people we can only say, "welcome to walking—but beware!" North Cascades weather, especially on the ocean side of the range, is notoriously undependable. Cloudless morning skies can be followed by afternoon torrents of rain or fierce squalls of snow. Even without a storm a person can get mighty chilly on high ridges when—as often happens—a cold wind rises under a bright sun and pure blue sky.

No one should set out on a North Cascades trail, unless for a brief stroll, lacking warm long pants, wool shirt or sweater, and a windproof and rain-resistant parka, coat, or poncho. And on the feet—sturdy shoes or boots with rugged lug soles and a 5-9-inch top to keep out mud and dirt plus two pair of wool socks and an extra pair in the rucksack.

As for that rucksack, it should also contain the Ten Essentials, found to be so by generations of members of The Mountaineers, often from sad experience:

1. Extra clothing—more than needed in good weather.
2. Extra food—enough so something is left over at the end of the trip.
3. Sunglasses—necessary for most alpine travel and indispensable on snow.
4. Knife—for first aid and emergency fire-building (making kindling).
5. Firestarter—a candle or chemical fuel for starting a fire with wet wood.
6. First-aid kit.
7. Matches—in a waterproof container.
8. Flashlight—with extra bulb and batteries.
9. Map—be sure it's the right one for the trip.
10. Compass—be sure to know the declination, east or west.

Camping and Fires

Indiscriminate camping blights alpine meadows. A single small party may trample grass, flowers, and heather so badly they don't recover from the shock for several years. If the same spot is used several or more times a summer, year after year, the greenery vanishes, replaced by the dusty, muddy barrens of "slum camps." The respectful traveler always aims to camp in the woods, or in rocky morainal areas. These alternatives lacking, it is better to use a meadow site already ruined rather than extend the destruction into a pleasanter place nearby. As time goes on and people pressure grows, more and more meadows necessarily will be posted against camping.

To protect water quality and particularly delicate plant communities, no camp should be placed within 200 feet of a lakeshore or riverbank; in many jurisdictions camping in this zone is now expressly forbidden.

Shelter cabins are on a first-come-first-served basis, so always carry a tent or tarp. Most shelters are crummy and foul from years of abuse and are best avoided. The bough bed, beloved of the frontier past, is so damaging to vegetation it is obsolete in areas worthy of preservation in a natural condition, including all the country covered by this book. Instead, carry an air mattress or a foam-plastic pad.

The wood fire, another age-old tradition, also should be considered obsolete in the high country. At best, dry firewood is hard to find at popular camps; the easy wood was burnt years ago. What remains now is from picturesque silver snags and down logs, and in using such material one erodes the very beauty that makes the hike worth taking.

Both for reasons of convenience and conservation, The Mountaineers strongly urge alpine hikers to carry a lightweight stove for cooking and to depend on clothing and shelter (and sunset strolls) for evening warmth. The pleasures of a roaring blaze on a cold mountain night are indisputable, but for the sake of these pleasures a single party on a single night may use up ingredients of the scenery that were long decades in growing, dying, and silvering.

At remote back-country camps, and in forests, fires may still be built (for a while, anyway) with a clear conscience. Again, one should minimize impact by using only established fire pits and using only dead and down wood. When finished,

be certain the fire is absolutely out—drown the coals and stir them with a stick and then drown the ashes until the smoking and steaming have stopped completely. Embers can smoulder underground in dry duff for days, spreading gradually and burning out a wide pit—or kindling trees and starting a forest fire.

Litter, Garbage, and Sanitation

Ours is a throwaway civilization, but it is bad wildland manners to leave litter for someone else to worry about. The rule among considerate hikers is: **If you can carry it in full, you can carry it out empty.**

On a day hike, take back to the road (and garbage can) every last orange peel and gum wrapper.

On an overnight or longer hike, burn all paper (if a fire is built) but carry back all unburnables, including metal, plastic, glass, and paper that won't burn.

Don't bury garbage. If fresh, animals will dig it up and scatter the remnants. Burning before burying is no answer either. Tin cans take as long as 40 years to disintegrate completely; aluminum and glass last for centuries. Further, digging pits to bury junk disturbs the ground cover, and iron often leaches from buried cans and "rusts" springs and creeks.

Don't leave left-over food for the next travelers; they will have their own food and won't be tempted by contributions spoiled by time or chewed by animals.

Especially don't cache plastic tarps. Weathering quickly ruins the fabric, little creatures nibble, and the result is a useless, miserable mess.

Keep the water pure. Do not wash dishes or bodies in creeks or lakes—haul water away from the shore to do the job. Do not swim in small lakes used for drinking water.

Finally, avoid "random elimination." Where privies are lacking, take care of toilet needs far from watercourses and cover the evidence. It's disgusting how many hikers don't have the manners of a cat.

Protect This Land, Your Land

The North Cascades country is large and rugged and wild—but it is also, and particularly in the scenic climaxes favored by hikers, a fragile country. If man is to blend into the ecosystem, rather than dominate and destroy, he must walk lightly, respectfully.

The public servants entrusted with administration of the region have a complex and difficult job and they desperately need the cooperation of every wildland traveler. Here, the authors would like to express appreciation to these dedicated men for their advice on what trips to include in this book and for their detailed review of the text and maps. Thanks are due the Superintendent of the North Cascades National Park, the Supervisors of the Mt. Baker, Snoqualmie, Wenatchee, and Okanogan National Forests, and their district rangers and other staff members.

On behalf of the U.S. Forest Service and National Park Service and The Mountaineers, we invite Americans—and Canadians, and all other citizens of Earth—to come and see and live in their Washington North Cascades, and while enjoying one of the world's finest wildlands, to share in the task of preserving the trails and ridges, lakes and rivers, forests and flower gardens for future generations, our children and grandchildren, who will need the wilderness experience at least as much as we do, and probably more.

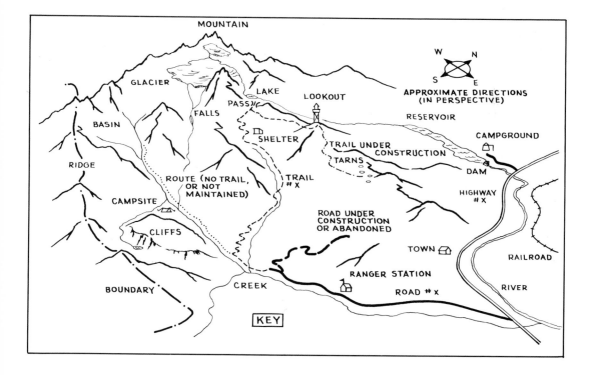

TABLE OF CONTENTS

	Page
NOOKSACK RIVER	
1 Bastile Ridge	16
2 Heliotrope Ridge	18
3 Skyline Divide	20
4 Excelsior Mountain	22
5 Gold Run Pass	24
6 Winchester Mountain	26
7 Table Mountain Loop	28
8 Ptarmigan Ridge	30
9 Lake Ann	32
10 Price Lake	34
11 Nooksack Cirque	36
12 Hannegan Pass and Peak	38
13 Copper Mountain	40
14 Easy Ridge	42
15 Whatcom Pass	44
BAKER RIVER	
16 Morovitz Meadow	46
17 Boulder Ridge	48
18 Baker River	50
SKAGIT RIVER-ROSS LAKE	
19 Finney Peak	52
20 Thornton Lakes-Trappers Peak	54
21 Sourdough Mountain	56
22 Thunder Creek	58
23 East Bank Trail	60
24 Crater-Devils Loop	62
25 Desolation Peak	64
26 Beaver Loop	66
27 Easy Pass	68
CASCADE RIVER	
28 Lookout Mountain-Monogram Lake	70
29 Hidden Lake Peaks	72
30 Kindy Ridge-Found Lake	74
31 Middle Fork Cascade River	76
32 South Fork Cascade River	78
33 Boston Basin	80
34 Cascade Pass-Sahale Arm	82
35 Trapper Lake	84
NORTH FORK STILLAGUAMISH RIVER	
36 Round Mountain	86
37 Squire Creek Pass	88
SUIATTLE RIVER	
38 Green Mountain	90
39 Bachelor Meadows	92

	Page
40 Sulphur Mountain	94
41 Milk Creek-Dolly Creek-Vista Creek Loop	96
42 Image Lake	98
43 Suiattle River to Lake Chelan	100
44 Around Glacier Peak	102
WHITE CHUCK RIVER	
45 Meadow Mountain	106
46 Kennedy Ridge and Hot Springs	108
47 White Chuck Glacier	110
48 Mount Pugh	112
NORTH FORK SAUK RIVER	
49 Lost Creek Ridge-Lake Byrne	114
50 White Pass-Red Pass	116
51 Pilot Ridge-Blue Lakes	118
52 Bald Eagle Trail	120
SOUTH FORK STILLAGUAMISH RIVER	
53 Goat Flats	122
54 Mount Pilchuck	124
55 Mount Forgotten	126
56 Mount Dickerman	128
SOUTH FORK SAUK RIVER	
57 Goat Lake	130
58 Bedal Basin	132
59 Gothic Basin	134
60 Poodle Dog Pass	136
61 Glacier Basin	138
SKYKOMISH RIVER	
62 Lake Blanca	140
63 Eagle Lake	142
64 Scorpion Mountain	144
NASON CREEK	
65 Lake Valhalla	146
66 Lake Janus and Grizzly Peak	148
67 Nason Ridge	150
LAKE WENATCHEE	
68 Dirtyface Peak	152
LITTLE WENATCHEE RIVER	
69 Minotaur Lake	154
70 Meander Meadow-Kodiak Peak	156
71 Cady Pass to White Pass	158

	Page
WHITE RIVER	
72 Mount David	160
73 Napeequa Valley via Bounder Pass	162
CHIWAWA RIVER	
74 Napeequa Valley via Little Giant Pass	164
75 Spider Meadow and Pass	166
76 Buck Creek Pass	168
ENTIAT RIVER	
77 Entiat Meadows	170
78 Larch Lakes Loop	172
79 Milham Pass-Emerald Park	174
80 Ice Lakes	176
LAKE CHELAN-STEHEKIN RIVER	
81 Chelan Lakeshore Trail	178
82 Chelan Crest Trail	180
83 McGregor Mountain	182
84 Agnes Creek	184
85 North Fork Bridge Creek	186
86 Park Creek Pass	188
87 Horseshoe Basin (Stehekin)	190
88 Lake Chelan to Cascade River	192
TWISP RIVER	
89 Twisp Pass-Stiletto Outlook	194
EARLY WINTERS CREEK	
90 Cutthroat Pass	196
METHOW RIVER	
91 Goat Peak	198
92 Grasshopper Pass	200
93 Windy Pass	202
94 Canyon Creek	204
95 Three Fools Trail	206
CHEWACK RVER	
96 Billy Goat Pass-Burch Mountain	208
97 Tiffany Mountain	210
SINLAHEKIN CREEK	
98 Horseshoe Basin (Pasayten)	212
99 Boundary Trail	214
100 Chopaka Mountain	216
101 CASCADE CREST TRAIL	218
Time of Year Trails are Passable	222
Still More Hikes	224
Index	228

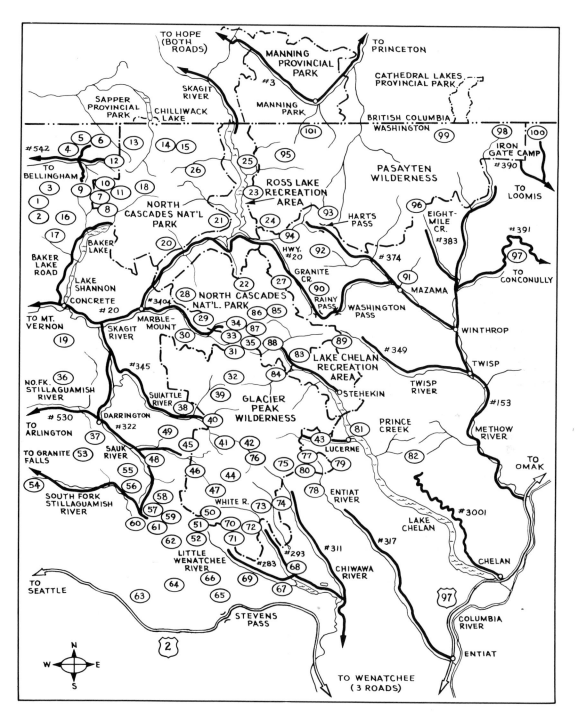

1 BASTILE RIDGE

This is **not** a beginners' hike. In fact, until suitable bridges are built across the raging torrents of Heliotrope and Glacier Creeks, the trail is impassable even to expert hikers. Too bad, for the ridge offers the most spectacular vista in the area.

Pound for pound, Mt. Baker is the iciest of all the Cascade volcanos. When the bridges are in place, hikers will be able to see for themselves by visiting the snout of the Coleman Glacier and then climbing meadows overlooking an empire of rough whiteness.

The Forest Service has proposed an "Around Mt. Baker Trail" which will bridge the two creeks. However, at the present rate of funding, the agency will be lucky to have the money by the late 1970s.

Present advice to those determined to explore Bastile Ridge is to wait until a low-water period and then wade the creeks. Both are fed by melting glaciers so the drier and warmer the summer the more tumultuous the floods; low water, if any, comes after the heat of summer is gone and before the fall rains. Before starting, call the Glacier Ranger Station and ask about the creeks. Also get explicit directions for finding the old trail.

There are two other alternatives. Make a 3-day cross-country hike from Skyline Divide (see Hike 3) across Chowder Ridge to Bastile Ridge. Or write your Congressman asking for more trail money. Don't blame the district ranger. It isn't his fault.

High point 5500 feet
Best late July through October
  (October only if creeks must be forded)
USGS Mt. Baker

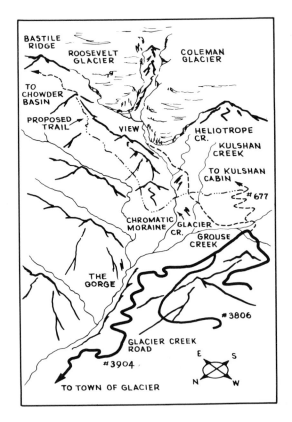

Roosevelt and Coleman Glaciers flowing from Mt. Baker. Black Buttes in distance

2 HELIOTROPE RIDGE

A splendid forest walk leading to a ramble-and-scramble on flowery moraines below (and above) the ice-chaos of the rampaging Coleman Glacier. See the mountain climbers—by the hundreds on many summer weekends, because this is the most popular route to the summit of Mt. Baker. They're a harmless and unobtrusive lot, boisterous in camp but sacking out early, rising somber-and-quiet in the middle of the night and spending all day on the glaciers, out of sight and sound. Along the trail, hikers can enjoy the colorful displays of tents and axes and ropes and helmets and ironware.

Drive State Highway 542 to the town of Glacier and about 1 mile beyond to Glacier Creek road. Turn right some 8 miles to a parking lot at a sign, "Mt. Baker Trail," elevation 3700 feet. Hike 2 miles, traversing and switchbacking through tree shadows, over cold little creeks, to Kulshan Cabin, built by the Mt. Baker Club and now maintained by the Western Washington Outdoor Club. (Respect the historic and deteriorating old cabin and the efforts of those who keep it going; don't use it unless necessary, and then only with care.) Note at the switchbacks how

shortcutting is ruining the new trail; the Forest Service would appreciate suggestions from hikers on how to save the trail.

The cabin is at 4700 feet, near but still below timberline, and camping inside and out is of the sort only a climber (his thoughts on high) can enjoy, so hike along and past. No reason to loiter.

The fun country is above. From the cabin the trail (such as it is, built by boots), climbs quickly out of trees and over a creek to a moraine crest, then continues upward in open land with wide views. Soon the trail ends—or rather, branches into innumerable tracks in all directions. Walk where you will on any of several bouldery moraines and into any of several intervening vales of flowers and brawling streams, rock slabs and waterfalls. Campsites everywhere.

The main-line climbers' route ascends an above-timberline moraine to Heliotrope Ridge, about 1 mile and 1300 feet above Kulshan Cabin. At 6000 feet the moraine touches ice-polished buttresses with a panorama of glaciers, Black Buttes, Baker, and the Nooksack valley. Hikers please note: be wary of the snow, which here merges indistinguishably into a crevassed glacier, strictly climbers' terrain.

For one among numerous other possible wanders: above timberline, drift left (east) on meager man-and-animal tracks over a moraine and a rocky draw whistling with marmots to an alpine-forested ridge (another moraine). Burst suddenly through old, old trees to the surprising brink of a gravel precipice falling down and down to the blue-white jumble of the Coleman Glacier. Good camps here. Then climb the ancient moraine—stopping well short of the living glacier above.

Because of the enormous snowfall on Mt. Baker, and because this is the north side of the mountain, hikers who come earlier than August are liable to be surrounded by snow—and potential danger—above Kulshan Cabin. The crevasses, of course, are always there, visible or invisible.

Round trip to Heliotrope Ridge 6 miles
Hiking time 5 hours
High point 6000 feet
Elevation gain 2300 feet
Best August to October
One day or backpack
USGS Mt. Baker

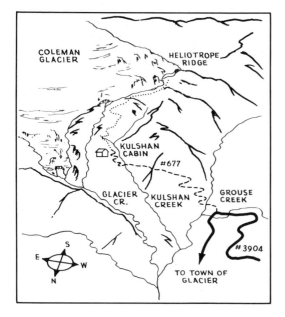

Coleman Glacier near Kulshan Cabin

Mt. Baker from Skyline Ridge trail. Black Buttes on right skyline

3   SKYLINE DIVIDE

A large green meadow. An enormous white volcano. Views of forests and glaciers, rivers and mountains. Miles of ridges and basins to explore.

Drive State Highway 542 1 mile beyond the town of Glacier. Turn right on the Glacier Creek road and within 100 yards turn sharply left onto Dead Horse road No. 3907. Follow the south side of the Nooksack River a pleasant 4 miles. The road then climbs abruptly. At 7½ miles pause to view a lovely waterfall splashing down a rock cleft. At 12 miles is a parking lot and trailhead, elevation 4000 feet.

The trail, moderate to steep, climbs 2 miles in subalpine trees to an immense meadow, the beginning of wide views. South are the vast glaciers of the north wall of Mt. Baker. North, beyond forests of the Nooksack valley, are the greenery of Church Mountain and the rock towers of the spectacular Border Peaks. Eastward is Mt. Shuksan, and for a gentle contrast, little Table Mountain, above Heather Meadows.

The meadow is superb but the supreme viewpoint is the 6200-foot knoll to the south. (From the meadow, it partly blocks out Baker.) Follow the trail ¾ mile along the ridge and around the knoll to the far side. Once the ridge crest is regained, walk back up the easy slope of the knoll to the summit. Sprawl in flowers and enjoy. (Note to photographers: generally the best pic-tures of Baker from here are taken before 10 a.m. or after 4 p.m.)

The trail continues along the meadow ridge another mile and then peters out. No matter; in these open highlands the roaming is easy, so walk where you will. There is enough country here to keep a party happy for several days of exploration. The trail, the big meadow, and Skyline Divide are waterless except in early summer. However, well-watered basecamps for wandering can be found in the flower gardens of Smith and Chowder Basins. Experienced alpine hikers can travel cross-country from here to Bastile Ridge (Hike 1).

Round trip to knoll 6 miles
Hiking time 4 hours
High point 6215 feet
Elevation gain 2200 feet
Best August to October
One day or backpack
USGS Mt. Baker

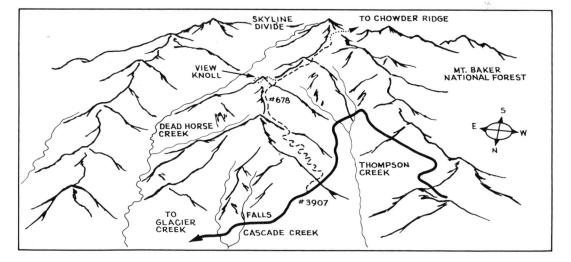

Mt. Baker from Excelsior Mountain

4 EXCELSIOR MOUNTAIN

Views from this meadow summit include Nooksack valley forests and Puget Sound lowlands, Mt. Baker and the Border Peaks, the southernmost portion of the British Columbia Coast Range, and more. Flowers in July, berries and colors in September. Three trails lead to the site of a recently-removed lookout cabin; the easiest is recommended here, but take your pick.

Drive State Highway 542 to the town of Glacier and 2 miles beyond to Canyon Creek road No. 400. Turn left 15 miles to the parking lot in a logged-off area at the start of trail No. 625; elevation, about 4000 feet.

Climb gently through forest ½ mile to the junction with Canyon Ridge trail No. 689 and a bit more to 4500-foot Damfino Lakes, two small ponds surrounded by acres of super-delicious blueberries (in season). Campsites and running water near the smaller lake.

Climb another timbered mile, then go up a narrow draw and shortly enter meadows rising in ½ mile to 5300-foot Excelsior Pass, some 2½ miles from the road. (Pleasant camps at the pass when there is snowfield water—perhaps until early August.) Leave the main trail at the pass and climb a way trail ¼ mile east to the 5699-foot peak.

Sit and look. See the glaciers of Mt. Baker across forests of the Nooksack. See more ice on Mt. Shuksan and other peaks east. See the steep-walled Border Peaks and snowy ranges extending far north into Canada. And see green meadows everywhere.

The summit is a magnificent place to stop overnight in good weather, watching a sunset and a dawn; no water, though, except possible snowmelt.

Two alternate trails can be used to vary the descent. (They can also be used to ascend the peak, but for reasons that will be obvious are not the best choices.)

Alternate No. 1. From Excelsior Pass, descend trail No. 670 4 miles and 3500 feet to the highway, reached 8 miles east of Glacier at a small parking area (with trail sign on opposite side of road) between the Nooksack Falls road and the highway overlook. The trail switchbacks steeply on south-facing slopes that melt free of snow relatively early in the season; an excellent hike from the highway in May or June, turning back when snowfields halt progress. In summer this route to high country is long and hot and dry.

Alternate No. 2. From the lookout, traverse the new High Divide trail No. 630 east 5 miles to Welcome Pass. At 4960-foot Welcome Pass, find a steep trail dropping south 2 miles to an unmaintained logging road; descend the road 2 more miles to the highway, reached at a point some 13 miles east of Glacier.

Someday the High Divide trail will extend the full length of the Nooksack Crest—and a famous highland tour **that** will be. Experienced off-trail travelers can follow the route now, starting at Church Mountain and running the ridge east to Excelsior Mountain, to Welcome Pass, to Gold Run Pass (Hike 5), to Twin Lakes (Hike 6), and perhaps all the way to Hannegan Pass (Hike 12). The Forest Service has completed a reconnaisance from Welcome Pass to Gold Run Pass; construction on this segment probably will begin in the mid- 1970s.

Round trip from Canyon Creek road 7 miles
Hiking time 4 hours
High point 5699 feet
Elevation gain 1700 feet
Best mid-July to October
One day or backpack
USGS Mt. Baker

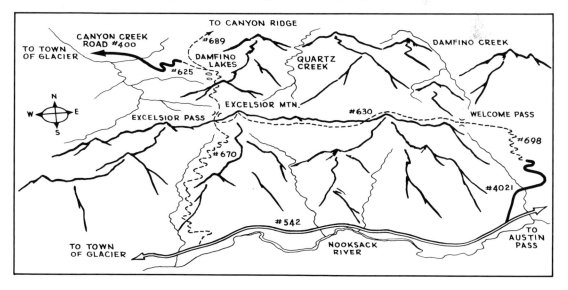

Mt. Shuksan from Yellow Aster Butte (John Spring photo)

5 GOLD RUN PASS

Views across the Nooksack valley to Mt. Baker and Mt. Shuksan. Views over the headwaters of Tomyhoi Creek to Tomyhoi Peak and the tall, rough walls of Mt. Larrabee and American Border and Canadian Border Peaks. Views down to a mile-long lake and north into Canada. Mountain meadows along a pretty trail—but a hot and dry trail on sunny days, so start early and carry water.

Drive State Highway 542 to Glacier and 13½ miles beyond to highway maintenance sheds and a small sign, "Twin Lakes Road." Turn left up the single-lane dirt road. At 2½ miles is the Keep Kool Trail to Yellow Aster Meadows and Tomyhoi Peak: keep driving; this is the wrong trail. At 3 miles is an intersection; go left. At 4½ miles is the Tomyhoi Lake trail sign, elevation 3600 feet; park here.

The trail switchbacks steadily up meadows, then trees, then meadows again. In 1½ miles the way leaves forest the last time and enters an open basin, snow-covered until July. South are Baker and a shoulder of Shuksan. Above is Yellow Aster Butte. The display of wildflowers begins here with avalanche lily and lanceleaf spring beauty in mid-June and continues with other species through the summer. At 2 miles is Gold Run Pass, 5400 feet.

Two further explorations are inviting. Tomyhoi Lake, 3800 feet, is 2 miles and 1600 feet below the pass. The lake is less than 2 miles from the border; Canadian logging roads can be seen. Avalanche snow floats in the waters until early summer. Good campsite. The trail from Gold Run Pass down to Tomyhoi Lake crosses a steep, hard-packed, north-facing snow patch that is often treacherous most of the summer.

The other choice is 6200-foot Yellow Aster Butte, 700 feet higher than the pass. The route to the summit is not difficult in a climbing sense, but definitely not easy walking; scrambling is required on loose rock. Go along the right or left side of the ridge and stick to the greenery; don't attempt to climb the bare rock—it becomes too steep. The views from the top are larger than from the pass, including a full look at Shuksan. Small flower gardens add color to the scene.

Experienced highland travelers can roam from the butte down the ridge crest south, then west, to a 5500-foot meadow basin dotted with a half-dozen small tarns; an intersection here with the Keep Kool Trail; lovely camps in the basin. Northward a long, broad ridge leads to the green slopes of Tomyhoi Peak and private camps below the glacier.

Round trip to Gold Run Pass 4 miles
Hiking time 4 hours
High point 5400 feet
Elevation gain 1800 feet
Best July through October
One day or backpack
USGS Mt. Shuksan

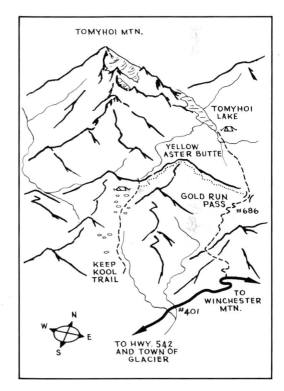

6 WINCHESTER MOUNTAIN

An easy and popular trail through alpine meadows to a summit view of Baker, Shuksan, Icy, Border Peaks, and Tomyhoi, with looks far down to Tomyhoi Lake and forests of Silesia Creek. Especially beautiful in fall colors.

Drive to Twin Lakes road (Hike 5). The first 4½ miles to the Tomyhoi Lake trail are in good condition, but the final 2 miles to Twin Lakes are something else: this section is a mine-to-market road, not built to customary forest road specifications and very steep and rough, culminating in five wickedly-sharp switchbacks. Many people prefer to protect cars and nerves from damage by driving 1 mile past the Tomyhoi Lake trail, parking near an old mine road, and walking the final mile (gaining 1000 feet) to the lakes. Road maintenance is so difficult this last stretch is not open to automobiles until the middle of August, some years not at all, and

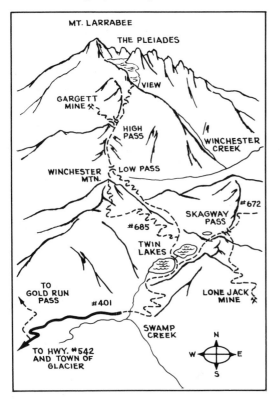

there is a possibility it may be officially abandoned, returning Twin Lakes to the realm of trail country. (A great idea.) However, the miners may start tearing up the terrain again.

The two lakes, lovely alpine waters at an elevation of 5200 feet, often are frozen until early August, though surrounding parklands melt free earlier. Between the lakes is an undeveloped campsite with a classic view of Mt. Baker.

Find the Winchester Mountain trail at the road-end between the lakes. Within ¼ mile is a junction with the High Pass (Gargett Mine) trail. Take the left fork and climb a series of switchbacks westerly through heather, alpine trees, and flowers. Near the top there may be a treacherous snow patch, steep with no runout, often lasting until late August. It may be possible to squirm between the upper edge of the snow and the rocks. Otherwise, drop below the snow and climb to the trail on the far side. Don't try the snow without an ice ax and experience in using it.

In 1½ miles the trail rounds a shoulder and levels off somewhat for the final ½ mile to the summit, site of an abandoned fire lookout cabin and a fine place to while away hours surveying horizons from Puget Sound lowlands to the Pickets and far north into Canada.

Twin Lakes makes a superb basecamp for days of roaming high gardens, prowling old mines, and grazing September blueberries. Even if the upper road must be walked, access is easy for backpacking families with short-legged members.

For one of the longer explorations of the many available, take the High Pass trail (see above). A steep snowfield near the beginning may stop all but trained climbers; if not, there is no further barrier to Low Pass (about 1½ miles) and 5900-foot High Pass (2½ miles). Splendid and private camps here. Follow an old miner's trail high on Mt. Larrabee to a close view of the rugged Pleiades. Investigate the junkyard of the Gargett Mine. Wander meadow basins and admire scenery close and distant.

Round trip from Twin Lakes 4 miles
Hiking time 3 hours
High point 6521 feet
Elevation gain 1300 feet
Best late July to October
One day
USGS Mt. Shuksan

Winchester Mountain trail. Goat Mountain across valley

Mt. Baker from Kulshan Ridge

7 TABLE MOUNTAIN LOOP

Alpine meadows loaded with blueberries (in season), a half-dozen small lakes, and at every turn of the trail a changing view, dominated by "the magnificent pair," the white volcano of Mt. Baker and the massive architecture of Mt. Shuksan. All this on an easy hike circling the base of a high plateau guarded on every side by impressive lava cliffs.

Drive State Highway 542 to Mt. Baker Lodge (Heather Meadows Recreation Area). Continue on gravel road 3 miles upward to the 5200-foot road-end on Kulshan Ridge. The winter snowpack here is often 25 feet deep on the level, with much greater depths in drifts, so the road commonly is snow-bound until late August. Drive as far as possible and walk the rest of the way.

Find the Chain Lakes trail on the west side of the road-end parking lot. In a few hundred feet keep left. (The right fork, the Table Mountain trail, climbs 500 feet through lava cliffs to grand views atop the plateau; to here, the walk is easy and rewarding. The trail then continues over Table Mountain and descends cliffs to meet the Chain Lakes trail. However, on the way it crosses a steep and dangerous snowfield and thus the summit traverse is not recommended for hikers.) The Chain Lakes trail makes an almost level traverse a short mile around the south side of Table Mountain to a saddle between Table Mountain and Ptarmigan Ridge. At the junction here take the right fork, dropping 300 feet to the first of the four Chain Lakes, tiny Mazama Lake. A bit beyond is aptly-named Iceberg Lake, which many years never melts out completely. (Halfway around the shore, one can take the left trail for a short side-trip on a narrow ridge between Hayes Lake and Arbuthnot Lake, rejoining the main trail at Iceberg Lake again.) Innumerable popular campsites throughout the Chain Lakes basin; firewood is becoming scanty at most, so carry a stove.

Climb 600 feet to 5400-foot Herman Saddle, a narrow slot whose cliffs frame Baker west, Shuksan east. Spend some time sitting and looking from one to the other. Then descend amid boulders, heather, and waterfalls, dropping 1100 feet to meadow-surrounded Bagley Lakes. Pause to wander flower fields of the inlet stream. Look

Iceberg Lake

for skiers on the north side of Table Mountain; diehards ski the permanent snowfields all summer and fall, until winter sends them to other slopes.

Between the Bagley Lakes find an unmaintained path (easy going even if the tread is lost) climbing to the Austin Pass warming hut and the Kulshan Ridge parking area, gaining 900 feet in 2 miles. If transportation can be arranged (by use of two cars, or by means of a helpful friend), this final ascent can be eliminated.

Round trip 6 miles
Hiking time 4 hours
High point 5400 feet
Elevation gain 1500 feet
Best late July through October
One day or backpack
USGS Mt. Shuksan

Mt. Baker from Camp Kiser

8 PTARMIGAN RIDGE

Begin in meadows, climb a bit to the snowy and rocky crest of a ridge open to the sky, and wander for miles on the high line toward the lofty white mass of Mt. Baker. This hike has no single destination; a party may go a short way until stopped by snow, or continue a long way to close-up views of the splendid Rainbow Glacier, or accept the invitation of side-trips. Everything is purely delightful.

Keep in mind, though, that Ptarmigan Ridge is basically "climbers' country." In late summer of light-snowfall years, in good weather, hikers can venture into the wild and lonesome highland, but even then they must be well-equipped and experienced. Indeed, climbers' gear and training are usually essential to get very far in safety.

Drive to Kulshan Ridge road-end at 5200 feet and hike 1 mile to the saddle between Table Mountain and Ptarmigan Ridge (Hike 7). At the junction take the left fork, Camp Kiser trail No. 683. The trail drops a bit and then climbs around the side of the 5628-foot hump marking the north end of Ptarmigan Ridge. Snowfields often linger here through the summer and may force casual walkers to turn back.

Beyond the hump the trail climbs (usually on snow) to a ridge crest and traverses some 2½ miles to Camp Kiser. The tread is sketchy, snow crossings are frequent, and the route becomes increasingly difficult to follow and increasingly easy to lose, despite rock cairns. In fog, even skilled alpine navigators get confused; spur ridges may be mistaken for the main ridge and lead a party far astray.

The Baker-Shuksan scenery is steadily dazzling and off-trail tours of high rocks and waterfall-loud basins are constantly tempting. Listen to marmots and conies whistling and squeaking. Watch for goats. And ptarmigan.

The trail swings around the south side of 6414-foot Coleman Pinnacle to Camp Kiser, which is not a specific place but rather a ½-mile stretch of ridgeslope benches sprinkled with alpine hemlock. Here is where the occasional climbers camp.

Camp Kiser offers many fine spots to stop overnight or longer. Water is plentiful but not wood; carry a stove. The place cries out for a basecamp to enjoy the explorations. Walk to near the top of Coleman Pinnacle—and scramble to the summit if competent to do so. Wander the climbers' track another mile or two closer to the glaciers. Or drop 500 feet down meadows to the cold little basin southeast of Coleman Pinnacle, only recently evacuated by a glacier, remnants of which linger; roam the shores of a new-born, ice-fed lakelet.

Round trip to Camp Kiser about 8 miles
Hiking time 8 hours
High point 6000 feet
Elevation gain about 1200 feet
Best August through September
One day or backpack
USGS Mt. Baker and Mt. Shuksan

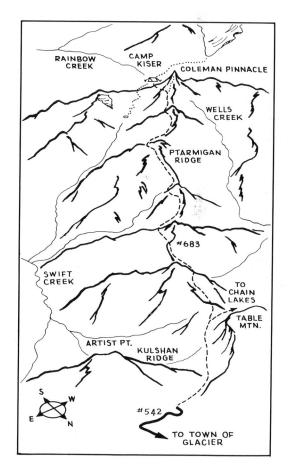

9 LAKE ANN

When North Cascades climbers and hikers compare memories of favorite sitting-and-looking places, Lake Ann always gets fond mention. The Mt. Shuksan seen from here is quite different from the world-famous roadside view, yet the 4500-foot rise of glaciers and cliffs is at least as grand. And there is much to do.

Drive State Highway 542 to Mt. Baker Lodge. Continue on gravel road about 1½ miles upward to the parking lot at Austin Pass, 4700 feet. Until August snow blocks the road somewhere above the Lodge, adding ½ mile or so of walking.

The trail begins by dropping 600 feet to a delightful headwater basin of Swift Creek. Brooks meander in grass and flowers. Marmots whistle from boulder-top perches. Pleasant picnicking.

From the basin the trail descends a bit more and traverses forest, swinging around the upper drainage of Swift Creek. At 2¼ miles is the lowest elevation (3900 feet) of the trip, an attractive camp in meadows by a rushing stream, and a junction with the Swift Creek trail.

Now starts a 900-foot ascent in 1½ miles, first in heather and clumps of Christmas trees, then over a granite rockslide into forest under a cliff, to a cold and open little valley. If the way is snow-covered, as it may be until mid-August, plod onward and upward to the obvious 4800-foot saddle, beyond which is Lake Ann. When whiteness melts away, the waterfalls and moraines and flowers and ice-plucked buttresses of the little valley demand a slow pace.

What to do next? First off, sit and watch the living wall of Shuksan. Then, perhaps, circumnavigate the lake, noting the contact between granitic rocks and complex metamorphics. In September, blueberry upward on the ridge of Mt. Ann. If time allows, go on longer wanders, splendid camps are everywhere around.

Recommended Wander No. 1. Follow the trail from Lake Ann as it dips into the headwater basin of Shuksan Creek (more campsites), then switchbacks up and up toward Shuksan. At a rocky gully a climbers' track branches steeply to the left. Just here the main trail may be nonexistent for a few yards; if so, scramble across gravel to regain the tread. Continue to a promontory a stone's throw from the snout of the Lower Curtis Glacier. Look up to the mountain. Look down forests to Baker Lake. Look beyond Swift Creek to the stupendous whiteness of Mt. Baker.

Recommended Wander No. 2. From the Lake Ann saddle climb the heathery spur to Shuksan Arm. No trail, but logic leads the feet. Views down to the Nooksack River and north to the splinter-summits of the Border Peaks.

Round trip to Lake Ann 8 miles
Hiking time 6-8 hours
High point (at saddle) 4800 feet
Elevation gain about 1000 feet in
    and about 1000 feet out
Best August to October
One day or backpack
USGS Mt. Shuksan

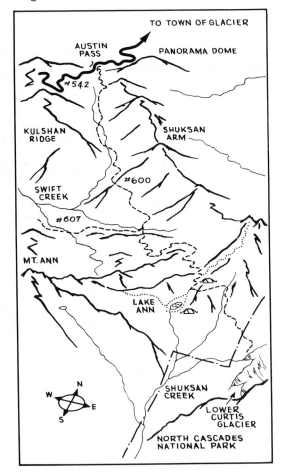

Curtis Glacier and Mt. Shuksan from Lake Ann

10 PRICE LAKE

A cold and rock-milky lake in a spectacular glacier-clad cirque under the north wall of Mt. Shuksan. Wild and lonesome and fiercely-beautiful country. No trail, and a bone-freezing river to ford, so definitely not for the casual hiker. Water, water, everywhere, but most of it so thick with glacier-milled rock flour there is scarcely a drop worth drinking; carry full canteens.

Drive State Highway 542 east from Glacier 12¾ miles to the Nooksack River bridge. Just before the bridge turn left on Nooksack River road No. 402. In about 1½ miles take the right fork, road No. 404. Go 4 miles to another fork; take the lower and most-used road and follow it 1 rough mile to end, elevation about 2400 feet. Road and trail should be marked "Nooksack Trail."

In ¼ mile leave the trail and beat a way down through trees to the river. One place is about as good as another. Lucky travelers may find a fallen tree over the river. But probably not—most years it is necessary to ford. To avoid wading both it is important to cross the river **above** the outlet of Price Creek.

The Nooksack River is about 30 feet wide here and even in low-water periods is cold, swift, and more than knee-deep. The bottom rocks are too sharp to allow barefoot wading, so either carry A pair of sneakers for the crossing or else take off boots and socks, put back on boots, wade river, drain boots, then put on dry socks and damp boots. A 120-foot climbing rope is helpful. Loop the rope around a tree. The first man carries both ends across and holds them tight as a support for the rest of the party. When every-

Fording the Nooksack River

one is over, the rope is recovered by pulling on one end.

Despite the lack of trail, walking is easy in the relatively-brushless forest; the route is obvious, climbing through woods near the east side of Price Creek and within sight of it. About halfway the creek is lost in a deep canyon. Stay within sound of the waterfalls, ascending steep but not difficult hillside between the canyon on one hand and a too-steep slope on the other. Once above the canyon stay in the woods 200-300 feet higher than the creek, emerging at last on a series of moraines at the level of the lake.

Price Lake is so loaded with rock milk from active glaciers it looks like pure mud. The color may be disappointing; not, though, the glaciers and peaks enclosing the cirque. Really good campsites are absent but several spots are level enough for sleeping. The only clear drinking water

is a small trickle on the south side of the lake; getting there requires a ford of Price Creek, which is less than knee-deep but so cold it hurts. Drinking the lake water won't kill you, though ingesting that much silt probably isn't the best way to treat a digestive system.

Hikers may be well content to sit and admire the spectacle of cliffs and glaciers. The more ambitious will enjoy a side-trip up the wooded ridge on the north side of the lake to open meadows and larger views.

Round trip 4 miles
Hiking time 8 hours
High point 3895 feet
Elevation gain 1100 feet
Best August to September
One day or backpack
USGS Mt. Shuksan
Park Service camping permit required

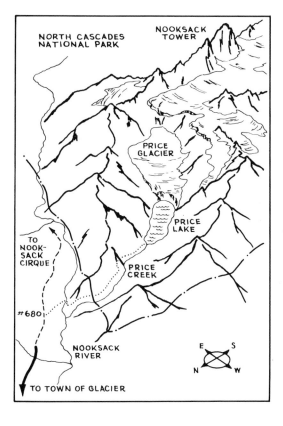

Price Glacier and Mt. Shuksan from Price Lake

Nooksack Cirque

11 NOOKSACK CIRQUE

A wild, lonesome cirque, a wasteland of glacial violence, one of the most dramatic spots in the North Cascades. Icefalls, waterfalls, moraines, a raging river, the stark pinnacle of Nooksack Tower, and the 5000-foot northeast wall of Mt. Shuksan. But not much trail, mostly miles of bushwacking and/or ankle-twisting boulders. The trip is best taken either in late spring when snow covers the brush or in fall when the river is low enough to fully expose gravel bars.

Drive to the start of the Nooksack trail, elevation about 2400 feet (Hike 10).

The trail goes 1 mile to an abrupt end at the river bank. From here on, lots of luck. No problems getting lost, just problems getting there.

When the river is low, as during extended periods of cool weather and in fall, gravel bars can be walked all the way from trail-end into the cirque. The bouldery travel is slow and occasional side-channels must be crossed by hopping or wading but the going is easy.

Not so when the river is high, covering some

or all the gravel bars, flooding the side-channels. A route must then be picked through the woods, which offers some open travel but a lot of brush, including patches of 6-foot-high huckleberry bushes. (More than one party has hiked into the cirque on gravel bars and been forced by a downpour and rising waters to beat brush to get out.)

In 2 miles, views of Icy Peak. In 3 miles, the hanging ice cliffs of the East Nooksack Glacier, falling from Cloudcap (Seahpo) Peak and Jagged Ridge. Now, rounding a bend in the valley, the way enters the cirque and at 4 miles reaches "the deepest, darkest hole in the North Cascades."

For the most impressive views climb a few hundred feet up slopes to the north. See the East Nooksack Glacier tumbling 5000 feet from the Summit Pyramid of Shuksan. See the startling thrust of 8268-foot Nooksack Tower. For higher views scramble to the 6000-foot saddle between Icy Peak and Cloudcap Peak.

Many campsites on gravel bars and moraines.

Within the cirque, several hundred feet above the river, is the famous Great Trog, well worth finding in bad weather, this overhang of a giant boulder offers comfortable camping, dry and protected, for as many as a dozen people.

The National Park Service plans to build a trail into the cirque. The trip will then be much easier but much less wild. Go now, before the crowds arrive.

Round trip 8 miles
Hiking time 6-10 hours
High point 3500 feet
Elevation gain 1100 feet
Best late May through October
One day or backpack
USGS Mt. Shuksan
Park Service camping permit required

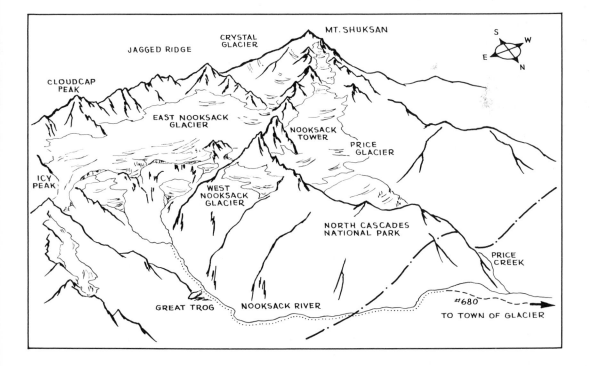

12 HANNEGAN PASS AND PEAK

A prime entryway to the Chilliwack and Picket section of the North Cascades National Park. The walk begins in a delightful valley dominated by the white serenity of Ruth Mountain and concludes with a relaxed wander to a meadow summit offering a panorama of the north wall of Shuksan, the Pickets, and wildness high and low.

Drive State Highway 542 east from Glacier 12¾ miles to the Nooksack River bridge. Just before the bridge turn left on Nooksack River road No. 402. In about 1½ miles take the left fork, Ruth Creek road No. 402, and continue 4½ miles to road-end at Hannegan Campground, 3000 feet.

The first trail mile ascends gently through trees and avalanche-path greenery near Ruth Creek, with looks upward to the waterfall-streaked cliffs and pocket icefields of Mt. Sefrit and Nooksack Ridge. At a bit more than 1 mile the snow dome of Ruth Mountain comes in sight— a startling expanse of whiteness for so small a peak. Now the path steepens, climbing above the valley floor.

Rest stops grow long, there is so much to see and so much good water to drink. At 3½ miles, 4600 feet, the trail swings to the forest edge beside a meadow-babbling creek; across the creek is a parkland of heather benches and alpine trees. Splendid campsites, the best on the route; sad to say, they are being mangled by thought-

Looking north from side of Hannegan Peak

less campers. The final ½ mile switchbacks in forest to Hannegan Pass, 5066 feet.

Views from the pass are restricted by trees; the camping is so poor (scarce wood, undependable water) and so damaging to the tiny meadow it doubtless will be forbidden before long. Hikers who come only to the pass will feel richly rewarded by scenes along the way but may be disappointed by the lack of a climactic vista. A side-trip is therefore recommended.

Visitors usually are drawn southward and upward on the climbers' track toward Ruth Mountain. This path leads to lovely meadows and broader views but dwindles to nothing before long, tempting the unwary onto steep and dangerous snow slopes. Leave Ruth to the climbers. There's a better and safer side-trip.

From the pass, saunter westerly up open forest, following game traces when available. Emerge into a steep, lush meadow (slippery when wet), at the top break through a screen of trees to heather and flowers, and wander wide-eyed up the crest of a rounded ridge to the summit plateau of Hannegan Peak, 6186 feet. Roam the meadow flats, looking down into valley forests of Ruth and Silesia Creeks and Chilliwack River, looking out to glaciers and cliffs of Baker, Shuk-san, Ruth, Triumph, Challenger, Redoubt, Slesse, and dozens of other grand peaks. Many of these peaks and valleys—including the entire route of this hike—have been omitted from the North Cascades National Park. This grievous error must be rectified.

In good weather a party can camp comfortably on the summit; carry a stove for cooking, collect water from snowfield trickles, and enjoy the panorama in sunset and dawn. Experienced highland travelers can run the open ridge north to connect with the Copper Mountain trail (Hike 13). The ridge-running west to Granite Mountain is also inviting.

Round trip to Hannegan Pass 8 miles
Hiking time 6 hours
High point 5066 feet
Elevation gain 2000 feet
Best mid-July to October
One day or backpack
USGS Mt. Shuksan

Round trip to Hannegan Peak 10 miles
Hiking time 8 hours
High point 6186 feet
Elevation gain 3100 feet
Best mid-July to October
One day or backpack

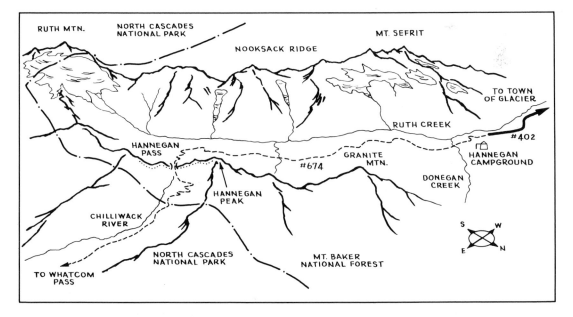

13 COPPER MOUNTAIN

A remote meadow ridge on the west edge of the North Cascades National Park, offering a rare combination of easy-walking terrain and panoramas of rough-and-cold wilderness. Views across far-below forests of the Chilliwack River to the Picket Range—and views west to other superb peaks and valleys proposed for addition to the Park.

Drive to Hannegan Campground and hike 4 miles, gaining 2000 feet, to Hannegan Pass (Hike 12). Descend forest switchbacks into avalanche-swept headwaters of the Chilliwack River, then side-hill along talus and stream outwash patched with grass and flowers. Note chunks of volcanic breccia in the debris and look up to their source in colorful cliffs—remnants of ancient volcanoes.

At the 5-mile marker, 1 mile and 650 feet below Hannegan Pass, is a 4400-foot junction. (Beside the nearby river is a nice campsite.) The Chilliwack River trail goes right, descending. Copper Mountain trail No. 675 goes left and up, entering forest and climbing steadily, switchbacking some, crossing the upper portion of Hells Gorge (sliced into volcanic rocks), and emerging into parkland.

At 7 miles the trail attains the 5500-foot ridge crest between Silesia Creek and the Chilliwack River. A memorable look back to Hannegan Pass, Ruth Mountain, and Shuksan—and the beginning of miles of constant views.

(From this point, experienced hikers can make an off-trail ridge-running return to Hannegan Peak and Pass; also, a short side-trip leads to a tiny cirque lake.)

The trail continues along the open crest, up a bit and down a bit, then climbs around a knob to a wide, grassy swale at 8 miles. Some 300 feet and a few minutes below the swale are campsites by little Egg Lake, 5200 feet, set in rocks and flowers.

The way goes up and down another knob to a broad meadow at 9 miles. Now comes the final mile, gaining 1100 feet to 6260-foot Cop-

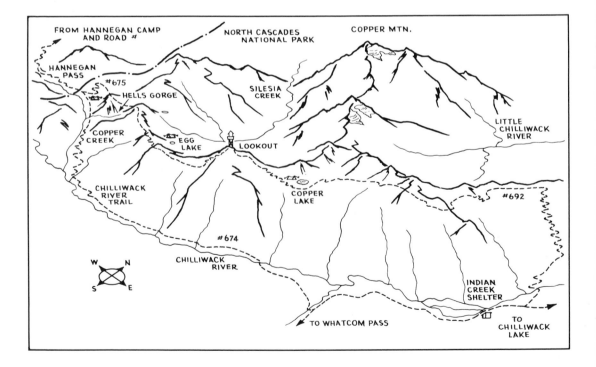

Mt. Shuksan from Copper Ridge

Mountain Lookout, the climax. Beyond the green deeps of Silesia Creek are the Border Peaks and the incredible fang of Slesse—and far-off in haze, ice giants of the British Columbia Coast Range. Look down and down to the white thread of the Chilliwack River and beyond its forest valley to Redoubt and Bear and Indian and the magnificent Pickets. Also see Shuksan and Baker. And more peaks and streams, an infinity of wildland.

Beyond the lookout the trail descends about 1½ miles to campsites at 5200-foot Copper Lake (blue waters under steep cliffs), then traverses and descends about 7 more miles (views much of the way) to the Chilliwack River trail at 2300 feet; this junction is 14.4 miles from Hannegan Pass. A 34-mile loop trip using this return route adds low-valley forests to the high-ridge wander.

For another exploration leave the trail before the steep descent to Copper Lake and investigate ridges and basins toward the 7142-foot summit of Copper Mountain. It'll be a few years before crowds are a problem here.

Round trip to Copper Mountain Lookout 20 miles
Allow 2-3 days
High point 6260 feet
Elevation gain about 4800 feet in, 1500 feet out
Best August to October
USGS Mt. Shuksan and Mt. Challenger
Park Service camping permit required

14   EASY RIDGE

A not-so-easy trail to a high green ridge surrounded by rugged and icy peaks. Wander amid picturesque alpine trees, fields of flowers, and small tarns, admiring the Chilliwack wilderness of the North Cascades National Park. The difficulty of the trip is compensated for by the privacy—and the views.

Drive to Hannegan Campground and hike 4 miles, gaining 2000 feet, to Hannegan Pass (Hike 12). Descend the Chilliwack River trail, dropping 2300 feet in 5½ miles. At 9½ miles, elevation 2800 feet, is the Easy Ridge trail junction. Go right, reaching a ford of the Chilliwack River in about ¼ mile. Except perhaps in late summer the river is too deep, swift, and cold to ford and a log must be found. Uusually one is available within ¼ mile of the ford, upstream or down. Give preference to searching upstream, since on the far side the trail parallels the river about ¼ mile before heading uphill along Easy Creek. If luck is bad in this direction, logs are generally abundant ¾ mile downstream, by the U.S. Cabin shelter; in this case the trail can be

regained without too much brush-beating if one stays near or on the valley wall. A good plan is to camp the first night by the ford, locating a footlog that evening for use the next morning. However, only fireless camps are permitted on the gravel bars here; if a fire is wanted the party must go ¾ mile downstream from the crossing to U.S. cabin.

The trail was built to service a fire lookout cabin, long since demolished. Park Service plans have not been settled at this writing but under Forest Service administration the trail was maintained only once every 4 years. However, brush is no problem and the travel is easy enough except for climbing over a few logs. The hillside forest is entirely dry so fill canteens at the bottom.

The trail switchbacks steeply 2½ miles, gaining 2600 feet, to the first views at a 5200-foot saddle in Easy Ridge. From the saddle the trail continues north ½ mile to the old lookout site on a 5640-foot knoll overlooking the junction of Brush Creek and the Chilliwack River; great looks down into valleys, across to the pleasant ridge of Copper Mountain, and off to rough, white

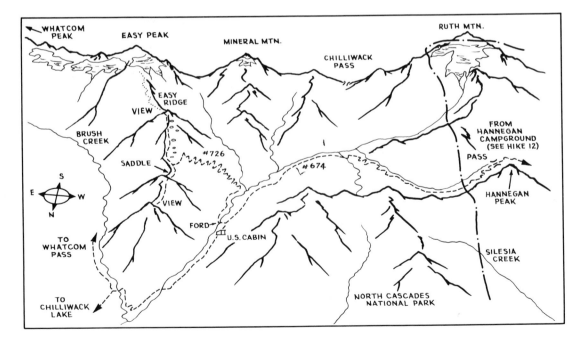

Whatcom Peak from Easy Ridge

peaks. For the broadest views, leave the trail at the saddle and walk the main ridge south, climbing open slopes, past a number of tarns, to a heather-covered knoll at 6100 feet. A tiny pool here, good for cold drinks while looking at Shuksan and Icy west, Canadian peaks north, Redoubt northeast, Whatcom Peak close by to the east, and mountains and valleys beyond number.

The route to the 6613-foot summit of Easy Peak may be blocked by a steep snow slope—don't try it without an ice ax and knowledge of self-arrest technique. When the snow melts away an equally dangerous slope of rotten scree is exposed. The view from the top isn't much better than from the heather knoll.

For a 3-day trip the best camp is on a gravel bar at the Chilliwack River ford. For longer trips, allowing more time to explore highlands, carry packs to wonderful camps near the small tarns.

Round trip 27 miles
Allow 3 days
High point 6100 feet
Elevation gain 5500 feet in, 2400 feet out
Best late July to October
USGS Mt. Shuksan and Mt. Challenger
Park Service camping permit required

15 WHATCOM PASS

A long hike on an old miners' route to the Caribou goldfields in Canada, entering the heart of the most spectacular wilderness remaining in the contiguous 48 states. Virgin forests in a U-shaped valley carved by ancient glaciers; rushing rivers; mountain meadows; and a side-trip to lovely Tapto Lakes, the ultimate blend of gentle beauty and rough grandeur. Whatcom Pass is the high point on the increasingly-popular walk across the North Cascades National Park from the Mt. Baker region to Ross Lake.

Drive to Hannegan Campground and hike 4 miles, gaining 2000 feet, to Hannegan Pass (Hike

12). Descend the Chilliwack River trail, which drops rapidly at first and then gentles out in delightful forest, reaching the U.S. Cabin shelter at 10 miles.

At about 11 miles, elevation 2468 feet (2600 feet down from Hannegan Pass), the trail crosses the Chilliwack River. The footbridge has been gone for several years and despite two drownings there are no immediate plans for replacement. Do not try to ford the river in high water; look downstream ½ mile for a footlog. The way now climbs moderately to the crossing of Brush Creek at about 12 miles. Here is a junction.

The Chilliwack trail goes north 9 miles to the Canadian border and about 1 mile more to Chilliwack Lake. The forest walk to the border is worth taking in its own right; parties visiting the region during early summer when the high country is full of snow may prefer pleasures of the low, green world.

From the 2600-foot junction the Brush Creek trail climbs steadily, gaining 2600 feet in the 5 miles to Whatcom Pass; the first portion may be quite brushy even a few weeks after the trail crew has passed by. At 14 miles is Graybeal Shelter, and at 17 miles 5200-foot Whatcom Pass; camping is not allowed at the pass or on the ridges immediately above.

Views from the meadowy pass are superb, but there is vastly more to see. Plan to spend at least a full day touring the area. The first thing to do is ramble the easy ridge south of the pass to a knoll overlooking the mind-boggling gleam of the Challenger Glacier.

Tapto Lakes are next. (However, don't bother if snow is still deep around the pass; the lakes will then be frozen and their basins solid white.) Climb steep slopes north from the pass, following obvious openings in alpine forest. When the hillside levels off continue left in meadows between little trees, crossing avalanche paths, to rocky ground above the lakes. Enjoy the waters and flowers, the stupendous view of Challenger. The steep bit above the pass may demand some scrambling but anyone able to get this far from civilization should find the going easy. Experienced alpine travelers can discover more lakes, more views, more lonesome wandering, northeast along Custer Ridge.

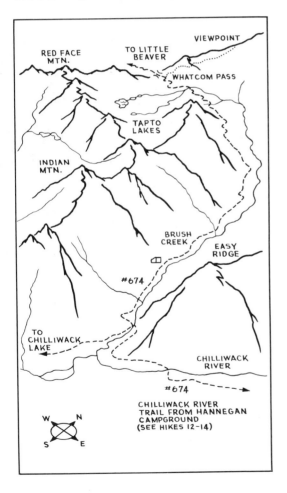

Mt. Challenger from Whatcom Pass

Good campsites on the trail include U.S. Cabin, Graybeal Shelter, a meadow about ¼ mile before Whatcom Pass, and on the trail ¼ mile beyond the pass.

The classic "across the National Park" hike from Hannegan Campground to Big Beaver Landing on Ross Lake covers 38½ up-and-down miles on easy trail beside wild rivers, through gorgeous forests, over three passes. Total elevation gain on the way, 5400 feet. To have time for side-trips a party should allow 7-9 days. From Whatcom Pass drop abruptly (56 switchbacks!) into headwaters of Little Beaver Creek, an en-chanting place where waterfalls tumble from cliffs all around. Good camping here at Twin Rocks Shelter, 3000 feet. At 6 miles from Whatcom Pass is Stillwell Shelter and the 2400-foot junction with the Beaver Pass trail. To conclude the cross-Park journey, see Hike 26.

Round trip to Whatcom Pass 34 miles
Allow 3-5 days
High point 5200 feet
Elevation gain 4600 feet in, 2600 feet out
Best late July to October
USGS Mt. Shuksan and Mt. Challenger
Park Service camping permit required

16 MOROVITZ MEADOW

Recommending any one hike in the parklands of Mt. Baker's southwest flank is like praising a single painting in a museum of masterpieces. There are days of wandering here, exploring meadows and moraines, waterfalls and lakes, listening to marmots and watching for mountain goats. The trail to Morovitz Meadow gives a good sampling of the country, with impressive near views of the glaciers of Baker, the towering Black Buttes (core of an ancient volcano), the Twin Sisters, and far horizons.

Drive State Highway 20 east from Sedro Woolley 14½ miles and turn left on the Baker Lake-Grandy Lake road. In 12½ miles, just past Rocky Creek bridge, turn left on Loomis-Nooksack road No. 3725, go 3 miles to Sulphur Creek road No. 372, and follow it 6 miles to the end in a logging patch (inside the Mt. Baker Recreation Area!) at about 3200 feet. Find the trail west of the road, near Sulphur Creek.

The trail immediately crosses Sulphur Creek into the heather and blueberries (in season) of Schreibers Meadow, passes frog ponds and a shelter cabin, then enters forest. In 1 mile is an interesting area where meltwater from the Easton Glacier has torn wide avenues through the trees. The drainage pattern changes from time to time; generally three torrents must be crossed by footlog or boulder-hopping.

Beyond the boulder-and-gravel area the trail enters cool forest and switchbacks steeply a long mile to lower Morovitz Meadow. The grade gentles in heather fields leading to upper Morovitz Meadow, 4500 feet. Pleasant campsites here, some in alpine trees, some in open gardens beside snow-melt streams.

At the trail junction in the upper meadow, go left to Park Butte, climbing to a ridge and in a mile reaching the 5450-foot summit. Views of Mt. Baker glaciers (and much more) are magnificent. Parties with spare time and energy may well be tempted to descend to the delightful basin of Pocket Lake, or roam the ridge to 6100-foot Survey Point.

There is another direction to go from Morovitz Meadow. Leave the trail near the junction and ramble upward to the intriguing crest of Railroad Grade, a moraine built by the Easton Glacier in more ambitious days. Look down the unstable wall of gravel and boulders to the naked wasteland below the ice. Walk the narrow crest higher and yet higher, closer and closer to the gleaming volcano. In late summer hikers can scramble moraine rubble and polished slabs to about 7000 feet before being forced to halt at the edge of the glacier.

From either Railroad Grade or Baker Pass, inventive walkers can pick private ways through waterfall-and-flower country to the edge of a startling chasm. Look down to the chaotic front of the Deming Glacier, across to stark walls of the Black Buttes. All through the wide sprawl of Mazama Park are secluded campsites, beauty spots to explore. Don't forget little Mazama Lake or nearby Meadow Point.

Round trip to Park Butte 7 miles
Hiking time 6-8 hours
High point 5450 feet
Elevation gain 2250 feet
Best mid-July through October
One day or backpack
USGS Hamilton and Mt. Baker

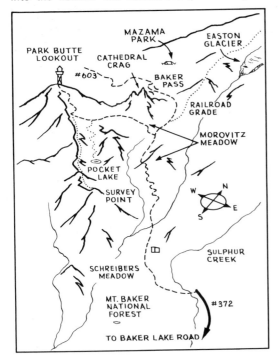

Morovitz Meadow and Mt. Baker from Park Butte

17 BOULDER RIDGE

A rough hike to one of the many beautiful alpine ridges radiating like octopus arms from the white heap of Mount Baker. The crest provides a magnificent overlook of the Boulder Glacier.

Drive State Highway 20 east from Sedro Woolley 14½ miles. Turn left on the Baker Lake-Grandy Lake road 14 miles to Komo Kulshan

Boulder Ridge trail and Mt. Baker (John Spring photo)

Guard Station and continue 4 miles to the Boulder Creek bridge. About $\frac{1}{4}$ mile beyond, turn left on the Baker Hot Springs-Boulder Ridge road. In 2 miles stay left again and drive $3\frac{1}{2}$ more miles to the road-end and trailhead, elevation 3200 feet.

The trail contours up and down, going through bogs and waist-high huckleberry bushes, gaining only 300 feet in 2 miles. Then, $\frac{1}{4}$ mile after crossing a little stream, the tread vanishes in a small, marshy meadow; no formal trail ever existed beyond here. At the far end of the meadow is an obscure blaze and the start of a very faint climbers' path angling to the right toward the ridge crest. Follow the blazes and plastic ribbons carefully. The track is steep, sometimes among evergreen trees and occasionally through slide alder. After climbing some 500 feet above the meadow, the way bursts from timber onto a moraine covered with knee-high firs and hemlocks.

From here there is a choice: an easy $\frac{3}{4}$-mile hike, the route obvious, to the top of the moraine and a close view of Boulder Glacier; or, an ascent of 500 feet in 1 mile to Boulder Ridge.

For the ridge, go back into forest, climb to a wooded saddle, and continue up the crest, scrambling to the left of a small lava cliff, to an overlook of both the Boulder and Park Glaciers, with Mt. Shuksan east and Whitehorse west, other peaks all around, and great white Baker above.

Weather-exposed but scenic camps are possible on the ridge; plan to cook on a stove and find meager water from snowfields, if any.

Other octopus arms (ridges, that is) radiating from Baker will surely intrigue the hiker. An especially inviting one to the east, between Park Creek and Rainbow Creek, can be reached by driving or walking the logging road past Rainbow Falls viewpoint to its very end at almost 4000 feet, then bushwacking the ridge crest a mile to open meadows.

Round trip 8 miles
Hiking time 7 hours
High point 4500 feet
Elevation gain 1300 feet
Best July through October
One day or backpack
USGS Mt. Baker

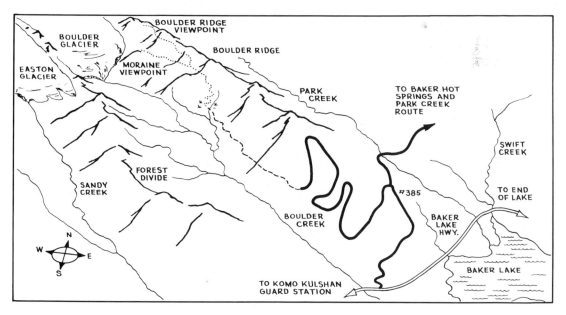

18   BAKER RIVER

Luxurious rain forest, a lovely green-milky river, and tantalizing glimpses of glacier-covered peaks. Because of the very low elevation (and such low-altitude virgin valleys are now rare indeed in the Cascades) the trail is open except in midwinter and offers a delightful wildland walk when higher elevations are buried in snow. Even bad weather is no barrier to enjoyment, not with all the big trees, understory plants, and streams. For a feeling of true lonesomeness, try the trip on a rainy day in early spring. It's also a good place to escape guns during hunting season, since the no-shooting North Cascades National Park is entered partway along.

Drive the Baker Lake road (Hike 17) 14 miles to Komo Kulshan Guard Station on Baker Lake and follow the Forest Service road 11½ miles to the lake head. Turn left ½ mile on a spur, passing several unmarked side-roads, to a shelter cabin and the start of Upper Baker trail No. 606, elevation 760 feet.

The first ¼ mile lies on and near an old logging road (which may be driven to shorten the walk), then civilization is left behind. In ½ mile is the first view—up and up the far side of the river to glaciers of 7660-foot Mt. Blum. At 1 mile the trail climbs a few feet above the river, a beautiful sight, and drops down again to go by large beaver ponds. In 2 miles, about where the National Park is entered, see Easy Ridge at the valley head, and a little farther on, the sharp outline of 7574-foot What-

Baker River

com Peak, northern outpost of the Picklets. In a short 3 miles the way reaches raging Sulphide Creek, dominated by Jagged Ridge and its small glaciers. Partly hidden by trees is the huge expanse of the Sulphide Glacier on the south side of Mt. Shuksan.

If Sulphide Creek is high and a bridge is lacking, this is far enough for most hikers. A trail shelter provides a snug bad-weather campsite, elevation 900 feet.

Trail continues another 2 miles to Crystal Creek and once went 3 more miles to Bald Eagle Creek, 1100 feet. Currently the upper section is lost in brush and the best route beyond Crystal Creek is on gravel bars of the river. However, the Park Service is considering reopening the way to a dead-end at Bald Eagle Creek.

Round trip to sulphide Creek 6 miles
Hiking time 3-4 hours
High point 900 feet
Elevation gain 200 feet
Best March through November
One day or backpack
USGS Lake Shannon, Mt. Shuksan, and Mt. Challenger
Park Service camping permit required

Sulphide Creek Shelter

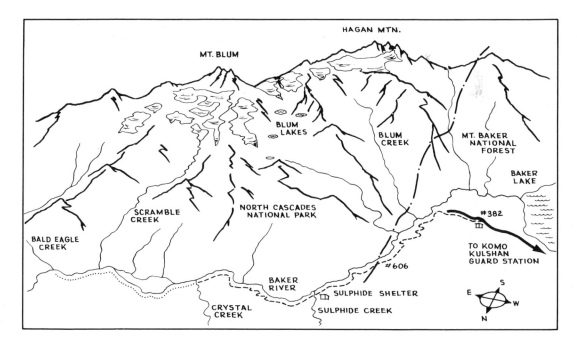

19 FINNEY PEAK

Site of an old lookout cabin—nothing left now except a few rusty nails. But the view remains. The peak stands near Puget Sound lowlands, in the center of a National Forest "island" of wooded ridges completely surrounded by wide valleys; its position on the west edge of the range provides an unusual perspective on the North Cascades. An exceptional opportunity, too, for close observation of logging past, logging in progress, and logging yet to come; the entire "island" is due to be clear-cut in the next few years.

Drive State Highway 20 to Concrete and turn south one mile, crossing the Skagit River bridge, to the South Skagit road. Turn left and continue east 8 miles to Finney-Cumberland road No. 353. In 11 miles turn left on road No. 3411 and go about 3 miles to the trailhead, elevation 2800 feet.

The trail switchbacks up to the top of a clear-cut and then follows the crest of a narrow wooded ridge with clearcuts on both sides. Timber sale signs indicate more logging to come.

Tantalizing glimpses through trees of distant peaks, but the best is saved for the top. North across the broad Skagit River valley are Mt. Baker, Mt. Shuksan, and Baker Lake—plus a near view of the green slopes of Sauk Mountain and a far view of the jagged Pickets. More to the east are the Eldorado massif, Dome Peak, and Glacier Peak. Close to the south is a neighbor peak of the "island," Round Mountain (Hike 36), and beyond the Stillaguamish River, the great north wall of Whitehorse. Carry a loaded canteen; there is no water on the route.

Under the concept of multiple use, Forest Service personnel had promised that the trail to Finney Peak would be kept open even though logging was taking place. However, during the short time the trail was hiked for this book and its going to the printer, the Forest Service officially announced the building of permanent logging roads which shorten the trail by 1½ miles. The logging could be done from a temporary cat road and when finished give the trail back to the hiker, but the Forest Service officials aren't yet oriented to that kind of thinking. New hikers may not have to huff and puff as much, but

there will be less solitude. The view from the top will be just as great but there will be a lot less satisfaction getting there. So much for the Forest Service's "multiple use."

If the Forest Service shortens the trail, it then will be reached from road No. 3407.

Round trip 9 miles
Hiking time 4 hours
High point 5079 feet
Elevation gain 2200 feet
Best June to November
One day
USGS none

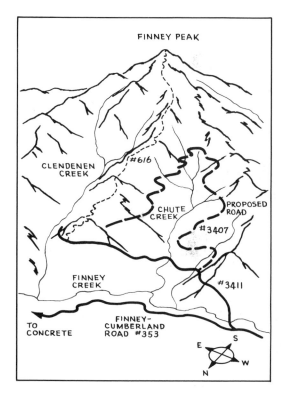

Mt. Baker from Finney Peak Trail

20 THORNTON LAKES— TRAPPERS PEAK

Three deep lakes in rock basins gouged by a long-gone glacier. Close by are living glaciers, still gouging. All around are icy peaks on the west edge of the North Cascades National Park. From a summit above the lakes, a splendid view of Triumph and Despair and the Picket Range.

Drive State Highway 20 to Marblemount and 11 miles beyond to Thornton Creek road No. 3745. Turn left 5 steep miles to a parking area, elevation about 2800 feet.

The first 2 miles are on an abandoned logging road. Then begins the trail, which was never really "built" in a formal sense, but just grew;

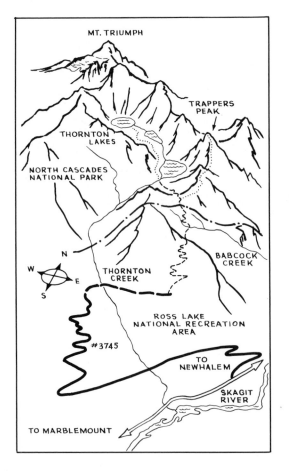

it's very steep in places and mucky in others. Except for the abandoned road across clearcuts, most of the way lies in forest. At a bit more than 1 mile from the abandoned road is a delightful opening and a small creek to jump. The trail then switchbacks up a forested slope to the ridge crest.

Recuperate atop the 4900-foot ridge crest. Look down to the lake basin and out to Mt. Triumph. Then drop 400 feet to the lowest and largest Thornton Lake. Across the outlet stream are several campsites.

To reach the middle and upper lakes, traverse slopes west of the lower lake. The middle lake usually has some ice until the end of July; the upper lake, at 5000 feet in a steepwalled cirque, ordinarily is frozen until mid-August.

If views are the goal, don't drop to the lakes. Leave the trail at the 4900-foot ridge crest and follow a faint climbers' track up the ridge to the 5964-foot summit of Trappers Peak. See the fantastic Pickets. And see, too, the little village of Newhalem, far below in the Skagit valley. The ridge route is steep in places and requires use of the hands, but is not really tough. Early in the season there may be dangerous snow patches; go above or below them. Turn around content when the way gets too scary for plain-and-simple hikers.

Round trip to lower Thornton Lake 9½ miles
High point 4900 feet
Hiking time 6-8 hours
Elevation gain 2100 feet in, 400 feet out
Best mid-July through October
One day or backpack
USGS Marblemount
Park Service camping permit required

Mt. Triumph and Thornton Lake

Diablo Lake from Sourdough Mountain

21 SOURDOUGH MOUNTAIN

No other hike from the Skagit River can match these views of the North Cascades National Park. Look down to Diablo Lake and Ross Lake and out to forests of Thunder Creek. Look south to the ice of Colonial and Snowfield, and southeast to Buckner, and the sprawling Boston Glacier. Look east to the king of the Skagit, Jack Mountain, and north to Canada, and northwest and west to the Pickets.

There are two routes to Sourdough Mountain. One is an extremely steep trail—a strenuous day trip and even with an overnight camp not an easy weekend. The other is a loop which can be done in an arduous 2 days.

Drive State Highway 20 to the Seattle City Light town of Diablo, at the base of Diablo Dam. Park in the main lot; elevation 900 feet.

Direct Trail: Walk back from the parking lot past the powerhouse and tennis court and find the signed trail behind the covered swimming pool. The trail starts steep and stays steep; countless short switchbacks gain 3000 feet in the first 2½ miles before the way "levels off" to an ascent of 2000 feet in the final 4 miles to the summit.

After 1½ miles of zigzags from the road up a forested hillside, an opening gives a sample of panoramas to come. At 3 miles is an unmarked junction. The left fork climbs a steep ½ mile to a TV antenna serving Diablo. For most day hikers this 4800-foot viewpoint is far enough, adding northern vistas to the southern. The way to this turnaround point often is free of snow in May, offering a spectacular springtime hike.

The main trail climbs from the junction, on a gentler grade than before, reaching a good campsite at Sourdough Creek, 4 miles, elevation 5000 feet. (Water and desperation camps can be found at several places before this point, but it's thirsty travel at best.) In another 1½ miles the summit and fire lookout cabin are attained, with all the previous views plus additional ones north up Ross Lake and west to the Pickets.

Loop Trail: From the parking lot, hike the unmarked ½-mile trail to the top of Diablo Dam and take the Diablo Lake passenger boat to the base of Ross Dam. (Boats leave 7:30 a.m. summer Saturdays only, 8:45 a.m. and 2:45 p.m.

daily; the fare is 50c.) Climb the road 400 feet in 1 mile to the top of Ross Dam (or ride a truck, fare $1.50), cross the dam, and find the Big Beaver Trail. In 3 miles is a junction. Turn left on the Sourdough Mountain trail (signed "Pierce Mountain Way") and climb 4000 feet in 5 miles to the 5985-foot lookout. Tread is indistinct or absent in the final rocky mile to the summit; watch for cairns. Descend to the parking lot via the "direct trail."

Round trip to TV tower 7 miles
Hiking time 7 hours
High point 4800 feet
Elevation gain 3900 feet
Best May through October
One day or backpack
USGS Diablo Dam and Ross Dam

Loop trip 14 miles
Allow 2 days
High point 5985 feet
Elevation gain 4500 feet
Best July through October
Park Service camping permit required

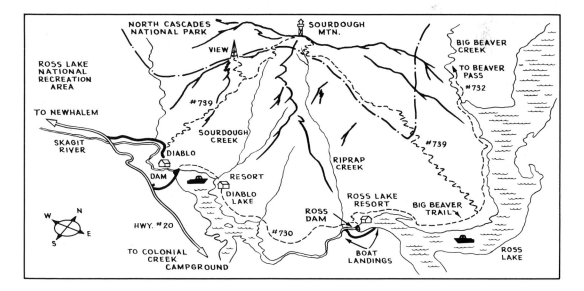

Thunder Creek trail

22 THUNDER CREEK

One of the master streams of the North Cascades, draining meltwater from an empire of glaciers. The first portion of the trail, easy walking, is nearly flat for miles, passing through groves of big firs, cedars, and hemlocks, with views of giant peaks. The route continues to a high pass amid these peaks; for experienced wilderness travelers, the trip from Thunder Creek over Park Creek Pass to the Stehekin River is a classic crossing of the range.

Drive State Highway 20 to Diablo Dam and 4 miles beyond to Colonial Creek Campground, where the trail begins, elevation 1200 feet.

The trail follows Thunder Arm of Diablo Lake

about 1 mile, then crosses Thunder Creek on a bridge and in another ½ mile comes to a junction with a trail climbing to Fourth of July Pass and Panther Creek; just beyond is a campsite. The Thunder Creek trail continues straight ahead on the sidehill, going up and down a little. To increase its hydroelectric capacity a minor amount, Seattle City Light is considering flooding this part of the valley, turning one of the few remaining examples of low-altitude virgin forest into another desolate mud flat and ruining one of the five remaining wilderness valleys in the North Cascades. Enough letters could change these plans.

At 5½ miles the way reaches campsites at and near the site of collapsed Middle Cabin. Along the trail are neck-stretching views to the summits of Snowfield and Colonial, and a look up the valley to Buckner, Boston, and Forbidden, some of the highest and grandest peaks in the North Cascades and carrying some of the largest glaciers in the range. The site of Middle Cabin is a good turnaround for a day or weekend trip. The trail to here offers one of the best forest hikes in the North Cascades and is open to travel early in the season and late.

At 7 miles the trail crosses Fisher Creek and climbs 1000 feet to a terrace above the valley floor, which here is a vast marshland. At 9 miles is a junction with Fisher Creek trail, left. Shortly thereafter a spur trail descends 1000 feet in 1 mile to the two Meadow Cabins, at the edge of the marsh with high and mighty peaks all around. The main trail goes along relatively flat to about 13 miles. Then, near where Skagit Queen Creek joins Thunder Creek, the way climbs steeply, gentles out somewhat in a hanging valley, and finally ascends steadily up and around the meadow flanks of Mt. Logan to 6040-foot Park Creek Pass, 18 miles, a narrow rock cleft usually full of snow. To continue down to the Stehekin River, see Hike 86.

Round trip to Middle Cabin site 11 miles
Hiking time 5-7 hours
High point 1800 feet
Elevation gain 600 feet
Best April through November
One day or backpack
USGS Ross Dam

Round trip to Park Creek Pass 36 miles
Allow 3-5 days
High point 6040 feet
Elevation gain 5000 feet
Best late July through October
USGS Ross Dam, Forbidden Peak,
Mt. Logan, Goode Mtn.
Park Service camping permit required

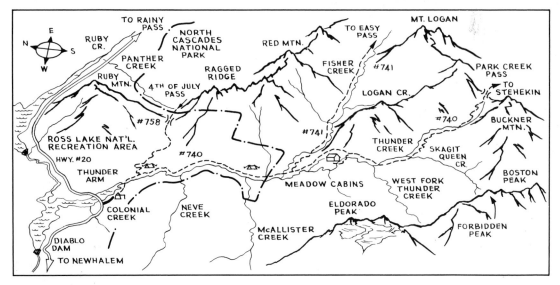

Lightning Creek bridge and Ross Lake

23 EAST BANK TRAIL

When full, the reservoir known as Ross Lake simulates nature and is, indeed, a beautiful inland fjord. Unfortunately, draw-downs for power production expose dreary wastelands of mud and stumps. Because of the low elevation, the hike along the lake is especially attractive in spring, when most mountain trails are deep in snow— sorry to say, that's when the lake is at its visual worst. Generally the reservoir is full from late June to October and at a lower level other months, the maximum draw-down of as much as 150 feet usually coming in March or April.

However, even when stumps are showing there still are grand views across the waters to high peaks. To learn the valley in all its moods, to enjoy the panoramas from end to end, hike the East Bank Trail, mostly through forest, a little along the shore, and finally detouring inland to reach Hozomeen Campground. The complete trip can be done in several days or any portion selected for a shorter walk.

Travel to Ross Dam (Hike 25) and arrange with Ross Lake Resort for water taxi service to the chosen beginning point and a pick-up at trip's end.

The trail starts at Ruby Creek Barn. From the boat landing, elevation 1600 feet, walk the old wagon road (which doesn't go anywhere anymore but once climbed from the now-drowned Ruby Inn on the Skagit River). The track soon becomes a trail. The first 5½ miles are in forest, ascending 900 feet to 2500-foot Hidden Hand Pass, then dropping near Rainbow Campground, reached by side-trail. Here begins the 6½-mile shore trail.

At 1½ miles from Rainbow Campground the way rounds a huge cliff; this section was blasted from solid rock a few feet from the full-reservoir line; the water is deep and when the lake is down it's an airy passage. The trail crosses Devils Creek Arm on a suspension bridge, passes campsites at Devils Dome Landing and Dry Creek Camp, and crosses Lightning Creek Arm on another suspension bridge; ¼ mile beyond is Lightning Creek Camp, where the lake trail officially ends. However, a way trail goes 3 more miles up the shore to the start of the Desolation Peak trail (Hike 25), a good side-trip for high views to complement the many low views gained thus far.

To continue to the north end of the lake, turn inland on the Lightning Creek trail, which climbs some 1000 feet of dry grass and pines to a magnificent overlook of the lake and peaks beyond, loses and gains elevation along an impressive and scenic gorge, and descends some 1000 feet to a campsite at Deer Lick Cabin beside the tumult of Lightning Creek, 4 miles from the lake.

Cross the creek on an enormous footlog flattened on the top. The trail proceeds upstream 3 miles to a junction with the Upper Freezeout trail; go left, fording (at least until a new bridge is built) Lightning Creek to the dark and spooky cedar groves of Nightmare Camp.

A steady, moderate ascent tops out in 3 miles at Willow Lake, a most unusual place. The lake gradually lowers once the snows are gone; by late summer, don't count on the polliwog-swarming water for drinkability. Around the shores are acres of muck stomped by herds of thirsty animals and also fields of tall grass and groves of aspen, a dramatic scene in a leaf-stirring breeze.

After an up-and-down walk through the forested trough of an ancient glacier, at 2 miles from Willow Lake is a side-trail going ¾ mile to the wooded shores and campsites of Hozomeen Lake, under towering cliffs of 8080-foot Hozomeen Peak. From the junction the trail descends gently 3 miles to the road-end at Hozomeen Campground, close to the waters (or, in season, an incredible vast desolation of mud and stumps) of Ross Lake. Hozomeen Campground is accessible from the Trans-Canada Highway via the 40-mile Silver Creek road starting 2 miles west of Hope.

One-way trip from Ruby Creek Barn to
Hozomeen 27 miles
Allow 3-4 days
High point about 3500 feet
Elevation gain about 5000 feet
Best mid-June to November
USGS map due 1974

One-way from Ruby Creek Barn to
Lightning Creek 13 miles
Best May to November

One-way from Rainbow to Lightning Creek 7¾ miles
Good all year except in midwinter
Park Service camping permit required

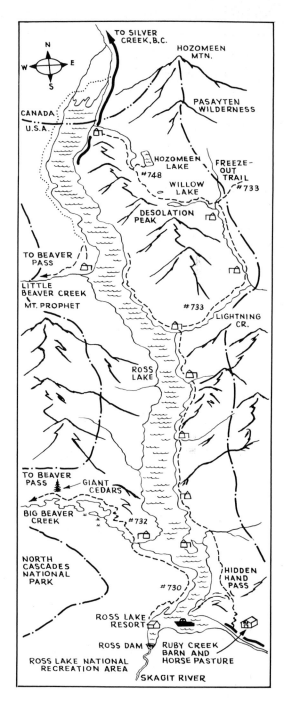

24 CRATER—DEVILS LOOP

Hoist packs and wander meadow ridges east of Ross Lake, encircling the far-below forests of Devils Creek and the cliffs and glaciers of 8928-foot Jack Mountain, "King of the Skagit," looking to peaks and valleys from Canada to Cascade Pass, the Pickets to the Pasayten. The trip is recommended as a loop but for shorter hikes the climaxes can be reached from either end.

Drive the North Cascades Highway 10 miles east from Colonial Creek Campground to the junction of Granite and Canyon Creeks (which merge to form Ruby Creek). The trailhead is across both creeks and, at the present time, there is no bridge across either of them. (Bridges are planned for 1975.) If lucky, a hiker may find a wobbly log across one or both of the creeks. During early summer the water is high, but by late August it is possible to ford. An alternative is to go back down the highway 3½ miles to the Panther Creek footbridge and return

up the north side of Ruby Creek in sight and sound of the highway. If the one-way trip to Devils Dome Landing is contemplated, starting at Panther Creek would be best. Either arrange for a boat to return you to White Water Landing at the head of Ruby Arm or hike the lakeshore trail 12 miles back to Panther Creek (Hike 23).

Once the trailhead is reached the work begins, as the trail gains 3400 feet in 4 miles. Fortunately the labor is mostly shaded by big trees and there is water at several well-spaced points and ultimately glimpses of peaks. At 4 miles, 5280 feet, is a junction.

For a compulsory side-trip, go left ¾ mile to the impressive cirque of 5800-foot Crater Lake. Just before the meadow-and-cliff-surrounded lake, a 2-mile trail climbs eastward to a lookout cabin on the broad 7054-foot east summit of Crater Mountain. From the lake a 2½-mile trail climbs westward to the site of a former lookout cabin on the 8128-foot main summit of Crater; the final ½ mile is for trained climbers only, but

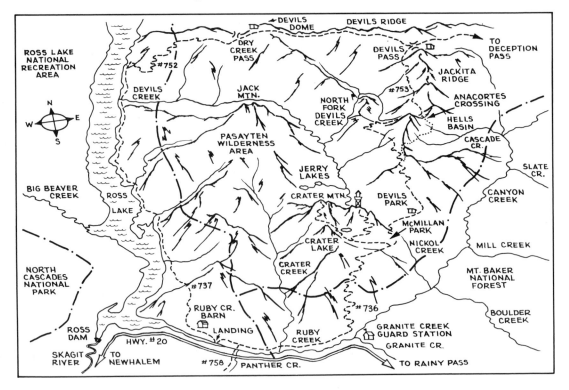

the panoramas are glorious long before difficulties begin.

From the 4-mile junction the trail descends the gently-sloping table of McMillan Park to Nickol Creek, 4900 feet, then climbs an old burn, loaded with blueberries in season, to Devils Park Shelter, 7 miles, 5600 feet. One can roam for hours in this plateau of meadows, clumps of alpine trees, and bleached snags.

The way now climbs northward along Jackita Ridge into a larch-dotted basin. At 9½ miles, some 6200 feet, is a junction of sorts. The well-maintained Jackita Ridge trail No. 753, the main route, continues up across the basin. The long-abandoned alternate trail, unsigned and with no tread at first, climbs to the 6700-foot ridge crest, drops more than 1000 feet into stark Hells Basin, regains the elevation to climb over Anacortes Crossing, and loses it again to rejoin the Jackita Ridge trail. The alternate "trail" is some 4 miles from junction to junction, shorter than the main route and infinitely scenic, but is so sketchy, rough, and tricky it is recommended strictly for experienced cross-country travelers.

From the unmarked junction at 9½ miles, the main route ascends a shoulder, switchbacks 800 feet down a slate scree to a rocky basin, rounds another shoulder and drops 300 feet into another open basin, climbs 500 feet to a third shoulder, drops 1000 feet through meadows and forest to the North Fork Devils Creek, and ascends upstream ½ mile to the 5500-foot junction with the trail to Anacortes Crossing—which is some 1500 feet and 1 mile from here, and another compulsory side-trip. Main-route distance to this junction, 14 miles.

The trail traverses sweeping gardens of Jackita Ridge, up some and down more, to Devils Pass, 20 miles, 5800 feet. The best camping is at Devils Pass Shelter, several hundred feet and ½ mile below the pass in a pretty meadow, reached via the Deception Pass trail and then a side-trail.

From Devils Pass the way turns west on the Devils Ridge trail, going through open woods near and on the ridge top, then climbing a lush basin to Skyline Camp, 18 miles, 6300 feet—a lovely spot for a campfire and a star-bright sleep, but with no water after the snows are gone.

A flower-and-blueberry traverse and a short

ridge-crest ascent lead, at 20 miles, to the 7000-foot site of the demolished Devils Dome Lookout, the highest elevation of the main-route trail.

Now down into a basin of waterfalls and boulders and blossoms and around the flowery slopes of Devils Dome, with time out for a compulsory, easy-walking, off-trail roaming to the 7400-foot summit and wide horizons. At 21½ miles is a ¼-mile side-trail to 6000-foot Bear Skull Shelter, the first possible camp if the loop is being done in the reverse direction and a long day— 5½ miles and 4500 feet—above Ross Lake.

At last the highlands must be left. The trail goes down the crest a short bit to Dry Creek Pass, descends forests and burn meadows to the only dependable creek (important for re-filling canteens when coming up this way!) at 28 miles, enters young trees (hot and grueling to climb in sunny weather) of an old burn, crosses the East Bank Trail and ¼ mile later, at 27 miles, ends at the lakeside camp of Devils Dome Landing.

One-way trip 27 miles to Devils Dome Landing,
complete loop 43 miles
Allow 5-9 days
Elevation gain 7500 feet or so
High point 7000 feet
Best mid-July through October
USGS Crater Mtn. (a portion only)
Forest Service wilderness permit required

25 DESOLATION PEAK

A forest fire swept the slopes bare in the 1920s, giving the peak its name. The lookout cabin on the summit gained fame in literary circles after being manned for a summer by the late Jack Kerouac, "beat generation" novelist and sometime Forest Service employee; some of his best writing describes the day-and-night, sunshine-and-storm panorama from the Methow to Mt. Baker to Canada, and especially the dramatic close-up of Hozomeen Peak, often seen from a distance but rarely from so near. Since Kerouac, the lookout frequently has been manned by poets. The steep trail is a scorcher in sunny weather; be sure to carry lots of water.

Drive State Highway 20 from Sedro Woolley through Newhalem and on to Diablo Dam and across the dam to the Seattle City Light dock. Take the boat up Diablo Lake to the foot of Ross Dam. Boats leave Diablo 7:30 a.m. (summer Saturdays only), 8:45 a.m., and 2:45 p.m. Boats leave Ross 8 a.m. (summer Saturdays only), 9:20 a.m., 2 p.m. (Sunday only), and 3:15 p.m. Ross Lake Resort meets all boats with a passenger truck providing a lift (for $1.50) 400 feet and 1 mile to the top of Ross Dam; one can, of course, hike the road if desired. Arrange with the resort for a water taxi ride up the lake to Desolation Landing and a pick-up at trip's end. For information in advance, write Ross Lake Resort, Rockport, Washington, or telephone Newhalem 7-4735. (Boat-owners can bring their own craft to Ross Lake via Canada but there is no safe moorage at the trailhead and the bank is too abrupt to pull a heavy boat out of the water.)

The trail starts steep and stays steep, climbing 1000 feet a mile. For such a desolate-appearing hillside there is a surprising amount of shade, the way often tunneling through dense thickets of young trees. This is fortunate, because the sun can be unmerciful on the occasional barren bluffs.

Views come with every rocky knoll. In ½ mile see a small grove of birch trees. In 2 miles re-fill canteens from a spring—which may, however, dry up in a rainless summer. At 3 miles the trail enters steep, open meadows and at 4 miles is the ridge crest. A high bump remains to be climbed over before the lookout is sighted. The flower fields include some species, sunflowers (balsam root) and erigonum, which properly "belong" on the east slopes of the Cascades.

The horizons are broad and rich. Only Mt. Baker stands out distinctly among the distant peaks, though those who know them can single out Shuksan, the Pickets, Colonial, Snowfield, Eldorado, and scores of other great mountains. Closer in, the spectacular glacier of 8928-foot Jack Mountain dominates the south. To the north rise the vertical walls of Hozomeen, the south

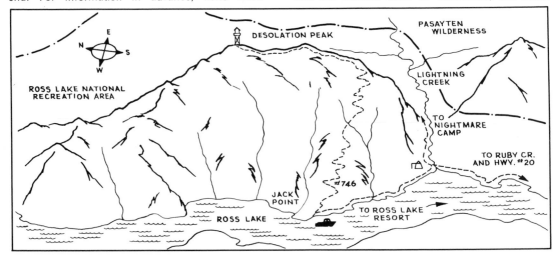

Jack Mountain, left, and Ross Lake from Desolation Peak

peak so far climbed by but a single route, with many virgin cliffs remaining to tempt the experts. West across Ross Lake are the deep valleys of Noname Creek, Arctic Creek, and Little Beaver Creek. East are the high, meadow-roaming ridges of the Cascade Crest and the Pasayten country.

The fjord-like Ross Lake reservoir, dotted by tiny boats of fishermen, is the feature of the scene. Unfortunately, from fall to spring miles of dreary mudflats are exposed as the reservoir is drawn down; plan the trip for summer, when the full reservoir adorns rather than desecrates the Ross Lake National Recreation Area.

Camping is splendid in the high meadows in good weather, but water is from snowfields only and usually rare or non-existent by late July.

Because of boat schedules, the best plan for a weekend trip is to travel the first day to Lightning Creek Campground, camp there overnight, and do the climb the second day, with an early enough start to be back at Desolation Landing (where camping is not permitted) in time to make connections down Ross and Diablo Lakes.

Round trip from Desolation Landing 9 miles
Hiking time 7 hours
Allow 2-3 days
High point 6085 feet
Elevation gain 4400 feet
Best mid-June to September
One day (from the lake) or backpack
USGS map due 1974
Park Service camping permit required

26 BEAVER LOOP

This loop hike from Ross Lake to close views of the Picket Range and back to Ross Lake offers perhaps the supreme days-long forest experience in the North Cascades. The 27-mile trip up the

Seattle City Light wants to flood this part of Big Beaver valley.

Little Beaver valley and down the Big Beaver passes through groves of enormous cedars, old and huge Douglas firs and hemlocks, glimmery-ghostly silver fir, lush alder, young firs recently established after a fire, and many more species and ages of trees as well. And there are brawling rivers, marshes teeming with wildlife, and awesome looks at Picket glaciers and walls.

Travel by car and boat to Ross Lake Resort (Hike 25) and arrange for taxi service up the lake and a pick-up at trip's end. The loop trip (or day or weekend hikes) can begin at either end; the Little Beaver start is described here.

After a scenic ride up Ross Lake, debark at Little Beaver Landing; a campground here, elevation 1600 feet. The trail starts by switchbacking 800 feet to get above a canyon, then loses most of the hard-won elevation. At 4½ miles is Perry Creek Shelter, an easy ford-or-footlog crossing of several branches of the creek, and a passage along the edge of a lovely marsh. At 9 miles is Redoubt Creek; scout around for a footlog. At 11½ miles is Stillwell Shelter, 2450 feet, and a junction.

The Little Beaver trail goes upstream 6 miles and 2800 feet to Whatcom Pass (Hike 15). Take the Big Beaver trail, which crosses Little Beaver Creek on a footlog and climbs a steep mile to Beaver Pass, 3620 feet. The trail goes nearly on the level a mile to Beaver Pass Shelter, the midpoint of the loop, 13½ miles from Little Beaver Landing and 13 miles from Big Beaver Landing.

An hour or three should be allowed here for an easy off-trail side-trip. Pick a way easterly and upward from the shelter, gaining 500-1000 feet through forest and brush to any of several open [1] slopes that give a staggering look into rough-and-icy Luna Cirque; the higher the climb the better the view.

Descend steeply from Beaver Pass into the head of Big Beaver Creek; two spots on the trail offer impressive glimpses of Luna Cirque. At 6 miles from Beaver Pass Shelter (7 miles from Big Beaver Landing on Ross Lake) the Big Beaver tumbles down a 200-foot-deep gorge; a good view here of Elephant Butte and up McMillan Creek toward McMillan Cirque. The moderately up-and-down trail crosses recent avalanches which have torn avenues through forest, passes enormous boulders fallen from cliffs above, and goes by a marsh.

At 7½ miles from Beaver Pass Shelter (6 miles from Ross Lake) is 10 Mile Shelter (10 miles from the old, drowned Skagit river trail), the only legal campsite between Ross Lake and Beaver Pass. The way now enters the glorious lower reaches of Big Beaver Creek, a broad valley of marshes and ancient trees, including the largest stand of western red cedar (some an estimated 1000 years old) remaining in the United States. Seattle City Light plans to flood the lower 6 miles of the valley by raising Ross Dam; this absolutely must not be allowed to happen.

Passing one superb marsh after another, one grove of giant cedars after another, the trail crosses Thirtyninemile Creek at 4 miles from Ross Lake. At 3 miles from Ross Lake the trail for the first time touches the banks of Big Beaver Creek, milky-green water running over golden pebbles. Finally the trail reaches Big Beaver Landing, from which a ¼-mile trail leads left to Big Beaver Campground.

There are two ways to return to Ross Dam. One is by hiking the 6-mile Big Beaver trail, which branches right from the Big Beaver trail at a junction ¼ mile before the landing. The second is to arrange in advance with Ross Lake Resort to be picked up at Big Beaver Landing; the pickup should be in time to make connections with the City Light boat on Diablo Lake.

Loop trip 27 miles
Allow 3-5 days
High point 3620 feet
Elevation gain about 3500 feet, including ups and downs
Best June through October
USGS map due 1974
Park Service camping permit required

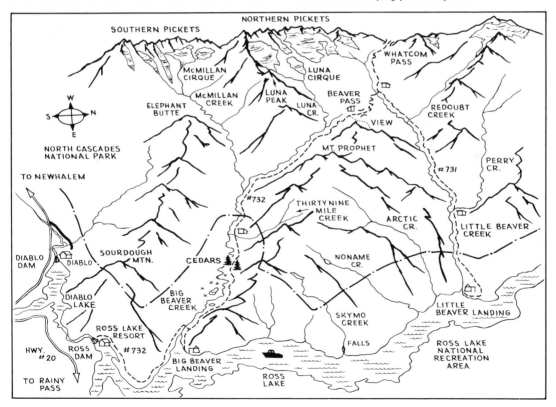

27 EASY PASS

Dramatic are the views, but the trail definitely is **not** easy. Prospectors found this the easiest (maybe the only) pass across Ragged Ridge, and thus the name. However, the tread is rough, at times very steep, in spots muddy, and if that's not enough, progress is blocked almost at the start by a raging creek. Finally, the pass area is very small, extremely fragile, and camping is not allowed.

Drive the ineffable North Cascades Highway 21.5 miles east from Colonial Creek Campground or 6.2 miles west from Rainy Pass to an unmarked spur road and tiny parking area, elevation 3700 feet.

A short 1/4 mile the trail blanks out on the bank of swift, cold Granite Creek. Lucky hikers may find a footlog a hundred feet upstream. If the log is too scary, or not there anymore, the alternatives are to risk the ford—or choose another destination.

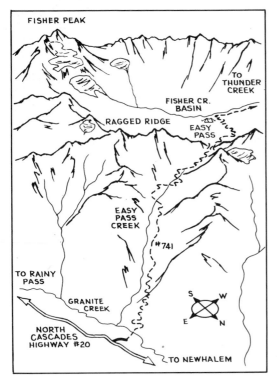

From the far bank the trail climbs for 2 miles in woods to the edge of a huge avalanche fan, 5200 feet, under the rugged peaks of Ragged Ridge. It now may become elusive, buried in snow or greenery. (Make very sure not to lose the path: cross-country exploration here is agonizing.) The way goes over the avalanche fan and Easy Pass Creek and begins a long, steep ascent along the south side of the valley to the pass. Flower gardens. Small groves of trees. Watercourses. Boulder fields. Up, always up. The route crosses Easy Pass Creek twice more and at about 6100 feet comes within a few feet of a gushing spring, the source of the creek. Tread shoveled from a steep talus slope leads to the 6500-foot pass, a narrow, larch-covered saddle.

For the best views walk several hundred feet beyond the summit and look down 1300 feet into Fisher Basin and out to glaciers and walls of 9080-foot Mt. Logan.

To reach permitted campsites, switchback down some 1½ miles to the edge of Fisher Basin (5200 feet), or descend Fisher Creek to Middle Cabin on Thunder Creek (Hike 22), or continue to Diablo Lake, 22 miles from Easy Pass.

Round trip 7 miles
Hiking time 7 hours
High point 6500 feet
Elevation gain 2800 feet
Best mid-July through September
One day or backpack
USGS Mt. Arriva
Park Service camping permit required

Douglas Glacier and 9081-foot Mt. Logan from Easy Pass. Glacier carved Fisher Creek valley in foreground

28 LOOKOUT MOUNTAIN— MONOGRAM LAKE

Take your pick: a fire lookout with a commanding view of North Cascades peaks and valleys, or a cirque lake, a fine basecamp for roaming, nestled in the side of a heather-covered ridge.

Drive State Highway 20 to Marblemount and continue east 7½ miles on the Cascade River road to the 1200-foot trailhead between Lookout and Monogram Creeks.

The trail climbs steeply in a series of short switchbacks along the spine of the forested ridge between the two creeks, gaining 2400 feet in the 2½ miles to a campsite at the first dependable water, a branch of Lookout Creek at 3600 feet. At 2¾ miles is a junction, elevation 4200 feet.

Lookout Mountain: Go left from the junction, shortly emerging into meadow and switchbacking relentlessly upward. The tread here may be hard to find and difficult to walk. In 1½ miles from the junction, gaining 1500 feet, the 5719-foot summit is attained.

Flowers all around—and views. Look north and

Eldorado Peak from Lookout Mountain

west to the Skagit River valley, southeast and below to the Cascade River. Mountains everywhere, dominated by giant Eldorado Peak. About ¼ mile below the summit, in a small flat, is a spring that runs most of the summer; magnificent camps here for enjoyment of the scenery in sunset and dawn—but disaster camps in a storm.

Monogram Lake: Traverse right from the junction, watching for blazes and strips of plastic tape, on a steep, lightly-timbered hillside. The unmaintained track may be faint in places. In about 1 mile from the junction the trail leaves trees for meadow and in another mile crosses a creek, climbs to a 5400-foot crest with broad views, and descends to 4800-foot Monogram Lake, usually snowbound through July. Nice campsites around the meadow shores but wood is scarce so carry a stove.

The lake is a superb base for wanderings. For one, climb open slopes to the southeast and then follow the ridge northerly to a 5607-foot knoll looking down into Marble Creek and across to the splendor of 8868-foot Eldorado—a closer and even better view of the peak than that from Lookout Mountain. Continue on the ridge for

more flowers, then drop through gardens to the lake. For a more ambitious tour, ascend meadows on the southern extension of Teebone Ridge and ramble to the 6844-foot south summit of Little Devil Peak, with looks down to small glaciers. Climbers can continue on and on along the rocky-and-snowy ridge, but hikers must stop when the terrain gets too rough for party experience.

Round trip to Lookout Mountain 10 miles
Hiking time 9 hours
High point 5719 feet
Elevation gain 4500 feet
Best mid-July through October
One day or backpack
USGS Marblemount

Round trip to Monogram Lake 10 miles
Hiking time 9 hours
High point 5400 feet
Elevation gain 4200 feet in, 600 feet out
Best mid-July through October
One day or backpack
Park Service camping permit required

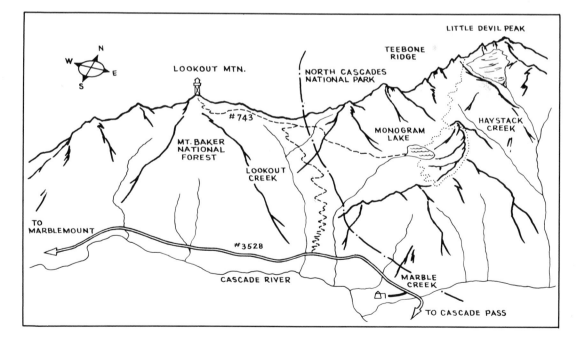

29 HIDDEN LAKE PEAKS

Flower fields, heather meadows, ice-carved rocks, and snow-fed waterfalls on an alpine ridge jutting into an angle of the Cascade River valley, providing an easy-to-reach viewpoint of the wilderness North Cascades from Eldorado on the north through the Ptarmigan Traverse to Dome Peak on the south.

Drive State Highway 20 to Marblemount and continue east on the Cascade River road 9½ miles (2 miles past the Marble Creek bridge) to Sibley Creek road No. 3503. Turn left 4.2 miles to road-end in a logging patch, elevation 3600 feet.

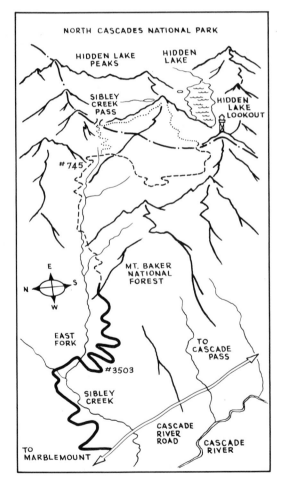

Trail begins on bulldozer track, entering forest in ¼ mile and switchbacking upward 1 mile. The way then emerges from trees into lush brush and crosses Sibley Creek. (Some years avalanche snow may linger in the creek bottom all summer, in which case look for obvious trail cut through very steep sidehill greenery.) The trail switchbacks up alder clumps and deep grass and flowers to a re-crossing of Sibley Creek at 2½ miles, 5200 feet. Note, here, the abrupt and striking transition from metamorphic to granitic rocks, the first supporting richly-green grassy-type flora, the other dominated by heather. Just pass the crossing is a minimal campsite.

Sibley Creek Pass: Leave the trail at the second crossing and follow your nose upward, scrambling very steep and slippery, then easy meadows ½ mile to 6100-foot Sibley Creek Pass on the exact boundary of the North Cascades National Park. The view is down to Cascade River forests and up the valley to Cascade Pass and out everywhere to alpine magnificence.

The pass is the recommended destination for short-trippers and hikers lacking experience in snow travel. The views are at least as glorious as those elsewhere on the ridge and the route is free of tricky snowfields much earlier in the summer. From the pass, a moderate rock scramble leads to the 7088-foot highest summit of the Hidden Lake Peaks.

Hidden Lake Lookout: From the second crossing the trail traverses wide-open heather-and-waterfall slopes (several nice good-weather camps), then rounds a corner and climbs. One snow-filled gully may be too treacherous for hikers lacking ice axes. If so, don't attempt to cross, but instead go straight uphill to find a safe detour, or turn back and visit Sibley Creek Pass. The trail may be snow-covered at other points but by proceeding straight ahead the tread can be picked up. At 3½ miles is a tiny basin, a lovely non-storm campsite. The abandoned lookout cabin can now be seen atop cliffs. Continue a short way, usually on a gentle snowfield, to the 6600-foot saddle and look down to Hidden Lake and out to a world of wild peaks.

Though it's only ½ mile and 300 feet from the saddle to the broader views of the 6890-foot lookout, parts of the trail may be lost in ex-

Snow-covered Hidden Lake and (left to right) Forbidden Peak, Boston Peak, Sahale Peak, Cascade Pass, and Mt. Johannesburg

tremely-dangerous snow, suited only for trained climbers. Even without snow the final section of trail is airy.

From the saddle an easy walk over loose boulders leads to the 7088-foot peak. Or descend rough talus to the 5733-foot lake, ordinarily snowbound through most of the summer. Good campsites on benches near the outlet, but as with all other camps in the area, wood is scarce so carry a stove.

Round trip to Sibley Creek Pass 6 miles
Hiking time 5 hours
High point 6100 feet
Elevation gain 2500 feet
Best mid-July through October
One day or backpack
USGS Eldorado Peak and Sonny Boy Lakes

Round trip to Hidden Lake Lookout 8 miles
Hiking time 8 hours
High point 6890 feet
Elevation gain 3300 feet
Best August through October
One day or backpack
Park Service camping permit required at Hidden Lake

Snowking Mountain and Snowking Lake from Kindy Ridge

30 KINDY RIDGE—FOUND LAKE

A close view of seldom-approached Snowking Mountain, high meadows to explore, and six alpine lakes for camping and prowling. **However, this is an off-trail route, not easy,** recommended only for experienced cross-country travelers.

Drive State Highway 20 to Marblemount and continue east 14½ miles on the Cascade River road. Turn right on Kindy Creek road No. 354, crossing the Cascade River and following road No. 354 to road No. 354A, which switchbacks to the road-end at a collapsed bridge and a patch of salvage logging in the Found Creek burn, elevation 2200 feet.

There are two ways to go. The most common is to cross the bridge on foot and proceed up the steep ridge to the west, there finding the long-abandoned Found Creek trail. The open areas are covered with brush and fallen logs so a party choosing this route should get into forest as quickly as possible. Be prepared for a very steep scramble near the ridge top.

The other way is to backtrack down the logging road ¼ mile or more to a point where the uphill bank can be easily climbed. Then strike directly up the moderately-steep forest. Brush is something of an obstacle, but game trails when headed in the right direction, are helpful. By keeping to the steepest part of the ridge, the old Found Creek trail is eventually intersected at the top of a 5116-foot wooded knoll.

It is probably best to return by the same route chosen for the ascent. Memorize the trail intersection in order to find the way. Don't clutter up the forest with plastic markers. Daniel Boone got around without them.

From the knoll, drop down on the trail 300 feet to the saddle, leave the trail, and climb 1000 feet to the 5791-foot viewpoint. Trees are few so the way is obvious; generally trend right for the easiest grade.

To see all the view, move about the broad summit—being careful of fissures, some of them deep, that split the rock. Snowking Mountain and its glaciers are the big reward but there are dividends in all directions—Eldorado, Boston, Formidable, and Resplendent. Four beautiful lakes lie below. Two of them—Neori, the lower, and Skare, the upper—are clear blue water. Snowking Lake, the largest, and a nameless pond above it are a striking turquoise. The other two lakes, Found and Cyclone, are out of sight.

Kindy Ridge is a splendid day hike but waterless and thus campless. For basecamps, since the country is of the kind that cries out for exploration, pick up the Found Creek trail at the 4800-foot saddle between the two knolls and descend 1 mile to 4000-foot Found Lake, gateway to the other lakes and the slopes of Snowking Mountain.

Round trip to Kindy Ridge viewpoint about 4 miles
Hiking time 8 hours
High point 5791 feet
Elevation gain 4000 feet in, 300 feet out
Best July through October
One day
USGS Sonny Boy Lakes and Snowking Mtn.

Round trip to Found Lake about 6 miles
Hiking time 12 hours
High point 4800 feet
Elevation gain 2900 feet in, 1100 feet out
Best mid-July through October
Backpack
Forest Service wilderness permit required

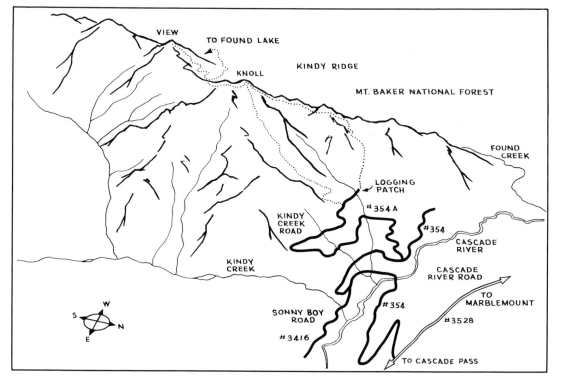

Cloud-capped Hurry-Up Peak from Middle Fork Cascade River Valley

31 MIDDLE FORK CASCADE RIVER

Standing on a high summit, looking out to horizons and down to valleys, expands the spirit. Standing in a low valley, looking up from forests to summits, gives humility. To know the North Cascades a person must walk low as well as high. This valley is one of the "great holes" of the range, lush with forests and avalanche greenery, offering awesome glimpses of splendid peaks and glaciers.

Drive State Highway 20 to Marblemount and continue east 16½ miles on the Cascade River road to South Fork Cascade River road No. 3404. Turn right 1½ miles to road-end in a logging patch, elevation 1800 feet.

Walk 500 feet up a logging spur to find an unmarked, miner-built path that traverses the hillside about ½ mile to intersect Middle Fork Cascade trail No. 767, the "Spaulding Mine Trail."

The trail climbs steeply through forest, the nearby river a steady roar of sometimes-seen, always-heard cataracts. At the 2400-foot lip of the hanging valley the way gentles out in a superb stand of big trees. At 2 miles, 2880 feet, is a small creek; for a side-trip leave the trail here, walk several hundred feet to the river, and look up avalanche-swept Cleve Creek to a glacier on the west ridge of Mt. Formidable.

Beyond the creek crossing the trail—apparently maintained only occasionally, and then by mine-stock salesmen—becomes a sometime thing, often requiring a bit of looking around to stay on the tread. Watch for blazes, sawn logs, plastic flags, and blotches of paint on trees. Though slow the walking is easy enough, in pleasant forest with glimpses of high ice.

At about 2½ miles is a short passage through alder and green stuff and views up the burned-off slopes of Mt. Johannesburg to the foot of tall cliffs. Now forest again, now a gravel wash sweeping down straight as a shot from Johannesburg, now more forest. The trail is still decent if sketchy. Then comes a monstrous swath of avalanche greenery, bracken fern, willow, alder, with exciting views up the valley. Somewhere around 3 miles, 3200 feet, perhaps on a gravel bar of the river, all pretense of trail is lost; the "Spaulding Mine" is in the vicinity.

Hikers of moderate ambition can turn back anywhere amid increasing difficulties, well-rewarded by the forests and the glimpses of the Middle Cascade Glacier, the cliffs of Johannesburg and Formidable, and the summits of Magic, Hurryup, and Spider.

Travelers experienced in off-trail bush-beating and meadow-scrambling and rock-hopping can see more. When the trail becomes too much trouble, climb boulders of a convenient tributary to a high viewpoint. Or follow gravel bars, with interludes of rough brush, to the toe of the Middle Cascade Glacier. Or ascend open slopes into the lonesome alpine basin beneath the summit of Johannesburg. Those with the energy and desire to explore can find campsites by the river.

A special tip: Until the Forest Service decides to maintain this trail, the best season for travel is early summer before the avalanche greenery achieves maximum growth.

This magnificent valley is in neither the adjoining Glacier Peak Wilderness Area nor the adjoining North Cascades National Park, a situation which **must** be rectified.

Round trip to trail's end 6 miles
Hiking time 6-hours
High point 3200-feet
Elevation gain 1400 feet plus ups and-downs
Best June through October
One day or backpack
USGS Sonny Boy Lakes and Cascade Pass

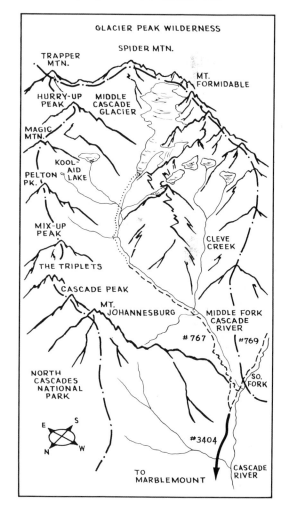

32 SOUTH FORK CASCADE RIVER

A superb wilderness valley. The first 3 miles offer an easy and rewarding afternoon stroll through forests beside a loud river; this portion of the walk can be done as early as June. Then the going gets tough, but experienced and energetic hikers able to follow the difficult trail to its end gain a dramatic view of the South Cascade Glacier flowing into a small lake.

Drive State Highway 20 to Marblemount and continue east 16½ miles on the Cascade River road to South Fork Cascade River road No. 3404. Turn right 1½ miles to road-end in a logging patch, elevation 1800 feet.

Find South Fork Cascade River trail No. 769

Puffball Mushrooms along South Cascade River trail

and hike an up-and-down ½ mile to a footlog crossing, 1800 feet, of the Middle Fork Cascade River.

The trail beyond here was abandoned for years, but in 1969 the first 2½ miles were cleared out and now will be maintained annually. There are no present plans to improve the rest of the trail or extend it.

The way meanders up and down the hillside above the river, occasionally plunging through patches of head-high brush, sometimes coming close to the river; gravel bars provide picnic sites for day-trippers and campsites for backpackers. At about 4 miles the trail climbs very steeply,

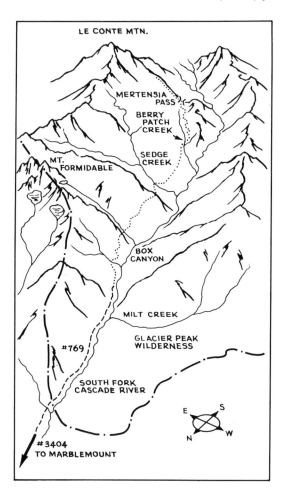

gaining some 800 feet in less than ½ mile to detour around the Box Canyon.

At 5 miles the trail crosses Sedge Creek on a log with a cable handrail and in ½ mile more climbs steeply along Berry Patch Creek to Mertensia Pass, 5000 feet.

Now the country is open and off-trail travel is relatively easy for the experienced hiker. To get the best views follow up the ridge from the pass toward LeConte Mountain. The higher the climb the more one sees of the South Cascade Glacier, 1½ miles away, with Mt. Resplendent above and chilly, moraine-surrounded South Cascade Lake below.

Up-and-down scrambling from Mertensia Pass leads to the shores of the 5292-foot lake; campsites amid the glacial debris.

Campsites in the first 3 miles, then none until the meadow below Mertensia Pass.

Round trip to South Cascade Lake 18 miles
Allow 2-3 days
High point 5292 feet
Elevation gain 3400 feet plus ups and downs
Best late July through September
USGS Sonny Boy Lakes, Cascade Pass, Dome Peak
Forest Service wilderness permit required

Middle Fork Bridge

Mt. Johannesburg from Boston Basin

33 BOSTON BASIN

One of the most spectacular alpine meadows in the Northwest, the flower fields surrounded by rugged peaks and topped by a vigorous glacier. However, the trail is hard to find, in poor condition, and recommended only for experienced hikers. (A new trail probably will be built ultimately, date unknown.)

Drive to the Cascade River road-end (Hike 34), elevation 3600 feet. Climb the new Cascade Pass trail about 17 switchbacks, roughly 1 mile, to a junction with the old, historic, and abandoned Cascade Pass trail at an elevation of about 4400 feet. Go left about ½ mile down the old trail, shortly crossing Soldier Boy Creek, then losing hard-won elevation to about 3800 feet. Watch carefully for a faint path, perhaps marked by plastic strips, going right and uphill from the trail.

Follow the boot-built track, and such blazes, rock cairns, and bits of colored tape as can be seen, up and along steep woods, across a large boulder field, over logs and through brush. In about ½ mile of rough, slippery walking look down to garbage of the Diamond Mine; soon thereafter intersect the old Boston Basin trail.

From the intersection things improve; old but good tread leads through a short bit of woods and then across a ½-mile-wide swath of avalanche greenery, down which roar Midas Creek and Morning Star Creek. Next come switchbacks in deep forest to a broken-down mine cabin; bad-weather campsites here, no scenery.

About ¼ mile from the wrecked cabin the trail emerges from timber and swings around the foot of an open moraine to a raging torrent; boulder-hop across and climb to a viewpoint atop the moraine. Look up to the fearsome cliffs and spires of Forbidden Peak and Mt. Torment, and to the nameless glacier falling from Boston and Sahale Peaks, and across the valley to the mile-high wall of Johannesburg and its finger-like hanging glaciers.

For one exploration of Boston Basin, traverse and climb westward over moraines and creeks to rich-green, marmot-whistling flower fields and beyond to waterfalls pouring down ice-polished buttresses under Mt. Torment.

For another exploration, look for intermittent tread of an old miners' trail that ascends a moraine crest to tunnels and artifacts close under Sharkfin Tower, right next to the glacier falling from Boston Peak.

And a spectacular for the experienced highland rambler only: climb moraines and meadows to Sahale Arm and descend to Cascade Pass; those capable of doing the tour need no further clues.

Enough said; there's a world of private wandering in Boston Basin. However, good campsites are rare and none are really comfortable. Water and scenery are plentiful but firewood is as scarce as the gold the miners sought—carry a stove and plan not to be here overnight in bad weather.

Round trip to first high moraine 7 miles
Hiking time 8 hours
High point 6200 feet
Elevation gain 3200 feet in, 600 feet out
Best July through October
One day or backpack
USGS Cascade Pass, Forbidden Peak
Park Service camping permit required

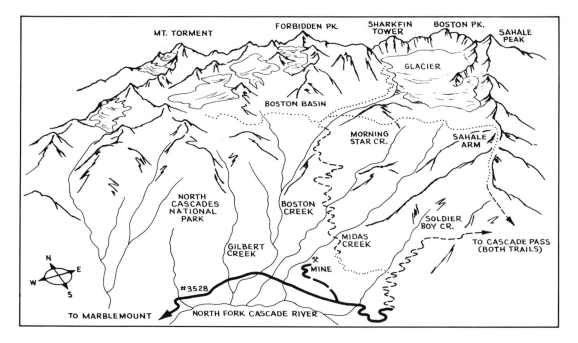

Cascade Pass and Eldorado Peak

34 CASCADE PASS—SAHALE ARM

An historic pass, crossed by Indians from time immemorial, by explorers and prospectors for a century, and recently become famous as one of the most rewarding easy hikes in the North Cascades. But the beauty of the pass is only the beginning. An idyllic ridge climbs toward the sky amid flowers and creeklets of sparkling water and views that expand with every step.

Drive State Highway 20 to Marblemount and continue east 25 miles on the Cascade River road to road-end parking lot and trailhead, 3600 feet.

Warning: At 21 miles the road makes a steep and rough double switchback that should stop the casual tourist inexperienced on mountain roads; the "mine-to-market" track stays rugged from here on and has torn the guts out of more than one car. Nevertheless, swarms of drivers, many of whom have no business here, take the risk. (If in doubt, park below the double switch-

back and walk the track, enjoying the views and the creeks without the hypertension caused by worrying about damage to the car and about the dangerous maneuvering required when you meet another car.) The road forks about 3 miles beyond the double switchback; ignore the left fork to the Diamond Mine and go right 1 mile to the parking lot, which usually is full-to-overflowing every summer weekend. (If possible, do the hike on a weekday. Traffic jams are already unpleasant on this nerve-wracking road and may soon force private autos to be barred on weekends, replaced by National Park Service shuttle-bus service.

Unlike the miserable road, which was not intended for heavy use and never should have been built in the first place, the wide, new trail, at an almost-flat 10 percent grade, was designed to accommodate the masses. In some 33 switchbacks the "highway" climbs forest about 2 miles, then makes a long, gently-ascending traverse through parkland and meadows to

Cascade Pass, 3½ miles, 5400 feet. Spectacular as the scenery is from road-end, the hiker runs out of superlatives before reaching the pass. The 8200-foot mass of Johannesburg dominates: hardly an hour goes by that a large or small avalanche doesn't break loose from its hanging glacier; several times a summer a huge section of ice roars all the way to the valley floor.

Cascade Pass retains its famous vistas, but in the past 20 years the meadows have been loved nearly to death. The National Park Service is now seeking to rehabilitate the flower gardens and thus camping and fires are forbidden. For campsites, descend ½ mile east of the pass to the forest near tiny Pelton Lake or climb to above 7000 feet on Sahale Arm.

One side-trip from the pass, easy and quick, is the wandering way south up the meadow crest of Mixup Arm. Another is to Trapper Lake (Hike 35).

To explore the sky, climb north on a steep and narrow trail through meadows; find the start a few feet over the east side of the pass below a rock outcrop. In 1 mile and 800 feet the trail reaches the ridge crest and a junction. The right fork descends heather 800 feet in 1 mile to 5385-foot Doubtful Lake, a great hike in its own right.

However, Sahale Arm calls. Walk the old prospectors' trail up and along the gentle ridge of flowers, and up some more. Look down to the waterfall-loud cirque of Doubtful Lake and east into the Stehekin River valley. Look west to Forbidden Peak and the huge Inspiration Glacier on Eldorado. Look south to nine small glaciers on the first line of peaks beyond Cascade Pass. Walking higher, see range upon range of ice and spires, finally including the volcano of Glacier Peak.

Round trip to Cascade Pass 7½ miles
Hiking time 5 hours
High point 5400 feet
Elevation gain 1800 feet
Best mid-July through October
One day
USGS Cascade Pass

Round trip to Sahale Arm 11 miles
Hiking time 10 hours
High point 7600 feet
Elevation gain 4000 feet
Best mid-July through October
One day or backpack
Park Service camping permit required

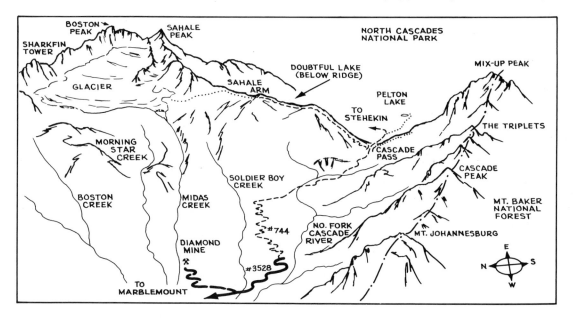

35   TRAPPER LAKE

An alpine jewel: a deep lake of blue-green water beneath tall cliffs of high and wild peaks, fed by a glacier whose snout nearly reaches the shore.

There are two approaches, one difficult, the other worse. The latter is from the Stehekin River trail, fording the lusty stream about 1/4 mile above Cottonwood Camp and climbing 1400 feet of tough brush on a faint, straight-up track beaten by hardy and hungry fishermen. The former, from Cascade Pass, is described here, being probably the most popular and most scenic.

Descend east from Cascade Pass (Hike 34) about 1/2 mile. Leave the trail just before it enters forest and drop down a boot-built path to campsites beside Pelton Creek. Cross the creek and follow the water to tiny Pelton Lake, 4600 feet. Climb open slopes to the east (on the north side of Pelton Peak), finding a faint and intermittent path up heather to a 5400-foot ridge. From the crest see a very steep green ridge, 300 feet higher, connecting Pelton Peak and a 5973-foot knob. This is the next objective. Where the hillside is the steepest there is an ancient and narrow but quite adequate trail.

The view from the 5700-foot ridge is tremendous, dominated by 7530-foot Trapper Mountain and a far-below corner of 4200-foot Trapper Lake. For most walkers the viewpoint is enough of a trip—especially when they think of the strenuous upward return should they go farther. Round-trip time from Cascade Pass to here is about 4 hours.

However, the sparkling water is enticing. The way to the lake is down a super-steep green wall. Be careful to stamp solid footholds—flowers and heather can be as slippery and treacherous as snow, especially when wet. The route moderates a bit, enters a jungle of mountain ash, and steepens again. Several paths are beaten through the brush. Be sure to find one—otherwise the thicket is impassable.

Bushes end abruptly at the valley bottom and all is easy to the lakeshore and numerous campsites. Not much further exploring is available to a hiker: a steep slope of hard snow effectively prevents circling the lake to the right and dense brush makes the left side unpleasant.

Round trip from Cascade Pass to lake 8 miles
Hiking time 7 hours
High point 5700 feet
Elevation gain 1200 feet in, 2400 feet out
Best mid-July through September
Backpack
USGS Cascade Pass and Goode Mtn.
Park Service camping permit required

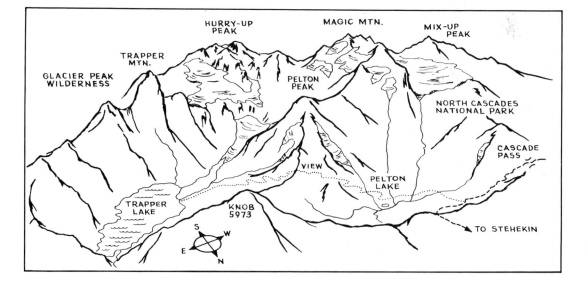

Hurry-Up Peak from trail to Trapper Lake

36 ROUND MOUNTAIN

A Swiss-type view of the Stillaguamish valley. Look down on farm pastures which from this distance seem as tiny as any in the Alps. Watch ant-sized cars creep along the highway. Trace meanders of the Stillaguamish River beneath the towering, glacier-hung peaks of Whitehorse and Three Fingers. The trail will be kept in a primitive condition with minimum maintenance as a hikers-only route.

Drive Highway 530 east from Arlington to 5 miles west of Darrington. Turn north on Swede Heaven Road (387th N.E.), cross the river, and go downvalley a short bit. Turn right on the first forest road angling upward, road No. 3403, and continue 12½ miles to a junction with spur road No. 3403E. Find the unmarked trailhead 500 feet along this spur, elevation 3500 feet.

The trail contours through woods, passing above several logging patches, and comes to a saddle in a ridge with an old clearcut on the north slope and possibly a new one on the south. The way follows the fire line along the narrow ridge crest to a high point, drops a few feet, goes by some ancient trail signs, and starts up a steep hillside. In some places the path is completely overgrown with huckleberry and young fir trees. If tread is lost, return to the last-for-sure spot and try again—once off the route, progress becomes hopeless.

After traversing the high-angle mountainside from east to west, climbing steadily, at about 1 mile the way heads sharply up, gaining a tough 300 feet; open meadows close above offer inspiration. With an abrupt transition from steep forest to rolling heather slopes, the trail enters a large basin and disappears beside a small creek and possible campsite, 4900 feet.

Some hikers will be content with a picnic by the stream and a good viewpoint at the basin edge. Others will want to scramble the last ½ mile and 500 feet to the summit. Just about any line of ascent works, but be careful of small cliffs. The best route is up the creek bed, then left to the sky-line and on to the approximately 5400-foot summit.

Views, views, views: Darrington and farms of the Stillaguamish, Whitehorse Mountain, Three Fingers Mountain, Glacier Peak, Dome Peak, Mt. Baker; and countless more.

Round trip 4 miles
Hiking time 4 hours
High point 5400 feet
Elevation gain 1900 feet
Best early June through October
One day or backpack
USGS Round Mountain and Fortson

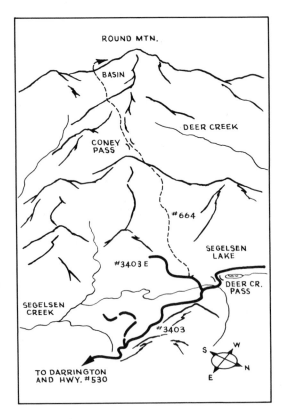

ROUND MTN.

BASIN

DEER CREEK

CONEY PASS

#664

#3403 E

SEGELSEN LAKE

DEER CR. PASS

SEGELSEN CREEK

#3403

TO DARRINGTON AND HWY. #530

Glacier Peak, in distance, from Round Mountain

37 SQUIRE CREEK PASS

Hike through lovely forest to a 4000-foot pass with a dramatic view of the seldom-seen cliffs of Whitehorse, Three Fingers, and Bullon—some of the steepest and grandest walls in the western reaches of the Cascades. Rambles and scrambles from the pass lead to meadowland and more scenery.

The trail was abandoned for many years but is now being reopened in response to the growing demand for hiking opportunities. In the fall of 1971 volunteers from Evergreen State College brushed out 2½ miles of the path and in 1972 the Forest Service started cutting through the

120 logs barring the way. The remaining 1½ miles still are clogged with brush, with many fallen trees and some tread missing, but are passable. The Forest Service plans to keep this a low-standard hikers-only trail.

From the business section of Darrington drive 5 miles on Squire Creek road No. 3203 to the road-end at a creek. Hike ¼ mile on the abandoned road, then follow the trail. Expect to crawl over and under logs the first 2½ miles and to fight brush and logs the last 1½ miles. But once to the ridge top the work will be forgotten amongst the towering walls of Squire Creek.

From the pass (camping space very limited) walk out the ridge 1½ miles to Cedar Flats, named for its numerous Alaska cedars. Find the great stone face of Old Man Jumbo on a 60-foot cliff.

A steep trail leads 2 miles from Clear Creek to the pass but is badly overgrown and very difficult to find.

The unlogged, unroaded portions of Squire Creek and Clear Creek are proposed by conservationists for inclusion in a Three Fingers-Whitehorse Wilderness Area which would also protect the magnificent Boulder River valley. (The Forest Service is considering a Scenic Area designation that would cover less of the region and give a much lower degree of protection.) Because of the spectacular peaks, the low-altitude forest and their long hiking season, and the quick access from population centers, this superb—but threatened—wilderness will surely become extremely popular if it is not crisscrossed with multiple-use roads and motorbike trails like the west side of Three Fingers and the valley of Crystal Creek. Only Wilderness Area classification will do the job.

Round trip to pass 8 miles
Hiking time 6 hours
High point 4000 feet
Elevation gain 2000 feet
Best June through October
One day or backpack
USGS Silverton

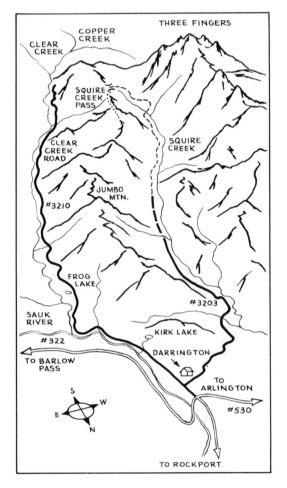

Three Fingers Mountain from Squire Creek Pass

38 GREEN MOUNTAIN

The name of the peak may seem banal, but probably no one has ever looked up its slopes from the Suiattle River valley without exclaiming, "What a **green** mountain!" The trail climbs through these remarkable meadows to a lookout summit with magnificent views to every point of the compass.

Drive north from Darrington or south from Rockport to the Suiattle River road and continue 18 miles to the Green Mountain road. Turn left 5 miles to road-end in a logging patch, elevation about 3500 feet. Find the trail sign above the road several hundred yards before the road-end.

The trail climbs a rather steep mile in mossy forest to a grubby hunters' camp with a year-around spring, then enters the vast meadow system admired from below. First are fields of bracken fern and other subalpine plants, then, on higher switchbacks, a feast (in season) of blueberries. Views begin—down to Suiattle forests

and out to Whitechuck Mountain and Glacier Peak. More meadows, and views of Mt. Pugh and Sloan Peak, seen beyond the intervening ridge of Lime Mountain.

At 2 miles, 5300 feet, the trail rounds a shoulder and in 1/2 mile traverses and drops 100 feet to a pair of shallow ponds amid gardens. Pleasant camps here, and all-summer water. Wood is scarce so carry a stove.

A short way above the pond basin the trail enters a larger, wide-open basin (great camps, but no water in late summer). The lookout cabin can now be seen directly above, and also Glacier Peak. Climb in flowers to the ridge and along the crest to the 6500-foot summit, 4 miles. A few yards below the summit ridge on the east is a small rocky-and-snowy basin; delightful and scenic good-weather camps with water but no wood.

Look north along the ridge to the nearby cliffs and glaciers of 7311-foot Buckindy (experienced highland travelers can wander there). Look up Downey Creek to peaks of the Ptarmigan Traverse from Dome north to Formidable. Look up Milk Creek to the Ptarmigan Glacier on Glacier Peak. Look to other peaks in all directions, too many to name.

Round trip 8 miles
Hiking time 6 hours
High point 6500 feet
Elevation gain 3000 feet
Best late June through October
One day or backpack
USGS Downey Mtn.

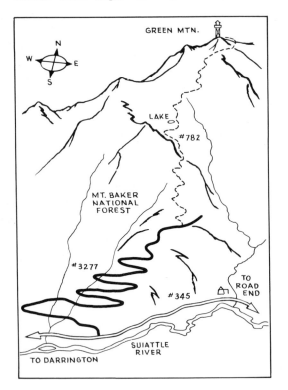

90

Suiattle valley, Glacier Peak, and old storage shed near the fire lookout. The shed was built during World War II when the lookout was manned the year-around for airplane watching. Since the taking of the photo the shed has been accidentally burned down.

39 BACHELOR MEADOWS

A pleasant hike through virgin forest along Downey Creek to 6 Mile Camp. For those with the energy and ambition, and experience in traveling rough wilderness, it's a tough climb some 5½ miles farther to meadows under 8264-foot Spire Point, with views of deep and blue Cub and Itswoot Lakes, Dome Peak, Glacier Peak, and other icy mountains.

Drive the Suiattle River road (Hike 38) 19½ miles to Downey Creek Campground and the trailhead, elevation 1450 feet.

The first mile climbs steadily, then the way levels into easy ups and downs amid tall firs, hemlocks, and cedars, crossing small streams, sometimes coming close to the river. At 6¼ miles, 2400 feet, the trail crosses Bachelor Creek and then Downey on a log jam leading to 6 Mile Camp, with numerous good campsites. The trip to here is a fine forest and river walk; for more of the same, the Downey Creek trail continues up the valley to a dead-end.

For Bachelor Meadows, follow the Downey Creek trail upstream ½ mile from 6 Mile Camp to the start of the Bachelor Creek trail. Cross Downey Creek on a narrow, slippery log—or perhaps scout around for a better and safer log. The first 1½ miles of trail are very old but well-graded. Then the way disintegrates into a route trampled out by boots, climbing over roots and plunging through gooey bogs. The worst windfalls have been cut but there are plenty of problems. In about 2 miles cross Bachelor Creek. The track becomes hard to follow through a boulder-strewn meadow deep in ferns and flowers. Views appear of Spire Point at the head of the valley. At about 3½ miles are a succession of good campsites.

Now the trail climbs a short but steep mile and at 5400 feet abruptly leaves forest and enters an improbable little valley at a right angle to the main valley and just under Spire Point. Water and flat campsites here in a scenic meadow.

For broader views continue up the trail ½ mile through heather, following the small valley south to a 6000-foot pass. The trail drops ½ mile to 5338-foot Cub Lake and on down to 5015-foot Itswoot Lake.

Rather than descend, walk ¼ mile westward from the pass along a narrow ridge to a superb view of Dome Peak and the glistening Dome Glacier. A stone's throw below are the two lakes. South is Glacier Peak. By camping at Cub Lake, one can explore meadow slopes eastward to a 6200-foot ridge with an even more complete view of Dome.

Round trip to 6 mile Camp 12½ miles
Hiking time 7-8 hours
High point 2400 feet
Elevation gain 1000 feet
Best June through October
One day or backpack
USGS Downey Mtn.

Round trip to Bachelor Meadows 23½ miles
Allow 2-3 days
High point 6000 feet
Elevation gain 4600 feet
Best mid-July through September
USGS Downey Mtn. and Dome Peak
Forest Service wilderness permit required

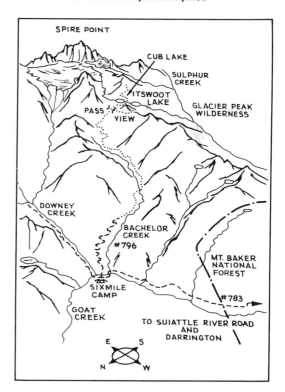

Cub Lake and Dome Peak

Sulphur Lake from Sulphur Mountain trail. The top of Dome Peak in clouds

40 SULPHUR MOUNTAIN

A long, steep climb to a green knoll on the ridge of Sulphur Mountain, with a striking view of Glacier Peak. Before setting out, sample the first 500 feet. If this seems easy, keep going. If not, consider taking some other hike in the vicinity (such as Green Mountain) because the trail has many, many pitches as tough as the first. Carry plenty of water—there is none on top.

Drive the Suiattle River road (Hike 38) 20 miles to Sulphur Creek bridge. Continue .3 mile to a small parking space and the trailhead, elevation 1800 feet. In less than ½ mile the trail descends sharply to cross a small stream. At about 1½ miles there may be a spring; if so, it's definitely the last water.

The trail ascends high-angle forest with very little underbrush. An altimeter is useful for keeping track of progress—or one can measure against the timberline on Lime Ridge, often seen across the Suiattle valley, through openings in the trees. At about 3½ miles the way briefly touches a ridge, then traverses, still climbing. The character of the vegetation changes at about 4 miles; the trees grow more alpine and the ground becomes covered with heather and blueberries.

The end of the grueling ascent is abrupt. The trail emerges from forest and reaches the ridge crest; the top is only a few hundred feet more up a flower-covered knoll.

Glacier Peak, rising over Milk Creek, rules the region. To the north, seen between two nearby pinnacles, are Dome Peak and its satellite, Sinister. West of them is Spire Point, and farther west, the brilliant green slopes of Downey Mountain and Green Mountain.

Assuming one has the energy to haul a pack here, Sulphur Lake, 800 feet below in lovely meadows, offers a delightful camp.

The summit of Sulphur Mountain is 700 feet higher and 2 hours farther. No trail: follow the ups and downs of the ridge, taking to easier slopes on the south side when the crest is too steep.

Round trip 10 miles
Hiking time 9 hours
High point 6000 feet
Elevation gain 4200 feet
Best mid-June through October
One day or backpack
USGS Glacier Peak
Forest Service wilderness permit required

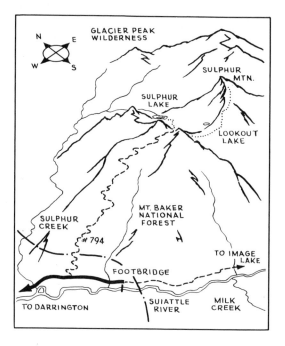

Glacier Peak and Milk Creek

41 MILK CREEK—DOLLY CREEK —VISTA CREEK LOOP

A section of the Cascade Crest Trail climbing high on the north flanks of Glacier Peak. Massive flower fields and close-up views of the mountain. Plan to spend an extra day, at least, roaming alpine ridges.

Drive the Suiattle River road (Hike 38) 24 miles to the end, elevation 1651 feet. (The final mile is rough and narrow and may soon be abandoned.) The Milk Creek trail drops a few steps from the parking lot, crosses the river on a bridge, and enters the Glacier Peak Wilderness Area. The way begins in glorious forest; at a mile or so is an awesome grove of ancient and huge

cedars, hemlocks, and Douglas firs. Going somewhat level, sometimes uphill, passing cold streams, the path rounds a ridge and enters the valley of Milk Creek.

A new trail is planned to cross Milk Creek at this point and continue up the valley. Day-hikers can follow the old trail to a broad field of greenery at 3 miles, 2400 feet, and a stunning look up to the ice, a satisfying reward for a short trip. A pleasant campsite in the forest ½ mile before the field.

The new trail soon rejoins the old and ascends gently, then steadily, passing campsites in the woods, and meets the Cascade Crest Trail at 6½ miles, 3900 feet. A short bit before the junction, under an overhanging rock, is Whistle

Pig Camp—a nice spot on a rainy night, though with room for only a few sleepers.

Turn left at the junction and plod upward on a series of 36 switchbacks (growing views of Glacier Peak and toward Mica Lake and Fire Mountain) to the crest of Milk Creek Ridge at 10½ miles, 6000 feet. The climbers' route to the summit of Glacier leaves the trail here; hikers can explore higher in flowers for hours before difficulties turn them back.

The trail traverses the flowery basin of the East Fork Milk Creek headwaters, crosses a ridge into the source of Dolly Creek, and at 13 miles comes to Vista Ridge and a shelter cabin, 5500 feet.

Flower gardens spread in every direction and views are grand north to Miners Ridge, Plummer Mountain, Dome Peak, and beyond. Glacier Peak is too close and foreshortened to be seen at its best. The trip schedule should include one or more walking-around days from the Vista Ridge camp. Wander up the crest to a 7000-foot knoll.

Even better, hike north in meadows to 6500-foot Grassy Point, offering impressive views up and down the green valley of the Suiattle River, but especially a mind-blasting spectacle of the white-glaciered volcano.

From the shelter the trail descends a long series of switchbacks into forest. At 19 miles, 3000 feet, is a campsite by the crossing of Vista Creek. At 20¼ miles is a junction with the Suiattle River trail and at 21 miles, 2700 feet, is a camp beside the Suiattle River. Here the trail crosses Skyline Bridge and proceeds 10 miles down the valley, in 31 miles reaching the road-end and completing the loop.

Loop trip 31 miles
Allow 3-5 days
High point 6000 feet
Elevation gain 4400 feet
Best mid-July to mid-October
USGS Glacier Peak
Forest Service wilderness permit required

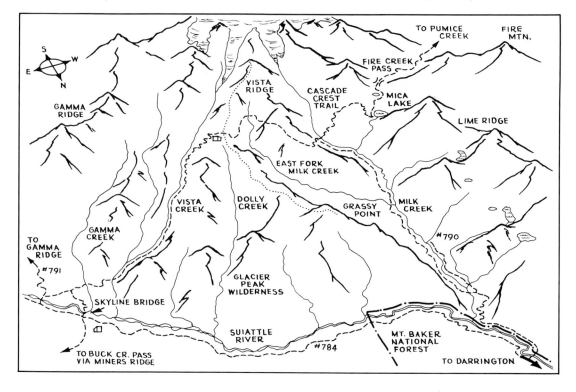

42 IMAGE LAKE

A 2-mile-high volcano, the image of its glaciers reflected in an alpine tarn. Meadow ridges for dream-walking. The long sweep of Suiattle River forests. Casting ballots with their feet, hikers have voted this a supreme climax of the alpine world of the North Cascades and the nation. (During July-August 1969, 1300 campers were counted at Image Lake; in a single day there have been more than 150.) Incredibly, Kennecott Copper Corporation may take advantage of a serious flaw in the Wilderness Act and dig a monstrous open-pit mine here, in the very heart of the Glacier Peak Wilderness Area.

Drive the Suiattle River road (Hike 38) 24 miles to the end, elevation 1651 feet. Find the Suiattle River trail above the parking area.

The trail has been rebuilt recently to Forest Service "superhighway" standards, including spots that are double-tracked for horses and hikers, and in the process the engineers have seriously damaged the wilderness walking experience. Be that as it may (and should not be) the way goes on a level grade near the Suiattle River 5½ miles, partly in ancient trees, partly in young trees, sometimes with looks to the river, crossing small tributaries, to Canyon Creek Shelter, 2300 feet. At about 8½ miles, 2800 feet, is

a creek with small campsites on both sides; be sure to fill canteens. Just beyond is a trail junction; go left on Suiattle Pass trail No. 784. The forest switchbacks are relentless and dry, but with occasional glimpses, then spectacular views, out to the valley and the volcano. At 11½ miles are two welcome streams at the edge of meadow country, and at 12 miles, 4800 feet, is a junction.

The Suiattle Pass trail goes straight ahead from the junction; take the left fork to Image Lake. Switchback up and up, into blueberry and flower meadows with expanding views, to a junction atop Miners Ridge, about 14 miles, 6150 feet. A ¼-mile trail leads left to Miners Ridge Lookout, 6210 feet. The main trail goes right ¾ mile, traversing, then dropping a bit, to 6050-foot Image Lake.

Don't come to Image Lake expecting privacy; for that, one must seek out other nooks and corners of the area. Indeed, over-use of the lake threatens its integrity and rules out any chance of lonesomeness. To protect especially fragile qualities, the Forest Service has prohibited camping within 200 feet of the shores and bans swimming in the lake—which is the water supply. Horses should be prohibited within ½ mile of the lake, but they are still allowed to contaminate the water.

Exploring the basin, climbing the 6758-foot

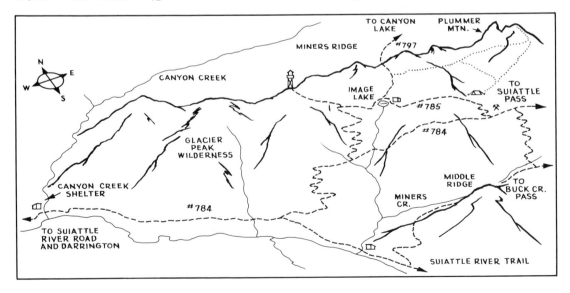

Glacier Peak and Image Lake, a small jewel in an emerald setting

knoll above, visiting the fire lookout, walking the Canyon Lake trail into the headwaters of Canyon Creek—thus one may fill memorable days. By no means omit the finest wandering of all, along the wide crest of Miners Ridge, through flower gardens, looking north to Dome Peak and south across Suiattle forests to Glacier Peak. Experienced scramblers can ascend steep heather to the 7870-foot summit of Plummer Mountain and wide horizons of wild peaks.

Also, hike the grassy trail east 1 mile to lovely Lady Camp Basin. Here is the west edge of the ½-mile-wide open pit mine Kennecott wants to dig; this blasphemy has been prevented so far by violent objections from citizen-hikers but can only

be stopped for good and all by your letters to congressmen and senators urging them to exercise the right of eminent domain and purchase the patented mining claims. From Lady Camp the trail drops some 500 feet in ½ mile to a junction with the Suiattle Pass trail, which can be followed 1¾ miles back to the Image Lake trail junction.

Round trip to Image Lake 30 miles
Allow 2-4 days
High point 6050 feet
Elevation gain 4400 feet
Best mid-July through October
USGS Glacier Peak and Holden
Forest Service wilderness permit required

43 SUIATTLE RIVER TO LAKE CHELAN

A rich, extended sampler of the Glacier Peak Wilderness Area, beginning in green-mossy west-side trees, rising to flowers of Miners Ridge and views of Glacier Peak, crossing Suiattle and Cloudy Passes, descending parklands of Lyman Lake to rainshadow forests of Railroad Creek and Lake Chelan. The traverse can be done in either direction; the west-to-east route is described here.

Drive to the Suiattle River road-end, 1651 feet, and hike 12 miles on Suiattle Pass trail No. 784 to the 4800-foot junction with the Image Lake trail (see Hike 42).

Continue straight ahead, climbing 1¾ miles to the east end of the Image Lake trail, 5500 feet. (The lake can—and should, if time allows—be included in the trip by taking the lake trail, which is 4½ miles long from end to end, thus adding some 3 extra miles and about 600 feet of extra elevation gained and lost.) In trees just

past the junction are two miners' shacks belonging to Kennecott Copper and a spring, a bad-weather campsite. The way now contours, crossing one huge and many small avalanche paths, entering open slopes with grand views to Fortress, Chiwawa, and other peaks at the head of Miners Creek, passing more miners' junk in a small flat, and at 16 miles reaches Suiattle Pass, 5983 feet. A bit before the pass and below the trail is a pleasant camp on a meadow bench.

The trail drops some 300 feet into headwaters of South Fork Agnes Creek (the drop can be avoided by taking a rough hiker-only alternate path) and climbs to the most spectacular views and gardens of the trip at 6438-foot Cloudy Pass, 18 miles. (From here, easy meadows demand a side-trip to 7915-foot Cloudy Peak and along the ridge to 8068-foot North Star Mountain.)

Descend magnificent flowers, then subalpine forest, to 5587-foot Lyman Lake, 20 miles. Beautiful as is the lake, its shores fringed by greenery, the campground, on a short spur trail west, is

Lyman Lake

marshy; camps above, under Cloudy Peak, have better views and fewer bugs. (From the lake, a steep path, rather obscure at the start, climbs 500 feet to Upper Lyman Lake, alpine camps, and a mandatory sidetrip to the toe of the Lyman Glacier. See Hike 75.

The trail drops past the outlet creek of Lyman Lake, where frothy water pours down long, clean granite slabs, and switchbacks into forests of Railroad Creek; views of Crown Point Falls and Hart Lake. After boggy walking and many bridges, at 23½ miles, 3989 feet, is Rebel Camp and at 24½ miles is Hart Lake. Good camping at both.

The last portion of the route is over blocks of rock under a tall cliff, past tumbling waterfalls, occasional views of high peaks, to beaver bottom and green jungle, and finally a jeep track and baseball field to the abandoned mining town of Holden 28½ miles, 3200 feet.

Holden, now owned by the Lutheran Church and used for various religious activities, is 12 miles by road from Lucerne, on the shores of Lake Chelan. Though not particularly pleasant, the road can be walked (a parallel trail is planned for future construction). In June-July-August a station wagon (capacity 6 passengers) from Lucerne Resort makes one trip daily from Holden to the lake, leaving just before noon, in time to catch the **Lady of the Lake,** which provides transit downlake from Lucerne to Chelan, from where bus connections can be made home (Hike 81). (If the Lucerne taxi is full up, the extra hikers must either walk the road or wait until next day.)

One-way trip 28½ miles
Allow 5-7 days
High point 6438 feet
Elevation gain about 5000 feet
Best mid-July through September
USGS Glacier Peak, Holden, Lucerne
Forest Service wilderness permit required

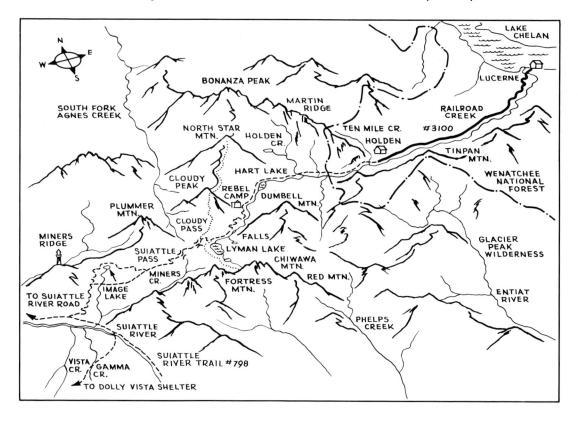

44 AROUND GLACIER PEAK

Mount Rainier National Park has the renowned Wonderland Trail; the Glacier Peak Wilderness Area offers an equally-classic around-the-mountain hike. Its fame lies in the future, but the pleasures are there now. The 94-mile circuit with an estimated 15,500 feet of climbing includes virgin forests, glacial streams, alpine meadows, and ever-changing views of the "last wild volcano."

The complete trip requires a minimum 10 days, and this makes no allowance for explorations and bad-weather layovers. However, the loop breaks logically into two sections which can be taken separately. Perhaps the ideal schedule is to do the entire circuit on a single 2-week jaunt, keeping packs to a reasonable weight by arranging to be met midway with additional supplies.

North and East Section

Begin at Suiattle River road-end. Hike 8 miles along the Suiattle River on trail No. 784 to a junction. Go right on trail No. 795 1¼ miles to Middle Ridge trail No. 2052 and climb 9½ miles to Buck Creek Pass.

(Two partial alternate routes can be taken; each adds a day and many extra rewards. One is the Milk Creek-Dolly-Vista trail (Hike 41), which starts at Suiattle River road-end and rejoins the main route near the 9-mile marker; this alternate adds 12 miles and 3200 feet of elevation gain to the total. The other is the Image Lake-Miners Ridge trail (Hike 42), which leaves the main route at 8½ miles and rejoins it 6 miles below Buck Creek Pass; this alternate adds 8 miles and 1700 feet of elevation gain. The two alternates can be combined on a single trip; first do the Milk

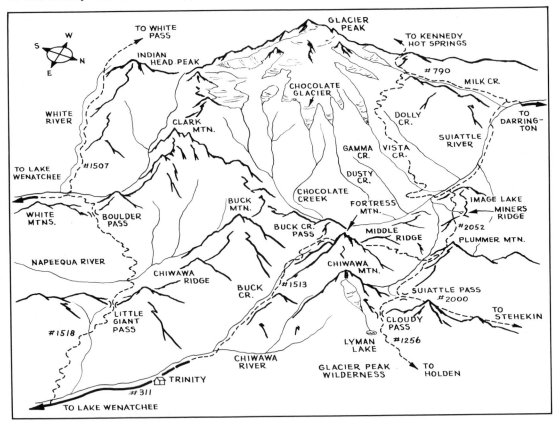

Creek-Dolly Vista trail, then backtrack 1 mile to begin the Image Lake-Miners Ridge trail.)

Descend 9½ miles from Buck Creek Pass to Trinity (Hike 76) and walk 5½ miles down the Chiwawa River road to Little Giant trail. Climb 4¾ miles to Little Giant Pass (Hike 74) and descend 1¾ miles into the Napeequa River valley and a junction with Boulder Pass trail No. 2176. Climb 6½ miles over the pass and down to the White River trail (Hike 73). If the trip is to be broken at this point, hike 3½ miles downriver to the White River road.

A possible itinerary (excluding the alternates) would be: Day One, 9 miles and a 1150-foot climb to Miners Creek Shelter; Day Two, 9½ miles and a 3200-foot climb to Buck Creek Pass;

Day Three, descend 3350 feet in 15 miles to Maple Creek; Day Four, climb 3900 feet, descend 2300 feet, in the 6½ miles to Napeequa River; Day Five, 10 miles to White River road-end, a climb of 1550 feet and a descent of 3350 feet. However, frequent campsites along the route allow shorter days or different days.

One-way trip 50 miles
Allow 5 days minimum
High point 6409 feet (Little Giant Pass)
Elevation gain 9800 feet
To: Buck Creek Pass 4100 feet
Little Giant Pass 3800 feet
Boulder Pass 1550 feet
Best late July through September
USGS Glacier Peak and Holden
Forest Service wilderness permit required

Ptarmigan in summer plumage

SUIATTLE RIVER

South and West Section

Begin at White River road-end. Hike 14¼ miles on White River trail No. 1507 to an intersection with the Cascade Crest Trail. Continue north on the crest 2 miles to White Pass (Hike 71).

From White Pass contour and climb to Red Pass in 2 miles, then descend the White Chuck River (Hike 47) 7 miles to a junction. For the main route, climb right on the Cascade Crest Trail, crossing headwaters of Kennedy Creek, Glacier Creek, Pumice Creek, and Fire Creek and reaching Fire Creek Pass in 8 miles (Hike 46).

(For an inviting alternate, go 1½ miles from the junction downriver to Kennedy Hot Springs, enjoy a hot bath, then continue a short ½ mile to the Kennedy Ridge trail (Hike 46) and climb to rejoin the main route; this alternate adds 1¼ miles and 800 feet of elevation gain to the total.)

From Fire Creek Pass, the snowiest part of the entire circuit, descend a valley of moraines and ponds, past the magnificent cold cirque of Mica Lake, reaching the Dolly-Vista trail junction in 4 miles. Continue 6½ miles down Milk Creek trail to the Suiattle River road-end (Hike 41).

A possible itinerary would be: Day One, 9 miles and climb 800 feet to Lightning Creek; Day Two, 9¼ miles, a gain of 2100 feet and a loss of 1000 feet, to Glacier Peak Shelter (the shelter is gone but the campsite remains); Day Three, drop 1700 feet and climb 2250 on the 9½ miles to Pumice Creek; Day Four, 500 feet up and 900 feet down on 4¼ miles to Mica Lake; Day Five, 10 miles and 3800 feet down to Suiattle River road. Again, frequent campsites allow shorter or different days.

One-way trip 42 miles
Allow 5 days minimum
High point 6450 feet (Red Pass)
Elevation gain 5700 feet
To: White Pass 3700 feet
Red Pass 700 feet
Fire Creek Pass 2000 feet
Best late July through September
USGS Glacier Peak and Holden
Forest Service wilderness permit required

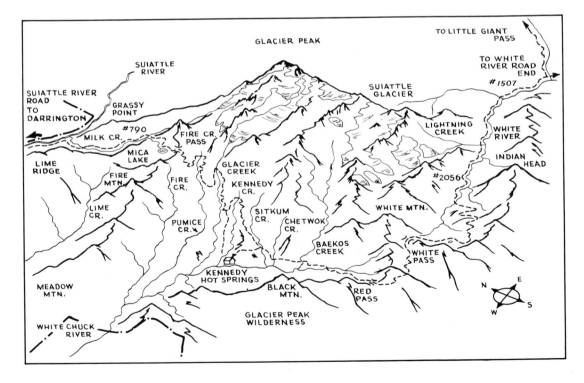

Indian Head Peak from White Pass

45 MEADOW MOUNTAIN

Meadows laced with alpine trees, views to White Chuck forests and Glacier Peak ice, and a long parkland ridge for roaming, with side-trips to cirque lakes.

Drive from Darrington on the Mountain Loop Highway $10\frac{1}{2}$ miles to the White Chuck River road. Turn left $5\frac{1}{2}$ miles to Straight Creek road No. 327, shortly beyond the crossing of the White Chuck River. Turn left, climbing and switchbacking, following "Meadow Mountain" signs at all junctions, 5 miles to road-end, elevation 3400 feet. Views of Glacier Peak, White Chuck Mountain, and Mt. Pugh even before leaving the car.

The trail climbs a steep $1\frac{1}{4}$ miles (but in deep, cool forest) to the first meadow. Cross a bubbling brook in an open basin and then choose either of two day-trip destinations, both offering splendid views down to the green valley and out to the peaks. For the easiest, follow a faint way trail 1 mile westward to a high knoll, about 5600 feet. For the best, and with the most flowers, hike the main trail 2 miles eastward, climbing to a 5800-foot spur ridge from Meadow Mountain.

For one of the great backpacking ridge walks in the Glacier Peak Wilderness Area, take the up-and-down trail traversing the ridge east toward Fire Mountain. Earlier camps are possible, but the first site with guaranteed all-summer water is Hunter's Camp at 4 miles, $\frac{1}{2}$ mile beyond the 5800-foot viewpoint, in a bouldery basin to which the trail drops to avoid cliffs of Meadow Mountain.

Going up, then down, then up again, at $5\frac{1}{4}$ miles the trail touches the 5850-foot ridge crest. From here, descend 1 mile northwest on a much-used but easily-lost path to 5300-foot Diamond Lake. From the east side of the lake climb a wide gully up the low ridge and descend extremely-steep slopes (no trail) to Emerald Lake, 5200 feet. Good camps at both.

Just past the Diamond Lake junction the main trail disappears for $\frac{3}{4}$ mile, but a meager way trail can be followed along the ridge to where tread resumes in a low saddle at about 6 miles. The path—still scanty, but now easy to find—

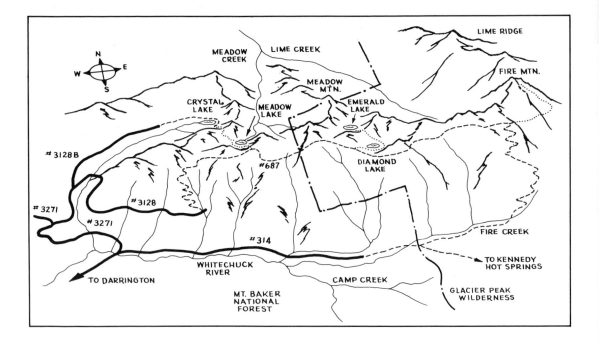

Flower fields on Meadow Mountain. Glacier Peak in distance

continues east through patches of trees, grassy swales, side-hill flowers, and views.

At 7½ miles is a magnificent camp in a cliff-walled basin and at 9 miles, beneath Fire Mountain, are charming garden camps near the broken-down Fire Chief Shelter. From this area experienced off-trail travelers can find an easy but not obvious route to the summit of 6591-foot Fire Mountain; if the terrain gets steep and scary, you're on the wrong route—turn back.

The trail descends an old burn to Fire Creek forests, joining the White Chuck River trail at 13½ miles, 1½ miles from the White Chuck River road. By use of two cars, one parked at each road-end, hikers can enjoy a 15-mile one-way trip along the full length of the ridge trail; a 3-day schedule allows for side-trips, but more days could easily be spent exploring.

Round trip to 5800-foot viewpoint 6½ miles
Hiking time 4-5 hours
High point 5800 feet
Elevation gain 2400 feet
Best July through October
One day
USGS Pugh Mtn. and Glacier Peak

One-way trip from Meadow Mountain road-end to White Chuck River road-end 15 miles
Allow 2-4 days
High point 5800 feet
Elevation gain 3500 feet, including ups and downs
Best July through October
Forest Service wilderness permit required beyond 5800-foot viewpoint

Glacier Peak and Scimitar Glacier on right, from Kennedy Ridge trail

46 KENNEDY RIDGE AND HOT SPRINGS

Two hikes which can be done separately or combined. A short-and-low trip leads through tall old trees, beside a roaring river, to a tingling bath in volcano-warmed waters. A long-and-high trip climbs to alpine flowers with a close-up look at icefalls tumbling from Glacier Peak.

Drive from Darrington on the Mountain Loop Highway 10½ miles to the White Chuck River road. Turn left 11 miles to the road-end parking area and campground, elevation 2300 feet.

The wide, gentle White Chuck River trail has become—deservedly—the most popular valley walk in the Glacier Peak area. The way goes through virgin forest always near and sometimes beside the ice-fed river, beneath striking cliffs of volcanic tuff, crossing the frothing tributaries of Fire, Pumice, and Glacier Creeks. At 5 miles, 3300 feet, is a junction with the Kennedy Ridge trail.

Kennedy Hot Springs: Continue 1/5 mile on the White Chuck River trail to a campground with two shelters and Forest Service station, 3300 feet. Cross the river on a bridge, turn left past the trail to Lake Byrne (Hike 49), and in a few yards come to steaming, mineralized waters seeping from the earth. A tub-like pool about 5 feet square and 5 feet deep has been dug, just big enough for three or four people. The water is not as hot as the Japanese like it, but the idea is the same—submerging to your chin and letting the bubbling heat relax your muscles. The water is usually a yellowish-reddish murk, but never mind; to clean away the iron oxide, one can always plunge into the icy river, several yards away. (This is the way the Finns like it—hot, then cold.)

Summer is not the best time for a bath; the trail remains superb in all seasons, but 1,992 people signed the Kennedy register in 1969, which means the waiting line gets long in good weather. For leisurely and private soaking, make an over-night trip in April or May, when weather is poor and the high country (and perhaps the trail too) is deep in snow.

Kennedy Ridge: From the junction at 5 miles,

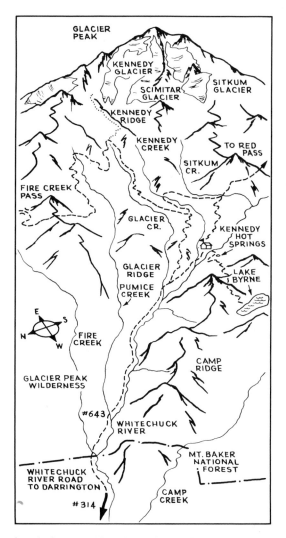

Glacier Peak from ridge above Pumice Creek

ests on the old moraine, then in ½ mile step suddenly out onto raw boulders of a much newer moraine. See the Kennedy and Scimitar Glaciers tumbling from the summit of the volcano. See glacial debris and cataracts below the ice. See valley forests, peaks beyond.

It's a shame to turn back at the edge of so much good highland roaming. Just 1 mile from Glacier Creek, over Glacier Ridge, are the splendid meadows and camps of Pumice Creek, and in 3½ miles more is Fire Creek Pass. With a schedule of 3 or more days, these and other delights can be enjoyed.

Round trip to Kennedy Hot Springs 10½ miles
Hiking time 5 hours
High point 3300 feet
Elevation gain 1000 feet
Best May through November
One day or backpack
USGS Glacier Peak

Round trip to Kennedy Ridge moraine 18 miles
Hiking time 8-10 hours
High point 6200 feet
Elevation gain 4000 feet
Best July through October
One day or backpack
Forest Service wilderness permit required

just before crossing Kennedy Creek, climb left on the Kennedy Ridge trail. (Fill canteens before starting up.) The steep forest way, with occasional glimpses of ice, joins the Cascade Crest Trail at 1½ miles, 4150 feet. The Crest Trail switchbacks through cliffs of red and gray andesite, then along heather parklands on a moraine crest, swinging left to reach the welcome wet splash (and campsite) of Glacier Creek at 5650 feet, 3½ miles from the White Chuck River trail.

Leave the trail and climb open subalpine for-

47 WHITE CHUCK GLACIER

Begin beside a loud river in deep forest. Walk miles through big trees, climb to little trees and wide meadows. Roam flowers and waterfalls and moraines to a broad glacier. Wander gardens and ridges. In the opinion of some experts, this is the supreme low-to-high tour of the Glacier Peak Wilderness Area.

Drive to the White Chuck River road-end, 2300 feet, and hike 5 1/5 miles to 3300-foot Kennedy

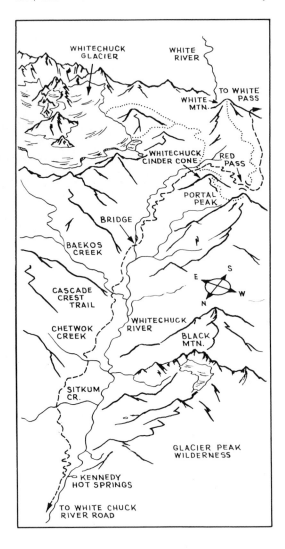

Hot Springs (Hike 46). Camp and take a hot bath. (Plan another for the return.)

Next day, ascend steeply then gently to join the Cascade Crest Trail at Sitkum Creek, 3850 feet, 7 miles from the road. The Crest Trail continues along the valley, passing the avalanche track and meadow-marsh of Chetwot Creek, fording Baekos Creek, and at 9½ miles, 4000 feet, crossing a high bridge over the rocky chasm and thundering falls of the White Chuck River.

Now the trail climbs a valley step. Trees are smaller and so is the river, assembling itself from snow-fed tributaries. A little meadow gives promise of what lies above. More subalpine forest. Then the way enters the tremendous open basin of Glacier Peak Meadows. At 12 miles, 5400 feet, is the site of the long-gone Glacier Peak Shelter, and magnificent campsites everywhere around.

As a base for easy hiker-type explorations, this highland valley of flowers and creeks and snowfields is unsurpassed in the North Cascades.

First off, if your hike is mid-August or later, visit the ice; before that it is covered with snow. Climb meadows around the valley corner east, taking any of many appealing routes to a chilly flatland of moss and meanders, to moraines and melt-water, and finally the White Chuck Glacier. The white plateau is tempting, but only climbers with rope and ice ax should venture onto its surface.

For another trip, investigate the intriguing White Chuck Cinder Cone, remnant of a volcano smaller and newer than Glacier Peak. Scramble meadows higher to the 6999-foot summit of Portal Peak.

If your visit is in late July or early August it is flower time on White Mountain. Therefore, hike the Crest Trail 2 miles up a wintry, rocky basin to 6450-foot Red Pass; from here, continue on the trail to White Pass (in early July be careful of the steep snow slopes) or leave the trail in about ½ mile and follow the flower ridge crest to the summit of 7030-foot White Mountain (Hike 50).

Every direction calls. Invent your own wanderings. The minimum trip to the glacier can be done in 3 days but any itinerary of less than a week will leave the visitor frustrated, determined

Glacier Peak from White Mountain

to return soon to finish the job at leisure.

Campsites other than those mentioned above are plentiful along the trail and throughout the high basin. However, as a conservation rule to be followed here and everywhere, camps should be placed in trees adjacent to meadows, not in the actual meadows, which are so fragile that only a few nights of camping can destroy nature's work of several years or more.

Round trip to White Chuck Glacier 28 miles
Allow 4 days minimum
High point about 6500 feet
Elevation gain 4200 feet
Best late July through September
USGS Glacier Peak
Forest Service wilderness permit required

48 MOUNT PUGH

A strikingly high and imposing peak, considering its position so far west from the main mountain mass; the height and the detachment make for an exceptional viewpoint. See out to Puget Sound lowlands. See the North Cascades from Baker to Eldorado to Dome to Bonanza. See nearby Glacier Peak standing magnificently tall above White Chuck River forests. Closer, see the superb horn of Sloan and the sharp peaks of the Monte Cristo area. A rare panorama indeed, but not for everyone—the upper portion of the trail once led to a fire lookout but has long been abandoned and now is climbers' terrain. However, hikers can go most of the way and see most of the horizons.

Drive from Darrington on the Mountain Loop Highway 14 miles to Mt. Pugh road No. 3131. Turn left 1 mile to Mt. Pugh trail sign, elevation 1900 feet.

The steep trail climbs cool forest 1½ miles to tiny Lake Metan, 3180 feet, and the first outward looks. Just before the lake are springs providing the last dependable all-summer water; fill canteens. Relentless switchbacks ascend to meadows, 3 miles, beyond which point the trail is not maintained. The only decent camps on the route are here, but water may be gone by late summer.

Three Fingers and Whitehorse appear beyond valley forests as the trail switchbacks up talus and flowers to the notch of Stujack Pass, 3¾ miles, 5500 feet. Inexperienced travelers should have lunch and turn back, content with a full bag of scenery.

Those who go beyond Stujack must be trained and equipped for steep snow travel (early summer) and for rock scrambling (all summer). The abandoned trail climbs abruptly from the pass to a knife-edge rock ridge, then picks a delicate way along cliffs above a glacier trough, perhaps vanishing occasionally in snowfields. Part of the trail was dynamited from rock to provide access to the summit lookout; the first cabin was destroyed by lightning, and its successor was

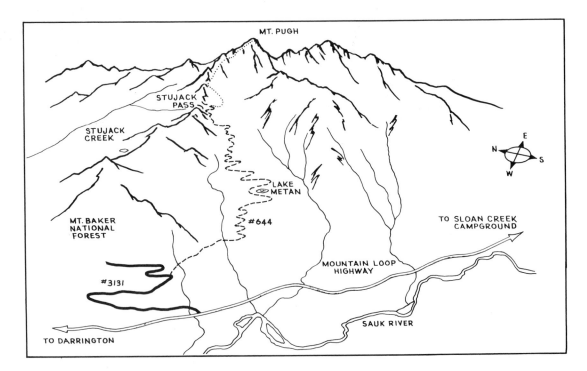

Mt. Pugh from Meadow Mountain

burned several years ago. (Note old lumber and ironware, remnants of a "tramway" used to haul building materials to the top). Steep heather and rock slabs lead to the summit, 5½ miles, 7201 feet.

The summit views are worth the effort for travelers who can use ice ax, hands and feet, and perhaps rope, and thus manage the upper "trail" in safety. The views short of the summit are also worthwhile; be sure to stop, satisfied, when the going gets scary.

Round trip to Stujack Pass 7½ miles
Hiking time 6-7 hours
High point 5500 feet
Elevation gain 3600 feet
Best mid-July through October
One day, possibly backpack
USGS Pugh Mtn., White Chuck Mtn.

Round trip to Mt. Pugh 10 miles
Hiking time 10-12 hours
High point 7201 feet
Elevation gain 5350 feet
Best August through October
One day, possibly backpack

Glacier Peak from Lost Creek Ridge trail

49 LOST CREEK RIDGE— LAKE BYRNE

A long ridge of green meadows, alpine lakes, and wide views of peaks near and far—one of the most memorable highland trails in the Glacier Peak region. The ridge can be ascended from either end for day trips or overnight camps, or walked the full length on an extended backpack. However, the middle section of the route is strictly cross-country travel, with no trail ever built and none planned; particularly in the fog, hikers must be careful not to get lost on Lost Ridge.

Drive from Darrington on the Mountain Loop

Highway 17 miles to North Fork Sauk River road No. 308. Turn left 3 miles to a small parking area and trail sign, elevation 2000 feet.

The trail goes gently along the valley ½ mile, then climbs steeply through open woods, with occasional views of impressive Sloan Peak, to 4425-foot Bingley Gap, 3 miles. The way continues some 2 miles up and along the ridge to meadows and a 5550-foot saddle overlooking Round Lake, 5100 feet. (A steep side-trail descends to the lake and good camps.) Scramble up the grassy knoll east of the saddle for more views of Sloan and a look at Glacier Peak. Here is the place for day-trippers to have lunch, soak up the scenery, and return home; generally the

114

trail is reasonably snow-free by early July.

Beyond this point the up-and-down trail is sketchy, very snowy until late July, and requires careful routefinding. (The section from ¾ mile past Sunup Lake to Hardtack Lake is only partly a "constructed" trail and is more of a high route with scattered sections of good tread and boot-built or hoof-built track. Daubs of orange paint on trees and rocks mark the route at both ends—but not the middle—of the "missing" section.) However, the going is easy and glorious —always near or on the crest, mostly in vast meadows, through open basins, near small lakes, with constant and changing views, and a choice of delightful camps. At 11 miles is 5650-foot Camp Lake, set in a cliff-walled cirque. From here the trail climbs to a 6000-foot knob, drops a few feet to the rocky basin of "Little Siberia," then descends to famous Lake Byrne, 12 miles, 5550 feet. Flowers and rocks and waterfalls of the basin and adjoining ridges demand leisurely exploration, ever dominated by the tall white volcano rising beyond White Chuck River forests.

From the lake the trail abruptly drops 2250 feet in 2 miles to Kennedy Hot Springs (Hike 46), 5 miles from the White Chuck River road. If Lake Byrne is the primary goal, the quickest route is from this road, gaining 3200 feet in 7 miles for a very long day or reasonable weekend. If transportation can be arranged, such as by use of two cars, a 19-mile one-way trip can be done from one road to the other; allow 3 days or more.

Round trip to Round Lake viewpoint 10 miles
Hiking time 6-8 hours
High point 5550 feet
Elevation gain 3550 feet
Best July through October
One day or backpack
USGS Sloan Peak

Round trip to Lake Byrne 24 miles
Allow 3 days minimum
High point 6000 feet
Elevation gain about 6500 feet, including up and
  downs in and out
Best August through October
USGS Glacier Peak and Sloan Peak
Forest Service wilderness permit required

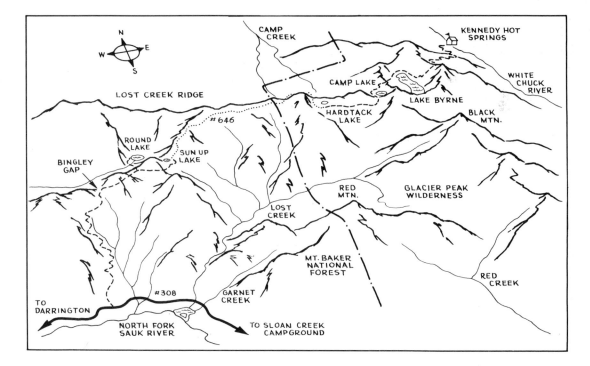

50 WHITE PASS—RED PASS

A cool, green forest for an easy afternoon stroll. Or vast meadows, attained by a grueling climb, for days of wandering flowers and views, always dominated by the grandeur of Glacier Peak.

Drive from Darrington on the Mountain Loop Highway 17 miles to North Fork Sauk River road No. 308. Turn left 7 miles to road-end at Sloan Creek Campground, elevation 2200 feet.

The North Fork Sauk River trail begins gently in rain forest, entering the Glacier Peak Wilderness Area at ½ mile. Ancient trees and a rusty-red mineral spring slow the pace. Day-trippers may turn back at about 1 mile, where the trail crosses a wide avalanche track and bouldery creek with a fine look at the north wall of

Yakbid (White Pass) Shelter, named for an Indian guide who led early surveyors through the region

Sloan Peak.

More forests and avalanche swaths lead to a campsite at Red Creek, 3¾ miles, 2800 feet, and onward to Makinaw Shelter, 5 miles, 2950 feet.

Now begins a stern 3000-foot climb. Fill canteens at the last dependable creek, 5½ miles. If the day is clear, the water will be badly wanted on the interminable switchbacks up an old burn regularly swept clean by avalanches, the whole south-facing slope open to the blazing sun. Flowers appear, and endless alpine meadows, and broad views, but no all-summer water.

However, at 5950 feet, 8½ miles, is a junction with the Cascade Crest Trail; shortly before or after there is water, a grand relaxation from the supreme effort, and full enjoyment of the hard-won scenery.

Two destinations, or a combination of both, now are offered.

For White Pass, go right in meadows an up-and-down ½ mile to the 5900-foot pass. The greenery is magnificent in every direction. Walk south along the Crest Trail. Wander northwest on sheep tracks to a 6500-foot saddle with staggering views of the White Chuck Glacier and Glacier Peak. Campsites at the Yakbid (White Pass) Shelter and nearby.

For Red Pass, go left from the junction, traversing steep meadows 1½ miles to the 6500-foot pass. Look down into headwaters of the White Chuck River (Hike 47) and across to Glacier Peak.

For the best views, hike partway (about ½ mile) toward Red Pass, leave the trail at a point where upward progress is obviously easy, and scramble meadows to the west ridge of White Mountain. Follow the flowery crest to the 7030-foot summit, then descend the south ridge to White Pass. Caution: this steep hill is too slippery for smooth-soled shoes. If the ridge is hiked in late July, there is a double reward: the view and the fields of flowers, including many, many white or cream-colored paintbrush.

Round trip to White Pass 18 miles
Allow 3 days
High point 5904 feet
Elevation gain 3700 feet
Best late July through October
USGS Glacier Peak
Forest Service wilderness permit required

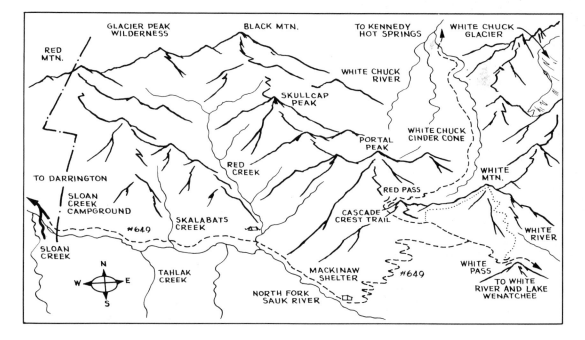

51   PILOT RIDGE—BLUE LAKES

A lonesome hikers-only trail along a high ridge, through meadows and all-directional views, to a grassy summit and alpine lakes. Connections can be made for loop trips and cross-mountain trips. Prime country for the experienced highland rambler seeking solitude and a bit of adventure.

Drive from Darrington on the Mountain Loop Highway 17 miles to North Fork Sauk River road No. 308. Turn left 7 miles to road-end at Sloan Creek Campground, elevation 2200 feet.

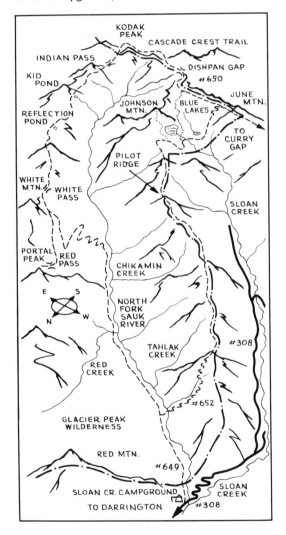

Walk the North Fork Sauk River trail (Hike 50) 2 miles to Pilot Ridge trail No. 652. Go right from the 2450-foot junction, crossing the river on a footlog. (If the log is missing, search for one up or down the stream.) The next 3 miles are why the ridge is so lonesome. The trail gains 3000 feet in a series of short switchbacks, the tread often destroyed by the trampling of sheep which once grazed the ridge. Fortunately there is little underbrush in the forest; when in doubt, simply continue upward. Be sure to fill canteens before starting the climb, which has drinking water at only two places, and these undependable.

Reaching the ridge crest, then traversing its slopes, at 6 miles the trail approaches a 5600-foot high point. Now the trees give way to meadows with views of Sloan Peak and glaciers falling from the Monte Cristo peaks into Pride Basin. And now the trail becomes very sketchy, often disappearing completely. Sometimes the track traverses around knobs, sometimes it goes over the tops. If the tread is lost, follow the ridge crest—you can't go wrong. On the trail or off, views of Glacier Peak are tremendous.

For the first good campsite, leave the trail at 8 miles, climb over the saddle east of a 6265-foot knob, and drop to a small 6159-foot lake on the north side of the ridge.

The trail abandons the crest to traverse a cirque on the west slopes of Johnson Mountain. At 10 miles is a side-trail climbing in 1 mile to the 6721-foot summit of the meadowy mountain, a splendid viewpoint to Red Pass, White Pass, and Ten Peaks—not to forget the omnipresent Glacier Peak. A party can make Johnson Mountain its destination, omitting the remainder of the ridge.

The main trail continues around a spur of the mountain and drops to a junction at 10½ miles. The left fork leads in a few hundred feet to upper Blue Lake, 5500 feet. Some camps by the cliff-walled lake, which usually is frozen until mid-August; better camps, and a shelter cabin, at lower Blue Lake, reached on the right fork, ½ mile beyond the junction.

The right fork is the main trail, which ends at June Mountain, 13 miles from the road, at a junction with the Bald Eagle trail (Hike 52). A two-ridge loop trip is possible if transportation can be arranged from one road to another.

Johnson Mountain and Pilot Ridge

The Bald Eagle trail can be followed 2½ miles to Dishpan Gap and a junction with the Cascade Crest Trail. However, if Dishpan Gap is the goal, a shorter route is available, going steeply up and down 1 mile (no real trail) from upper Blue Lake to the Crest Trail at a point ¾ mile south of the Gap. Distance from upper Blue Lake to the Gap via the Bald Eagle alternate, about 4¼ miles; via the shortcut, about 2 miles.

For a splendid loop with no extra transportation needed, go 6¾ miles on the Crest Trail (Hike 71) from Dishpan Gap to White Pass, then 9 miles down the North Fork Sauk River trail (Hike 50). Total distance 28 miles; allow 3 days.

Or, one can cross the Cascade Crest and descend to the Little Wenatchee River road-end on the east side of the range (Hike 70).

Round trip to Blue Lakes 21 miles
Allow 3 days
High point 6200 feet
Elevation gain some 5000 feet, in and 800 feet out
Best August through October
USGS Bench Mark Mtn., Glacier Peak, and Sloan Peak
Forest Service wilderness permit required

52 BALD EAGLE TRAIL

Begin the hike on a remnant of the old miners' route over Curry Gap, then climb a wooded ridge to flower meadows and broad views. This trip, like the one along neighboring Pilot Ridge (Hike 50), follows a lonesome trail used more by deer and marmots than people—which is surprising, considering the beautiful alpine terrain.

Drive the Mountain Loop Highway 17 miles from Darrington. Turn left 9 miles on North Fork Sauk River road No. 308, then right 2¾ miles on road No. 308A to the road-end and trailhead, elevation about 3200 feet.

Monte Cristo peaks from Bald Eagle trail

Start by walking a cat road 300 feet. Find the trail which traverses a clearcut, enter the woods, and climb a wet and sometimes muddy 1½ miles to Curry Gap, 4000 feet. Turn left on steep and dry Bald Eagle trail, ascending the forested ridge eastward. In 3½ miles is a good view of Sloan Peak and the Monte Cristo peaks. Eventually the path levels somewhat and contours around 5668-foot Bald Eagle Peak.

Beyond Bald Eagle the way drops 400 feet, steadily and gently ascends the wooded ridge, and contours the south side of Long John Mountain through large meadows. At 5½ miles is Long John Camp and at 6½ miles Spring Camp —the only certain late-summer water supply on the trip. Again on the wooded ridge, the trail climbs 800 feet to within a few yards of the top of 5946-foot June Peak. Be sure to take the short side-trip to the top for views of the two Blue Lakes (Hike 51), Glacier Peak north, Monte Cristo peaks and Sloan south, and Mt. Rainier far southeast.

The tread on the north side of June Mountain may be covered by steep, hard snow. If so, climb above, but be careful—the heather is steep and slippery too. In a few hundred feet the trail passes the junction with the Blue Lake trail, which leads in 1½ miles to lower Blue Lake.

The final 3 miles traverse steep alpine parkland, mostly in blueberries and heather with occasional patches of brilliant flowers. At 5600-foot Dishpan Gap, 10 miles from Curry Gap, is the junction with the Cascade Crest Trail.

If transportation can be arranged, a number of alternate exit routes are available, among them the Cascade Crest Trail north to White Pass (Hike 71), then out either the North Fork Sauk River or the White Chuck River; the Cascade Crest Trail south to Stevens Pass; and the little Wenatchee River of Cady Ridge or Cady Pass trails out to Little Wenatchee Ford (Hike 70).

Round trip to Dishpan Gap 23 miles
Allow 2-3 days
High point 5946 feet
Elevation gain about 3500 feet
Best late July through September
USGS Blanca Lake, Bench Mark Mtn.
Forest Service wilderness permit required
**   beyond June Mountain**

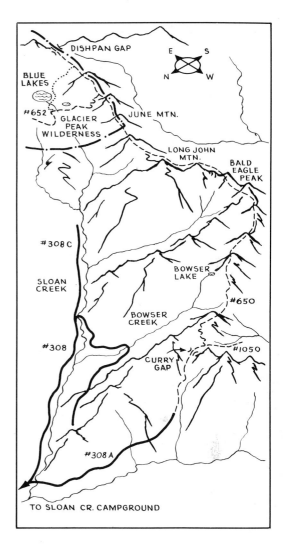

53 GOAT FLATS

The rock spires and icefields of Three Fingers Mountain stand near the west edge of the North Cascades, rising above lowlands and saltwater, prominent on the skyline from as far away as Seattle. On a ridge of the mountain are the lovely alpine meadows of Goat Flats, the most beautiful in the Verlot area. Once upon a time a great network of trails linked the North and South Forks of the Stillaguamish River. Now most of the forest land is chopped up by logging roads, the trails ruined or abandoned or neglected. The hike to Goat Flats follows a small remnant of the old pedestrian network.

Drive the Mountain Loop Highway 6½ miles east from Granite Falls to Forest Service road No. 320 and turn left 1½ miles to a major junction. Go left on road 320, passing several side-roads and also the Meadow Mountain trail. At 17 miles from the Mountain Loop Highway turn right on road No. 320B and in ¼ mile find the trailhead, elevation 2800 feet.

The trail climbs along the forested side of the ridge 2 miles and emerges into subalpine meadows of 3800-foot Saddle Lake. Just before the lake outlet is a three-way junction. The right leads to Meadow Mountain, a tree-covered hill. Straight ahead are campsites and a shelter on the far side of the lake. Take the left fork to Three Fingers and Goat Flats.

From the lake the trail ascends steep slopes above Saddle Creek forests and in 1 mile enters rolling meadows with acres and acres of blueberries and heather. The meadows are broken by groves of alpine trees and dotted with ponds —one in particular, several hundred feet below the trail, offers an excellent camp.

Some 2½ miles from Saddle Lake the trail reaches the meadow plateau of 4700-foot Goat Flats. Near the center is a very old and decrepit log shelter once used as a patrol cabin; good camps are all around. Sad to say, the heather and huckleberries are being trampled to death by hikers who refuse to stay on the trail; leaving the trail to pick berries or enjoy viewpoints is expected, but otherwise parties should keep to the beaten path. For most hikers the Flats are far enough, offering a close-up view of the cliffs and ice of Three Fingers, looks south to Pilchuck, north to Whitehorse and Mt. Baker, west to Puget Sound and the Olympics. Campers get the best: sunsets on peaks and valleys, farm and city lights in the far-below lowland night, a perspective on megalopolis and wildness.

For hikers who want more, the trail goes on, traversing meadows and then climbing steeply up a rocky basin to 6400-foot Tin Can Gap, above the Three Fingers Glacier. From here the way weaves along an airy ridge to the foot of the pinnacle of the 6854-foot South Peak of Three Fingers, atop which is perched a lookout cabin built in the 1930s. The pinnacle once was mounted by a series of ladders, long since rotted away.

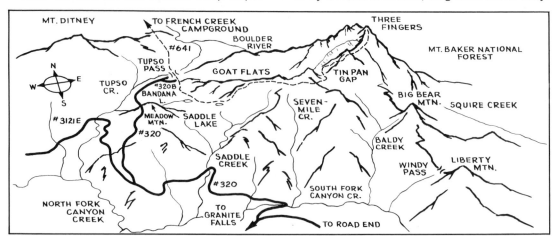

Fogbound Goat Flats

In order to build the cabin, the Forest Service dynamited a platform on the summit; tradition says the original summit never was climbed before it was destroyed. Tradition also says one lookout was so stricken by vertigo he had to telephone Forest Service supervisors to come help him down the ladders. Casual hikers will not want to go beyond Tin Can Gap.

There is an alternate route to Saddle Lake and Goat Flats, longer but richer. Drive east from Arlington to French Creek Campground and hike gorgeous forests of the Boulder River trail 8 miles to Saddle Lake. To preserve intact this superb combination of low forest and high meadow, The Mountaineers proposes a Three Fingers-Whitehorse Wilderness Area. The Forest Service suggests, instead, a ''scenic area'' classification that would cover less of the region and give a lower degree of protection.

Round trip to Goat Flats 9 miles
Hiking time 6 hours
High point 4700 feet
Elevation gain 2000 feet
Best early July through October
One day or backpack
USGS Granite Falls and Silverton

Three Fingers Mountain from Mt. Pilchuck

54 MOUNT PILCHUCK

A peak at the very west edge of the range, prominent on the mountain horizon seen from Puget Sound lowlands, offering broad views west over farms, towns, cities, and saltwaterways to the Olympics and views east to Cascades from Baker to Rainier.

Before logging roads and a ski area intruded, the summit was a splendid all-day trip from

124

valley forests. Now the short trail is traveled as heavily as any path in the Northwest, yet was ignored and neglected by public agencies for many years; since 1971, however, the route has been maintained by Washington State Parks with the help of volunteer work parties.

Drive from Verlot on the Mountain Loop Highway a short mile to the Mt. Pilchuck State Park road. Turn right 7 miles to the road-end parking lot at the ski area, elevation 3200 feet.

The trail starts at the lower end of the parking lot. The way skirts the right (south) edge of the ski area, ascending in forest, then switchbacks across the top of the ski slopes to the upper terminal of the chair lift. Many confusing paths and many dabs of paint all lead to the same place; if in doubt, aim for the lift terminal.

The trail rounds the base of Little Pilchuck, climbing heather and ice-polished rock slabs to a saddle. The main route drops under a cliff

and switchbacks ½ mile up southwest slopes to the summit. (A scramblers' route, marked with paint—which, incidentally, is an obnoxious way to smear up a mountain—goes straight up the ridge over huge blocks of granite.)

Views from the long-abandoned summit lookout cabin are magnificent—lowland civilization in one direction, mountain wilderness in the other. Immediately below sheer cliffs is Frozen Lake, set in a snowy and rocky cirque. For those with left-over energy, an easy way trail descends east along the ridge to a group of small, picturesque tarns perched on the ridge-top.

Round trip 4 miles
Hiking time 4 hours
High point 5324 feet
Elevation gain 2100 feet
Best late June to early November
One day
USGS Granite Falls

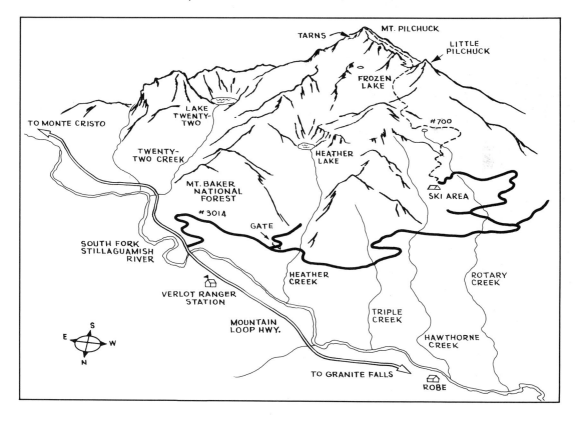

55 MOUNT FORGOTTEN

A valley forest, a waterfall, a small alpine meadow, and views of the impressive wall of Big Four Mountain and the white volcano of Glacier Peak. Come early for flowers, come late for blueberries.

Drive from Verlot on the Mountain Loop Highway 15 miles to Perry Creek road No. 3010, about 1 mile beyond Big Four Campground and just after the crossing of Perry Creek. Turn left 1 mile to the cramped parking area at road-end, elevation 2100 feet.

The trail traverses a steep hillside, now in forest, now in flowered greenery, boulder-hops a frenzied creek, and at 2 miles climbs above Perry Creek Falls. Pause to look over the top of the falls—but don't trust the handrail. A few feet farther the way crosses Perry Creek on boulders. A campsite here.

Elevation is gained steadily to a small field of heather and lupine dotted by alpine trees. The trail switchbacks up forests on the slopes of Mt. Forgotten, enters lush meadows, and disappears at about 5200 feet, 4 miles.

Novice hikers should turn back here, well-rewarded by views of Glacier Peak, seen at the head of the long valley of the White Chuck River, and closer views of Big Four, Twin Peaks, Mt. Dickerman, and the long ridge of Stillaguamish Peak.

Experienced off-trail travelers can continue onward and upward a mile, climbing very steep heather slopes, then scrambling broken rock, to the 6005-foot summit of the peak and more views.

Round trip to meadows 8 miles
Hiking time 7 hours
High point 5200 feet
Elevation gain 3100 feet
Best mid-June through October
One day or backpack
USGS Bedal

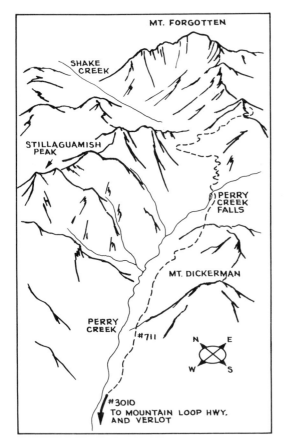

White Chuck Valley and Glacier Peak from Mount Forgotten

56 MOUNT DICKERMAN

All too few trails remain, outside Wilderness Areas and National Parks, which begin in valley bottoms and climb unmarred forests to meadows. The way to Dickerman is strenuous, but the complete experience of life zones from low to high, plus the summit views, are worth every drop of sweat.

Drive from Verlot on the Mountain Loop Highway 16½ miles to a small parking area and easily-overlooked trail sign, elevation 1900 feet, about 2¼ miles beyond Big Four Campground.

The trail doesn't waste time: switchbacks instantly commence climbing up and up and up through lovely cool forest; except perhaps in late summer, several small creeks provide pauses that refresh. Tantalizing glimpses through timber give promise of scenery above. A bit past 2 miles lower-elevation trees yield to Alaska cedars and alpine firs. Then the forest thins as the trail traverses under towering cliffs onto flatter terrain; near here, in a sheltered hollow to the west, is a little lakelet and possible campsites, reached by a faint path.

The next ½ mile ranks among the most famous blueberry patches in the Cascades; in season, grazing hikers may find progress very slow indeed; in the fall, photographers find the blazing colors equally obstructive. Now, too, the horizons grow.

The final mile is somewhat steeper, switchbacking meadows to the broad summit, as friendly a sack-out spot as one can find.

Abrupt cliffs drop toward Perry Creek forests, far below. Beyond are Stillaguamish Peak and Mt. Forgotten. To the east rise Glacier Peak and the horn of Sloan Peak and all the Monte Cristo peaks. And across the South Fork Stillaguamish River are rugged Big Four Mountain and the striking rock slabs of Vesper Peak. But this is only a small part of the panorama which extends in every direction.

Round trip 8 miles
Hiking time 8-9 hours
High point 5723 feet
Elevation gain 3800 feet
Best July through October
One day or backpack
USGS Bedal

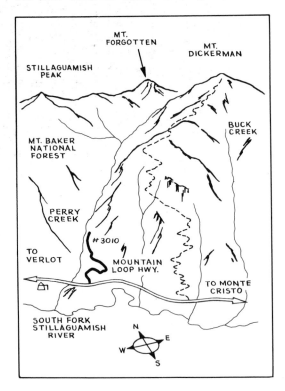

October snowfall on Mt. Dickerman. Del Campo Peak in distance

57 GOAT LAKE

A subalpine lake beneath cliffs and glaciers, a popular destination with hikers of all ages. Wander beside clear, cold water, investigate artifacts of long-ago mining, and admire snow-fed waterfalls frothing down rock walls. The trail (foot travel only) partly traces the route of a wagon road dating from the late 19th century.

Drive from Verlot on the Mountain Loop Highway 19½ miles to Barlow Pass, then north about 4 miles to Elliott Creek road No. 309.

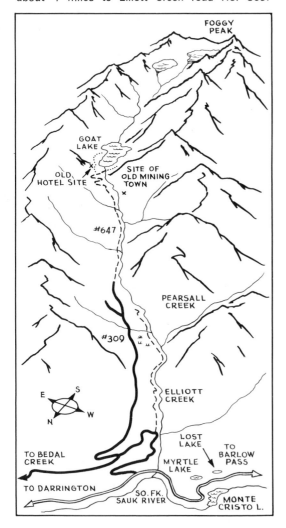

Turn right 2 miles to a junction; go right 1 mile to a parking area large enough for 80 cars and a trail sign, elevation 2500 feet.

(**Note:** At ¼ mile from the Mountain Loop Highway is a trail sign, "Goat Lake." Though this lower 2-mile section of the Elliott Creek trail is now paralleled by road, and thus is not the short way to the lake, it offers a pleasant forest walk along the old wagon track, beside the tumbling creek, for about 1½ miles. The last ½ mile has not yet been reconstructed, but will be in future when funds are available.)

The first ¾ mile or so of the trail from the parking area follows the wagon road, climbing rather gently through cool forest up the valley of Elliott Creek, passing tributary streams at intervals convenient for slaking thirst on a hot day. The next and final ¾ mile switchbacks more steeply, leaving the wagon road and then rejoining it just before the lake outlet.

For an interesting side-trip, at about the ¾-mile mark, the wagon road diverges rightward from the trail and crosses Elliott Creek to decrepit remains of a mining settlement. The road then switchbacks and in roughly ½ mile recrosses the creek on risky remnants of a bridge to meet the trail.

Enjoy the views of Foggy Peak. Prowl relics of what was, some 75 years ago, a busy mining town. In summer sunshine, take a brisk swim.

Beyond the outlet is a nice spot to picnic. The trail continues left around the shore, eventually disappearing in alder and vine maple. On a rocky knoll before the brush begins is a particularly fine place to sit and stare and eat lunch before going home.

Because campers have over-used the lake-shore areas, these are now restricted to picnicking. Camping is permitted only at the old hotel site on a knoll above the outlet.

Round trip 3 miles
Hiking time 2 hours
High point 3162 feet
Elevation gain 700 feet
Best mid-June through October
One day or backpack
USGS Sloan Peak and Bedal

Goat Lake and a shoulder of Foggy Peak

Bedal Peak and the remains of Harry Bedal's cabin

58 BEDAL BASIN

Lovely and lonesome alpine meadows beneath the towering south wall of Sloan Peak, reached by an ancient miners' trail that is missing some of its tread and has boggy sections and steep pitches. A great place for experienced hikers who don't mind sweating for the sake of solitude.

Drive from Verlot on the Mountain Loop Highway 19½ miles to Barlow Pass, then north about 4 miles to Elliott Creek road No. 309. Turn right 2 miles to a junction; go left on Bedel Creek road No. 309A, signed "Bedel Creek Trail." In 2 miles, about ¼ mile beyond the crossing of Bedel Creek, is a sign marking Bedal Basin trail, elevation about 2800 feet. (The road isn't always passable to cars the whole way, adding extra hiking distance.)

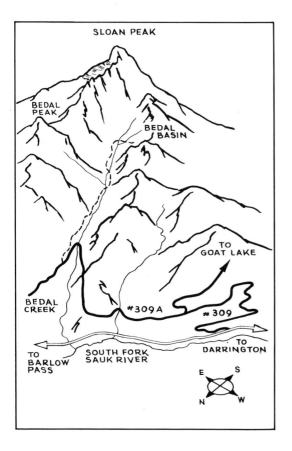

The trail gains altitude constantly, alternating between cool forest and sun-hot avalanche tracks choked with ferns, salmonberry bushes, and a spicing of nettles. At 1½ miles, amid big trees beside the creek, is a campsite much-used by Sloan climbers of years past, before another summit approach became more popular. Cross Bedal Creek here—hopefully on a log. The way gentles out in a broad avalanche area of alder and vine maple and a gathering of tributaries. At 2 miles re-cross the creek.

The trail becomes steep and elusive, sometimes vanishing. The way again crosses the creek, now quite small, loses itself under a huge snow avalanche near an old mine adit, then switchbacks through the woods to the lip of the meadow basin, 5000 feet.

Above is the wall of Sloan. Monster boulders fringe the heather-and-flower floor. Near a great block of rock on the right side of the meadow are rotten logs of Harry Bedal's Cabin, which along about 1940 succumbed to the crushing winter snows. Splendid camps all around. From the pass at the basin head are broad views.

Round trip 6 miles
Hiking time 6 hours
High point 5000 feet
Elevation gain 2200 feet
Best July through October
One day or backpack
USGS Sloan Peak and Bedal

59 GOTHIC BASIN

A glacier-gouged basin designed for wandering. Rounded buttresses polished and scratched by ice, sparkling ponds in scooped-out rock, an Arctic-barren cirque lake, loud waterfalls, meadow nooks, old mines, ore samples, and views of Monte Cristo peaks. The miner-built trail is steep from start to end, and often extremely steep, but mostly in reasonably decent shape.

Drive from Verlot on the Mountain Loop Highway 19½ miles to Barlow Pass. Go straight ahead on the Monte Cristo road 2 miles; ¼

mile beyond the bridge over the South Fork Sauk River, park in a small lot, elevation 2400 feet. A sign marks the beginning of the route.

From the sign, follow boot tracks downstream on gravel several hundred feet to get around an alder patch. Proceed to the river at a point a few yards below the mouth of Weden Creek. Here is a large, time-bleached footlog, chopped flat on top for easy crossing—but unfortunately it no longer reaches the far bank. A newer footlog is so high in the air acrophobics may prefer to go upstream to just above Weden Creek and ford—but in high water this is virtually impossible. The river crossing is the toughest

Sheep Gap Mountain from Gothic Basin

part of the hike and effectively stops casual walkers. Tread starts beyond the footlogs.

The sturdy miners didn't waste effort on switchbacks and the trail is steep all the way. The first 1½ miles are waterless, but luckily shaded by superb big trees. At 1½ miles is a series of three streams rushing down slot gorges; here too are flowers, a mine, and views across Weden Creek to Silvertip Peak.

The gorges may be snow-filled and dangerous until early August; if so, the hiker without ice ax should turn back, content. Beyond, the trail enters brush, the tread gets skimpy and requires some careful walking, and the grade is at least as grueling as ever. A magnificent waterfall, "King Kong's Showerbath," demands a halt amid unpleasantness. Another mine invites a side-trip to inspect rusted garbage. After an especially straight-up and rock-scrambling stretch, the way emerges into a final ½ mile of heather and flowers, traversing the valley wall on meadow shelves, gradually nearing the ridge crest.

At 3 miles, 5000 feet, the trail cuts through the ridge into Gothic Basin and ends in a meadow among buttresses. A good campsite here and many others throughout the basin.

Now explorations. In the lower basin are flower gardens, artifacts of oldtime mining, waterfall gorges, and views down to Weden Creek and across to the Monte Cristo group. Especially fascinating are the rocks: limestone, sandstone, conglomerate, granite, and iron-red mineralized zones, all plucked and polished by the ice, the dominant brownish limestone weathered into oddly-beautiful forms. Follow the stream bed or the buttress crest 300 feet higher to Foggy (Crater) Lake, in a solemn cirque under Gothic Peak and Del Campo. Scramble slabs and talus and blossoms to the ridge of Gothic, or to 5500-foot Foggy Pass between Gothic and Del Campo, or to the ridge east of the lake, for higher views of the Monte Cristos, Sultan Basin, Sloan Peak, and more.

Round trip to basin entrance 6 miles
Hiking time 7 hours
High point 5000 feet
Elevation gain 2600 feet
Best late July through October
One day or backpack
USGS Monte Cristo

Gothic Basin rocks scratched and polished by glaciers

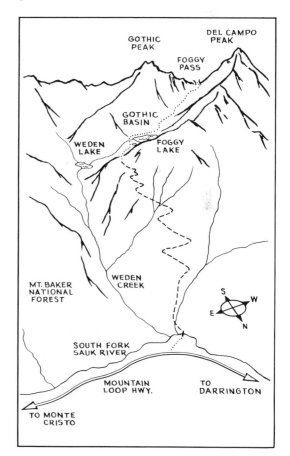

60 POODLE DOG PASS

A deep alpine lake in a cirque of cliffs, waterfalls, and meadows, especially beautiful during fall colors. Because of private land ownership dating back to the 1890s, when Monte Cristo was a roaring mining town, the trail is poor much of the way. However, the difficulties are worth it, as thousands of hikers testify with their feet each summer.

Drive from Verlot on the Mountain Loop Highway 19½ miles to Barlow Pass. Go straight ahead on the Monte Cristo road 4 miles to the entrance to Monte Cristo, now a privately-owned resort. Either park at the crowded Forest Service campground and walk into town for free, or drive ¼ mile into town and pay a fee.

Find the trail between two bridges, elevation 2800 feet, at a Forest Service sign marked "Silver Lake." The first ¼ mile goes along an abandoned truck road up to a mine. The next ½ mile is very poor trail climbing through a logging patch—but don't blame the Forest Service, because this is private land. The way now enters unmolested trees and ascends steeply, in the fashion of no-nonsense miners intent on gaining elevation with minimum fuss. The tread is slippery when wet and always rocky and rough.

At 1½ miles from Monte Cristo is Poodle Dog Pass, 4350 feet. Views of Wilmon Spires through subalpine trees; a good spot for lunch before going home. However, trails beckon beyond the four-way junction at the pass.

The main trail, an historic miners' route, descends Silver Creek to Mineral City. A way trail goes left from the pass 3 up-and-down miles to

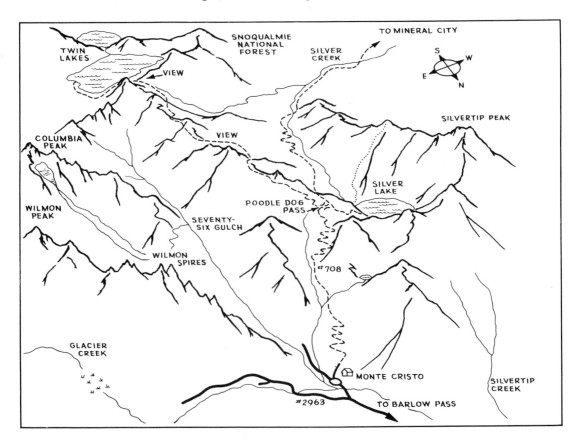

Silver Lake and Silvertip Peak

4560-foot Twin Lakes and a wealth of campsites amid a world of alpine roaming.

Most short-trippers choose Silver Lake, descending the right fork from the pass ¼ mile to the 4260-foot shore. Camping is possible by the outlet but the space is cramped and abused.

For the best views and picnics, cross the outlet and climb open slopes 700 feet to a shoulder of Silvertip Peak. Look down Silver Creek toward Mineral City, look beyond Silver Lake to the Monte Cristo peaks. In season, graze blueberries.

Round trip to Poodle Dog Pass 3 miles
Hiking time 4 hours
High point 4350 feet
Elevation gain 1600 feet
Best July through October
One day
USGS Monte Cristo

61 GLACIER BASIN

Meadows and boulders, flowers and snowfields, cold streams for wading and soft grass for napping, all in a dream basin tucked amid fierce peaks. The miner-built trail is extremely steep and rugged, but short.

Drive from Verlot on the Mountain Loop Highway 19½ miles to Barlow Pass. Go straight ahead on the Monte Cristo road 4 miles to the Monte Cristo parking area (do not confuse with the resort), elevation 2800 feet.

Begin by walking along an abandoned mining road 1½ miles, much of the way through clearcuts on private land, to the start of the true trail, which ascends at a moderate grade through open greenery, then enters alders and Alaska

cedars and becomes steep. Stop for a rest on a rock outcrop above a loud waterfall. The next stretch is the worst, blistering hot in sunny weather, and the straight-up "trail" eroded to a deep rut by years of snowmelt and boots. The rock slabs and mud slopes are slippery, often requiring use of alder handholds. Going down is even messier than going up. But in ½ mile unpleasantness is over, the track easing out on remnants of an old mining road and entering a gulch filled with talus, snow, and whistling marmots.

Below the waste rock and rusted garbage of a mine, the trail divides. (Good campsites here on grassy stream-side flats.) The low route lies beside the creek, on snowfields in early summer, through brush patches later on. For the high route, walk beyond the mine a few yards and climb about 50 feet on dirt and boulders to a rock causeway carrying a large pipe—formerly the water supply for the mine.

With startling abruptness the way opens into the basin—the meandering creeks, the flat fields of grass and blossoms, the many and delightful camps, and the cliffs and glaciers of Cadet and Monte Cristo and Wilmon Peaks, the sharp thrust of Wilmon Spires.

What to do now? Sit and look, have lunch, watch the dippers. Or roam among boulders and wade sandy creeks and maybe organize a snowball fight. Or climb scree slopes to explore old mines. Or take a loitering walk to Ray's Knoll (named for climber Ray Rigg) and views over the basin and down the valley. Scramblers can continue up an easy gully to a higher cirque with glaciers, moraines, waterfalls, and broader views.

Round trip from parking area 5 miles
Hiking time 5 hours
High point 4500 feet
Elevation gain 1700 feet
Best July through October
One day or backpack
USGS Monte Cristo and Blanca Lake

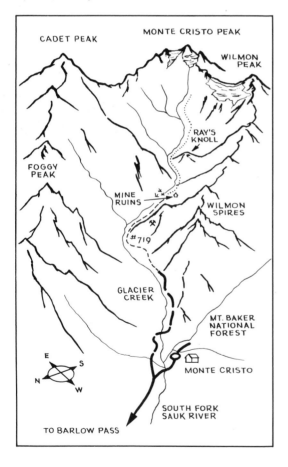

Glacier Basin and Monte Cristo Peak

62   LAKE BLANCA

The rugged cliffs of Kyes, Monte Cristo, and Columbia Peaks above, the white mass of the Columbia Glacier in the upper trough, and the deep waters of ice-fed Lake Blanca filling the lower cirque. A steep forest climb ending in a grand view, with further explorations available to the experienced off-trail traveler.

Drive US 2 to Index junction and turn left on the North Fork Skykomish River road 14 miles to Garland Mineral Springs. At a junction ½ mile

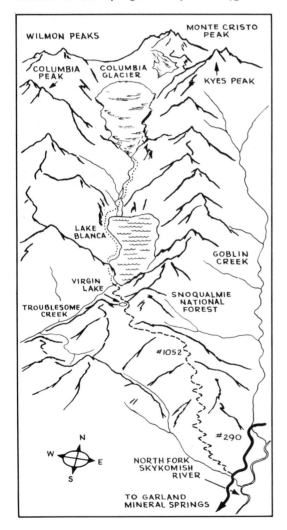

beyond the springs, turn left 2 miles to Lake Blanca trail sign and parking area, elevation 1900 feet.

The trail doesn't mess around with preliminaries, but starts steep and stays that way, switchbacking up and up in forest, eventually with partial views out to Glacier Peak. At 3 miles the way reaches the ridge top at 4600 feet, the highest point of the trip. In a few hundred yards is shallow little Virgin Lake, amid meadows and trees of a saddle on the very crest. Acceptable camping here for those who don't wish to carry packs farther.

Now the trail goes down, sidehilling through trees with glimpses of blue-green water, dropping 600 feet in 1 mile and reaching the 3972-foot lake at the outlet. Relax and enjoy the wind-rippled, sun-sparkling lake, ¾ mile long, the Columbia Glacier, the spectacular peaks. Where the trail hits the lake, and across the outlet stream on the west shore, are a number of over-used but fairly decent campsites. Don't expect to find any easy wood; carry a stove.

Experienced hikers can explore along the rough west shore to the braided stream channels and waterfalls and flowers at the head of the lake. Those with proper mountaineering background and equipment can climb the Columbia Glacier to the col between Columbia and Monte Cristo Peaks and look down to Glacier Basin. The descent into the basin is not technically difficult, but strictly for parties skilled in use of the ice ax.

Round trip to lake 8 miles
Hiking time 6-8 hours
High point 4600 feet
Elevation gain 2700 feet in, 600 feet out
Best July through October
One day or backpack
USGS Blanca Lake

Air view of Lake Blanca and Monte Cristo Peak. Glacier Peak on right

63 EAGLE LAKE

For many years, until very recently, Barclay Lake ranked among the most popular low-elevation hikes in the Cascades, passing through pleasant old forest to the base of the tremendous north wall of Mt. Baring, a trip good in early spring and late fall when higher country was deep in snow. The wall remains, and the brush-bordered lake, but not much forest. Tragically, the walk to Barclay Lake no longer deserves, by itself, inclusion in this book. However, there is still Eagle Lake, offering a staggering view of the Baring nordwand.

Drive US 2 some 6 miles east from Index junction. Turn left on the road signed "Baring," cross railroad tracks, and go 4½ miles to the well-signed trailhead, elevation 2200 feet.

The trail, with minor ups and downs and numerous mudholes, meanders through what remains of the recently-virgin forest of Barclay Creek, in 1½ miles reaching Barclay Lake, 2422 feet, and at 2¼ miles ending on the eastern shore. Camping here, and also a neck-stretching look up and up the precipice of 6123-foot Mt. Baring.

From near the trailend a fishermen's scramble route, unmarked and hard to find, ascends the northern slope to Eagle Lake. The route goes straight up a steep, forested hillside to a rockslide where the tread is lost. Climb the rocks to about 3600 feet and then veer slightly right to another rockslide directly below Stone Lake. From Stone Lake the route contours the edge of marshy Paradise Meadow to 3888-foot Eagle Lake.

By the open shore is a private cabin, kept locked; the owner maintains a nice campsite for public use near the outlet.

The special feature of the trip is the cross-valley look at the Baring wall, a legend among climbers for difficulty and treachery and nastiness; so far it has been ascended only once. For more views, and for meadow-roaming, wander up the easy slopes of 5936-foot Townsend Mountain.

Round trip to Eagle Lake 8½ miles
Hiking time 6 hours
High point 3888 feet
Elevation gain 1700 feet
Best late June through October
One day or backpack
USGS Baring

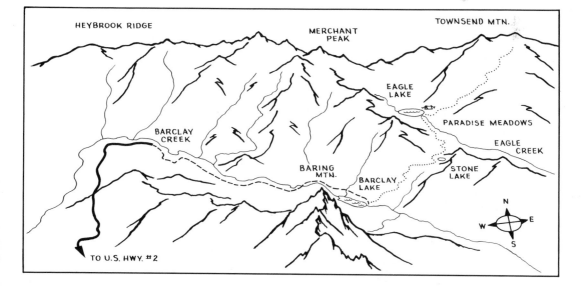

North wall of Baring Mountain and Barclay Lake

64 SCORPION MOUNTAIN
(Johnson Ridge Trail)

Looking for views from an easy trail? Try Evergreen Mountain. Looking for a pleasant family walk? Choose any other destination but Scorpion! Even the access road, carved into a steep hillside stripped bare of trees, is difficult.

And there is no water on the path, making at least one loaded canteen essential. However, hikers seeking solitude and a nice view at the end of a tough trail will find Scorpion worth a day's effort.

This hike was selected to replace Evergreen Mountain, which between writing and publication of the first edition of this book was so

6190-foot Mt. Fernow on right from Scorpion Mountain. Mt. Daniel, Mt. Hinman, and the Dutch Miller Gap peaks in the distance

vandalized by logging roads that the former 6-mile trail shrank to less than a mile. Undoubtedly Scorpion Mountain is slated for the same fate, so go now before the bulldozers and chainsaws arrive.

Drive US 2 to Skykomish. Just beyond town turn left on Beckler River road No. 280. At 7 miles turn right on road No. 273, signed Johnson Creek and Johnson Ridge Trail. At 1.7 miles from Beckler River road keep straight ahead at a junction, and at 5.6 miles turn right onto road No. 273A and continue to its end at 7 miles and about 3500 feet. If the going is too hairy, park and walk the last mile.

There is no formal trailhead. From the road-end climb 3/4 mile up a shadeless clearcut, picking from the maze of cat roads one that can be followed to the ridge top, where the trail starts.

The trail is seldom used and practically never maintained. It was cleared in 1967 in the process of fighting a series of little fires, all fortunately extinguished before reaching proportions of the devastating Evergreen Mountain fire which occurred at the same time. The trail is obscured here and there by windfalls but there is no problem detouring around them. If the tread is lost just follow the ridge top.

The heavily-wooded ridge crest occasionally offers glimpses of rocky 6190-foot Mount Fernow to the south. At 2 1/4 miles the trail passes over the top of 5056-foot Sunrise Mountain, with a view of Glacier Peak, and then drops about 300 feet before climbing nearly to the top of 5540-foot Scorpion Mountain at 4 miles. Leave the path at its highest point and follow the ridge a few hundred feet to the summit, flanked by a lush carpet of grass and flowers and surrounded by a panorama of the Cascades.

The trail continues around the southern shoulder of the mountain and drops 500 feet to tiny Joan Lake at 4 1/2 miles.

Round trip 8 miles
Hiking time 6 hours
High point 5540 feet
Elevation gain 2300 feet in, 300 feet out
Best July through October
One day
USGS Evergreen Mountain and Captain Point

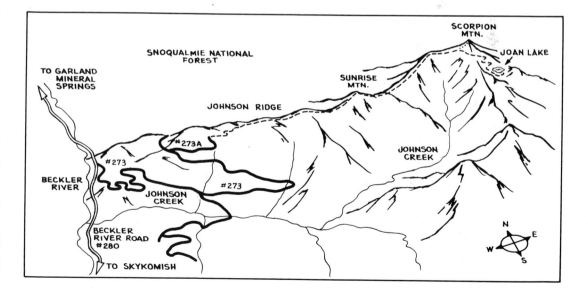

65 LAKE VALHALLA

North from Stevens Pass the Cascade Crest Trail roams by a splendid succession of meadowy alpine lakes. First in line is Lake Valhalla, set in a cirque under the cliffs of Lichtenberg Mountain.

Drive US 2 to Stevens Pass, elevation 4061 feet, and park in the lot at the east end of the summit area. Behind some buildings is the start of the Cascade Crest Trail.

The way begins along the original grade of the Great Northern Railroad, used when trains went over the top of the pass, the right-of-way was abandoned upon completion of the first Cas-

cade Tunnel (predecessor of the present tunnel) early in the century.

From the open hillside, views extend beyond the pass to ski slopes and down Stevens Creek to Nason Creek and far east out the valley. Below is the roar of highway traffic. In 1½ miles the gentle path rounds the end of the ridge and enters the drainage of Nason Creek. Here, a side-trail drops east ½ mile to the old Cascade Tunnel, now employed as a research station by University of Washington geophysicists.

The main trail descends a bit to cross a little stream, climbs a ridge, and at 3½ miles enters a basin of meadows and marsh. Staying east and below the Cascade Crest, the way ascends easily to a 5100-foot spur, then drops to the rocky shore of the 4830-foot lake.

Heavily-used and frequently-crowded camps lie among trees near the outlet; wood is hard to come by, so carry a stove. For explorations, climb heather meadows to the summit of 5920-foot Lichtenberg and broad views, or continue north on the Cascade Crest Trail (Hike 101) as far as time and energy allow.

A much shorter (5 miles round-trip) but less scenic approach is via the Smith Brook trail (Hike 66) which joins the Cascade Crest Trail at Union Gap ½ mile from the road. The Crest Trail leads south from the Gap 2 miles to Lake Valhalla.

Round trip 11 miles
Hiking time 6 hours
High point 5100 feet
Elevation gain 1100 feet
Best mid-July through October
One day or backpack
USGS Labyrinth Mtn.

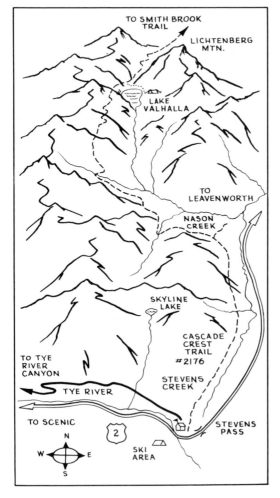

Lake Valhalla from Crest Trail near Lichtenberg Pass

Lake Janus and Mountain Memorial Cabin

66 LAKE JANUS AND GRIZZLY PEAK

A strikingly-beautiful alpine lake and a long ridge trail, sometimes in Western Washington and sometimes in Eastern Washington and sometimes straddling the line. An easy but spectacular stretch of the Cascade Crest Trail. The trip can be done in a day but at least a weekend should be planned—the lake is inviting and "looking around the next corner" is bound to be irresistible.

Drive US 2 east 4½ miles from Stevens Pass and turn left on Smith Brook road. Cross Nason Creek bridge, turn left, and follow the road 3¼ miles toward Rainy Pass to the Smith Brook trailhead, elevation 3800 feet. There is no space for cars so drop passengers and packs here and drive another ½ mile to the Rainy Pass parking area. (Eventually the Forest Service will build a trail from the pass.)

Climb a long ½ mile on trail No. 1590 to 4680-foot Union Gap and the junction with the Cascade Crest Trail. Turn right, dropping 700 feet down the west side of the crest to round cliffs of Union Peak, then regaining part of the elevation before reaching 4146-foot Lake Janus, 2½ miles from the Gap. The trail goes through pleasant forest with the far-off sound of Rapid River. Though the grade is gentle, the tread is badly water-eroded in places from years of heavy use, making walking a little difficult.

The lake is everything an alpine lake should be—sparkling water surrounded by meadows and tall trees and topped by the bright green slopes of 6007-foot Jove Peak. Numerous camps are available, including a mountain memorial cabin that has not been treated kindly by the public. Wood is scarce so carry a stove.

From the lake the trail enters forest on smooth and easy tread, climbs 1100 feet in 1½ miles to the Cascade Crest, contours around the Eastern Washington side of a small hill and then ducks around a corner back into Western Washington, a process repeated frequently on the way to Grizzly Peak.

Every turn of the crest-wandering trail offers new views. Look east down into Lake Creek and Little Wenatchee River drainage and across to nearby Mt. Labyrinth. Look north to Glacier Peak.

Look west down to the Rapid River and out to peaks above the Skykomish. At 2 miles from Lake Janus is a glimpse of Margaret Lake, some 400 feet below the trail. A short ½ mile beyond is a view down to Glasses Lake and larger Heather Lake; this is a good turnaround point for day hikers.

At about 4½ miles from Lake Janus the trail climbs within a few feet of the top of 5597-foot Grizzly Peak and more panoramas—but unfortunately not of Glacier Peak, cut off by a nameless peak ½ mile north. The trail also goes close to the summit of the nameless peak, with a view of Glacier Peak; succumbing to this temptation will lead to further temptations, on and on along the Cascade Crest Trail.

Round trip to Grizzly Peak 15 miles
Hiking time 6-8 hours
High point 5597 feet
Elevation gain 2200 feet in, 800 feet out
Best mid-July through October
One day or backpack
USGS Labyrinth Mtn. and Captain Point

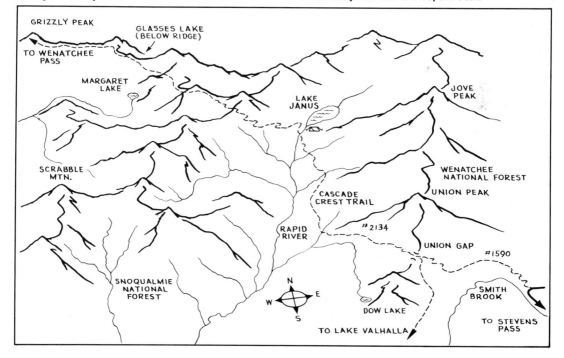

Mountain goat at Alpine Lookout

67 NASON RIDGE

A magnificent journey 26 miles through wide-sky highlands from near the Cascade Crest to near Lake Wenatchee. The full length of the ridge can be walked on a single long trip, or the climaxes attained on day or weekend hikes via four access trails.

Drive US 2 east 4.2 miles from Stevens Pass and turn left on Smith Brook road. Cross Nason Creek bridge, turn left, and continue 3½ miles to 4600-foot Rainy Pass. Go 100 feet beyond the lily pond at the top of the pass and on the right side of the road find a faint track crossing the small meadow. The poorly-maintained route goes straight up, gaining some 600 feet to about 5200 feet, holding elevation around the south side of the first peak and the north sides of the next two peaks, then dropping into Snowy Creek and at an estimated 4 miles reaching the end of the Snowy Creek trail at a point 2¼ miles from the road.

Snowy Creek access: For this pleasant way to Nason Ridge through cool forest, by many small creeks, drive 6 miles from the Little Wenatchee River road (Hike 69) on the Rainy Creek road. (Logging will disrupt the trail in 1973. Afterward, a spur road will shorten the trail by 1 mile.)

Starting at 3640 feet, climb 2¼ well-graded but sketchily-maintained miles on trail No. 1531 to the 4640-foot junction with the trail from Rainy Pass.

In 1 mile east from this junction, 5 miles from Rainy Pass, is a 3800-foot campsite in a large, level meadow below cliffs of Rock Mountain. Tread vanishes in the meadow but re-appears halfway across, on the left. The next 2 miles are grueling, entering trees and leaving them, climbing 1800 feet to the ridge of Rock Mountain. (From the junction on the ridge it's a 1/3-mile, 300-foot detour to the 6852-foot summit lookout cabin.) From the lookout junction at 7 miles, the way drops ¾ mile to the 6200-foot intersection with the Rock Mountain trail.

Rock Mountain access: For this popular approach, drive US 2 east from Stevens Pass 9 miles (½ mile east of Highway Department sheds) to Rock Mountain trail No. 1587, elevation 2700 feet. The trail ascends endless short switchbacks 4 miles to Nason Ridge trail, gaining 3500 feet.

From the Rock Mountain trail junction the Nason Ridge trail descends ½ mile to a campsite at 5800-foot Rock Lake, 8¼ miles from Rainy Pass. At 9½ miles is the tiny Crescent Lake and more camping. At 12¼ miles pass the junction with the west branch of Merritt Lake trail No. 1588. (At 13½ miles a fisherman's path leaves the main trail, going over the ridge top and down in 1½ miles to Lost Lake.) At 13¾ miles the main trail passes above 5003-foot Merritt Lake to a junction with the east branch of Merritt Lake trail No. 1588.

Merritt Lake access: Drive US 2 east 12½ miles from Stevens Pass to the trailhead beside the highway, elevation 2700 feet. The trail climbs 2600 feet in 4 miles to either the lake or Nason Ridge.

From Merritt Lake the Nason Ridge trail continues 3 high miles to a junction, 16¾ miles, with the Alpine Lookout trail. (For the side-trip, climb west 1/3 mile to the 6200-foot lookout cabin.) The main trail goes eastward along the crest, very gradually losing elevation, 2½ miles to a junction with Round Mountain trail No. 1529.

Alpine Lookout access: Drive US 2 east from Stevens Pass about 17 miles to a Highway Department rest area. A few hundred feet beyond, turn left on Butcher Creek road No. 2717. Cross Nason Creek, avoid spur roads, turn right at 2½ miles, and drive almost to road-end. Find the trailhead (Round Mountain trail No. 1529) at 4100 feet. Climb 1000 feet in 1½ miles to the junction with the Nason Ridge trail and continue west 2½ miles to the lookout.

From this junction the main trail follows the crest, coming to 5500-foot Dishpan Camp at 21½ miles, Kahler Creek trail at 22½ miles, and at 26½ miles the 1900-foot road-end. To reach this road-end by car, drive from US 2 on Highway 207 toward Lake Wenatchee State Park. Enter Nason Creek Campground and just across Nason Creek bridge turn left and hike a service road (gated) about ½ mile to the east end of Nason Ridge trail No. 1583.

One-way from Rainy Pass to Lake Wenatchee 26½ miles
Allow 3-5 days
High point (Rock Mountain) 6852 feet
Elevation gain about 4800 feet
Best mid-July through October
USGS Wenatchee Lake and Labyrinth Mtn.

Round trip to Alpine Lookout via Round Mountain trail
 8 miles
Allow 6 hours
High point 6200 feet
Elevation gain 1700 feet
Best August through October
One day
USGS Wenatchee Lake

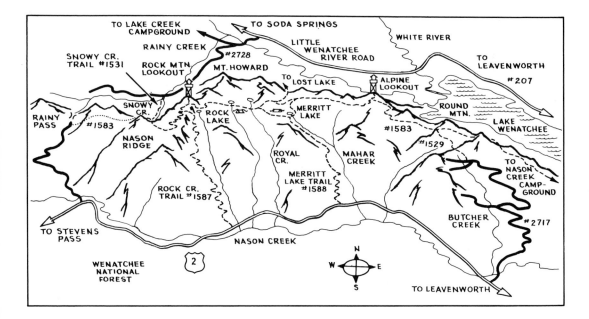

Wenatchee Lake and the meanders of the Little Wenatchee and White Rivers, from Dirtyface Lookout

68 DIRTYFACE PEAK

A stiff climb, cruelly hot in summer and wind-less weather, to an airy view over Lake We-natchee and into the Glacier Peak Wilderness Area. The last 2½ miles are dry so carry lots of water. For hikers who don't mind a few small snowpatches, this is a fine mid-June trip.

Drive US 2 east from Stevens Pass 19 miles and turn left to Lake Wenatchee. Pass the state park road, the roads to Plain and Fish Lake, and continue to Lake Wenatchee Ranger Station. Turn right to the small campground behind the station; just before the first campsite is the trailhead, elevation 1900 feet.

The trail is mostly in very good shape, wide and smooth, but steep, very steep, gaining about 1000 feet a mile. (The trail sign says the peak is 4 miles, but the distance is definitely 4½ miles or more.) In the first mile are several creeks. At 1½ miles is an abandoned logging road. Fol-low it a short ½ mile to its end and pick up the trail again. Here is a good campsite in the woods, and also the last water.

The way relentlessly climbs 70 exasperating switchbacks (we counted them) to the summit ridge. At about switchback 45 the trail leaves tall Ponderosa pine and enters alpine trees and flowers—and glorious views of the lake. Near the ridge crest is a small sign pointing to "Last Water." Ignore it; the water is over the ridge and down the other side. From the crest it is almost ½ mile and 11 more switchbacks (for a total of 81) to the 6193-foot summit.

Enjoy views west to Nason Ridge (Hike 67), north up the Napeequa River to Clark Mountain, Chiwawa Ridge, and the Chiwawa valley, and east to endless hills. Below to the left is Fish Lake and directly beneath, Lake Wenatchee. At the head of the latter note the vast marshes and the meandering streams: at one point the White River comes within a few feet of the lake but snakes back another ¼ mile before entering. (All this magnificence of marshland and meanders, all the wildlife range, would be endangered if a dam now being plotted is allowed to materialize.) Ant-size boats can be seen on the lakes, and cars on the highways.

In early July the summit is a striking rock garden of blossoming phlox. In late summer and fall the upper trail offers blueberries to sate a perhaps gigantic thirst.

Round trip 9½ miles
Hiking time 7 hours
High point 6193 feet
Elevation gain 4300 feet
Best mid-June through October
One day or backpack
USGS Wenatchee Lake

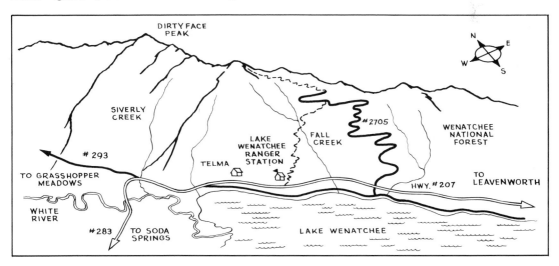

69 MINOTAUR LAKE

Minotaur Lake lies in a Grecian setting. Above and beyond are the rock walls of 6376-foot Labyrinth Mountain. Below is Theseus Lake. Heather meadows and alpine firs complete the mythological scene. No longer are seven girls and seven boys annually given in sacrifice to Minotaur, but each year visitors pay (in season) a tribute to the gods as the bugs take a libation of blood.

Drive to Lake Wenatchee Ranger Station (Hike 68) and continue 1½ miles to a junction. Turn left on the Little Wenatchee River road 6 miles to Rainy Creek road No. 2728. Turn left 6 miles to the trailhead, elevation 3520 feet, a couple hundred feet after crossing a small creek.

The first 2 miles are on North Fork Rainy Creek trail no. 1517, maintained but muddy. The trail switchbacks up a hill, drops to cross an unnamed creek, and follows this stream ¾ mile. The North Fork trail goes on, but at about 2 miles find an unmaintained fisherman's path shooting straight up. There is no formal tread, only the groove pounded by many boots. The route gains 1500 feet in the next 2 miles. The track is well-marked and has plenty of water; views are limited to a few glimpses out through trees. At the end of the long, steep ascent the trail turns down valley ½ mile, losing 100 feet, then turns again and heads up Minotaur Creek. Forest gives way to highland meadows and at 4 miles is 5550-foot Minotaur Lake.

Around the shores are several good campsites. Cross the outlet and walk a few yards northeast to see 5060-foot Theseus Lake; a very steep path leads down to its shores and more good camps.

For broader views of mountains west to Stevens Pass, north to Glacier Peak, and east beyond Lake Wenatchee, scramble easily to open ridges above the lakes and wander the crests.

Round trip to Minotaur Lake 8 miles
Hiking time 5 hours
High point 5550 feet
Elevation gain 2000 feet
Best mid-July through October
One day or backpack
USGS Labyrinth Mtn.

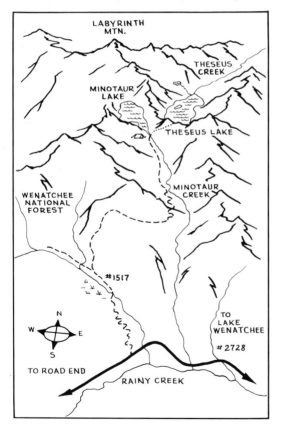

Theseus Lake (John Spring photo)

70 MEANDER MEADOW— KODAK PEAK

A forest-and-meadow valley floor, a steep-and-hot struggle, and finally a superb little basin of grass and flowers and slow, deep meanders of the headwater stream. Above lie parklands of the Cascade Crest and endless easy wandering with views to everywhere.

Drive to Lake Wenatchee Ranger Station (Hike 68) and continue 1½ miles to a junction. Turn left on Little Wenatchee River road 14½ miles to the end at Little Wenatchee Ford Campground and trailhead, elevation 3000 feet.

In ¼ mile the trail passes a junction with the Poe Mountain trail, which climbs steeply right in about 2½ miles to a 6015-foot summit of "Poet Ridge"—see below for a possible alternate return route. (Poe also makes a good day hike from the road.)

The first 4 miles are gently up and down, with a net gain of only 700 feet, alternating between forest and glade and frequently crossing creeks. The easy part ends at the edge of a vast meadow; here are a small creek and a campsite. The next 2 miles, gaining 1300 feet, may require courage and fortitude when the sun is blazing and flies are biting, especially if the sheep have been here recently. The way climbs grass and brush, becoming confused in a maze of sheep paths through sometimes-soggy greenery; look sharp to stay on the track. Once above the vast meadow, in mixed trees and avalanche paths, the tread is distinct but steep. Fortunately there is a spring just where needed most. And views grow with every step. At 6 miles the trail drops a short bit into the basin of 5000-foot Meander Meadow; the camps are splendid and so are the hours of flower walking.

The trail crosses a meandering highland fragment of the Little Wenatchee River and climbs another open mile and 500 more feet to a ridge and trail fork. Go either way—north or south of a small hill—to the Cascade Crest Trail at 5450-foot Sauk Pass.

The junction with the Crest Trail gives the first view of Glacier and marks the boundary of the Glacier Peak Wilderness Area. Walk the trail north ½ mile to a 5630-foot saddle above Meander Meadow, on the east ridge of 6121-foot Kodak Peak. Climb blossoms ½ mile to the summit panorama and start cranking film through the Kodak.

For a loop trip, three alternate routes can be taken back down to Little Wenatchee Ford:

Casy Pass: See Hike 71.

Cady Ridge: From the junction with the Cascade Crest Trail at Sauk Pass, go 2 miles south and turn left on Cady Ridge trail. Tread is often

Meander Meadow

lost in meadows, but the way climbs and contours rather obviously to the south of the highest point on the ridge and then follows ups and downs of the crest 2½ miles before starting a long, steep, dusty descent. Within ½ mile of the bottom intersect a new, 10 percent-grade trail. Take your choice: the old too-steep track, or the new frustratingly-flat zigzag which adds an extra mile. Both trails join the Cady Creek trail a few hundred yards from the road-end. There is no water on the ridge, which is not recommended for an up-hike. Total distance from the Crest to the road, about 5 miles.

Poet Ridge: From the 5630-foot saddle below Kodak Peak, traverse open highlands, mostly without tread, eastward past 6401-foot Bryant Peak and 6577-foot Longfellow Peak to 6015-foot Poe Mountain. The trail, though signed Bryant Peak trail No. 1544, has not been maintained for decades and is recommended only for experienced cross-country travelers. There is, however, no danger of getting lost—either stay on the ridge-top or on the south side. In about 7 miles from the Kodak Peak saddle is Poe Mountain Lookout, from which good trail descends some 2½ miles to the road.

Round trip to Meander Meadow 12 miles,
  Kodak Peak 16 miles
Allow 2-3 days
High point (Kodak Peak) 6121 feet
Elevation gain 2000 feet to Meander Meadow,
  3100 feet to Kodak Peak
Best mid-July through October
USGS Poe Mtn. and Bench Mark Mtn.

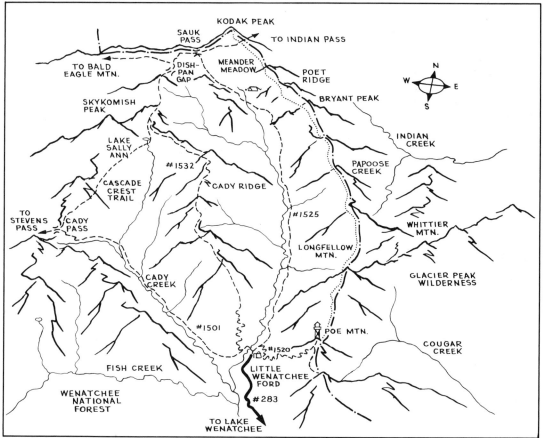

Sauk River valley from Crest Trail on side of Indian Head Peak. Sloan Peak on left

71   CADY PASS TO WHITE PASS

Some argue this is the most beautiful segment of the entire Cascade Crest Trail. Certainly it offers one of the longest gentle meadow walks anywhere in the range. Where else can hikers wander at and above timberline a dozen miles, seldom dropping or climbing more than a few hundred feet, never with any difficulties, and always with views?

Any part of the ridge route is worth a visit— the problem is that none of the many accesses is quick and easy, and once on the crest it's excruciatingly painful to stop short of the climax. Therefore the best plan is to do the whole walk on a single trip.

Drive to Little Wenatchee Ford Campground, elevation 3000 feet (Hike 70). Park here and walk back down the road a short bit to the trailhead.

The trail drops to a bridge over the Little Wenatchee River. In 1/4 mile more keep left at the junction with the Cady Ridge trail and follow Cady Creek 5 miles, gaining 1700 feet (including ups and downs), to wooded and waterless 4300-foot Cady Pass. Turn right on the Cascade Crest Trail, passing a possible camp in 1/2 mile, climbing 1300 feet in 2 miles to break out above timberline on the divide between Cady Creek and Pass Creek. Now the way goes around this side or that of one small knoll after another, alternating between Eastern and Western Washington. Then comes a traverse along the east slope of 6368-foot Skykomish Peak. At 2½ miles from Cady Pass (8 miles from the road) is 5479-foot Lake Sally Ann, a charming little tarn amid cliff-bordered meadows; this is the first dependable campsite on the trip, a strenuous day from the cars but with a delightful ending.

Less than ½ mile north from the lake is an intersection with the Cady Ridge trail (Hike 70); another camp here in a broad meadow. Climb a waterfall-sparkling basin to 5680-foot Wards Pass and roam parkland atop and near the crest to 5600-foot Dishpan Gap at about 4¼ miles from Cady Pass. Here is a junction with access trails from the west (Hikes 51 and 52).

The Crest Trail contours on in picturesque alpine trees and heather meadows to 5450-foot Sauk Pass, 5½ miles from Cady Pass, and the two junctions with the little Wenatchee River trail (Hike 70). Traverse the green slopes of Kodak Peak to a 5630-foot saddle above the flat basin of Meander Meadow; the short side-trip to the 6121-foot summit of Kodak gives big views.

A descent across a gorgeous alpine basin and down forest leads to partly-grassy, somewhat-boggy, mostly-wooded Indian Pass, 5000 feet, 7 miles from Cady Pass, and the junction with Indian Creek trail. Pleasant campsites in the pass—but usually no potable water except in early summer.

Climb forest, climb gardens around the side of Indian Head Peak to tiny Kid Pond (camping) and beyond to 5378-foot Lower White Pass, 8½ miles from Cady Pass, and the junction with the White River trail.

The final 1½ miles are the climax, past Reflection Pond (camping) into magnificent flower fields culminating at 5904-foot White Pass, 10 miles from Cady Pass, 15½ miles from the start. Just west below the pass is a shelter cabin; all around are good camps.

For dramatic views of Glacier Peak and the White Chuck Meadows, walk the trail west to Red Pass or climb 7030-foot White Mountain. (For details, see Hike 50.)

If transportation can be arranged, a party can continue out to civilization via the North Fork Sauk River (Hike 50) or the White Chuck River (Hike 47). The simplest plan is to return

south on the Cascade Crest; for variety, drop back to Little Wenatchee Ford via Poet Ridge, Meander Meadow, or Cady Ridge (for all these, see Hike 70).

Round trip 31 miles
Allow 4-6 days
High point (White Pass) 5900 feet
Elevation gain about 4000 feet in, about 1200 feet out
Best late July through September
USGS Bench Mark Mtn., Poe Mtn., and Glacier Peak
Forest Service wilderness permit required
beyond Kodak Peak

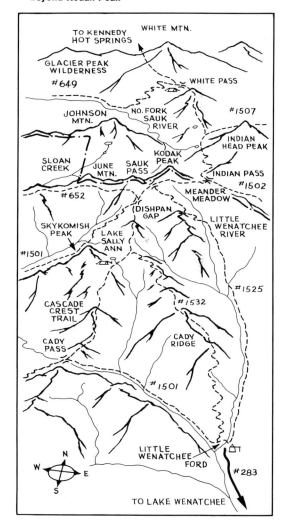

72 MOUNT DAVID

Climb a real mountain, 7431 feet high. As with any other main-range Cascade peak of such elevation, the ascent is lengthy and strenuous. However, the cliffy summit, where otherwise climbers would rope up, has a trail blasted to a long-abandoned lookout cabin. Panoramic views of countless peaks, and almost a vertical mile below is the river bottom. The trail is dry so carry plenty of water. It's best not to try the hike until August, when snow has melted from the steep and potentially-dangerous gullies.

Drive to Lake Wenatchee Ranger Station (Hike 70) and continue 1½ miles to a junction. Keep right on the White River road 10 miles to the

Abandoned lookout on top of Mt. David

end and trailhead, elevation 2200 feet. (Do not attempt to cross the river at White River Falls—there is no bridge.)

Take the Indian Creek trail, crossing the White River on a large bridge. On the far side turn left, downstream. In about ½ mile watch for a fork. The left leads to an overlook of White River Falls. The right, less used, is the main trail. In a short mile from the bridge is another junction. Turn right on the Mount David trail—subsequent mileages are calculated from this beginning.

There is a big bundle of altitude to gain and the trail gets at it immediately. At 1/3 mile cross the last reliable stream; fill a canteen or two. In 1 mile the tread is difficult to find in buckbrush and vine maple of an avalanche slope. From here the trail is well-graded, though with a few fallen trees. Relentless switchbacks grind up and up through forest to the ridge crest at 3½ miles.

The final 3½ miles follow ups and downs of the ridge, sometimes contouring below high points, switchbacking up one gully then moving into the next. Around several cliffs the trail has been eroded away, but is still safe. Views grow: south to Lake Wenatchee, Mt. Daniels, and Mt. Rainier and north to Clark Mountain. Frequent glimpses of the lookout cabin ahead.

Snow remains on slopes directly under the summit rocks until late August—a good reason for doing the trip no earlier. Tread is very obscure in a talus here and easily may be lost. If so, climb to the ridge and find the way where it crosses to the south side of the peak. The last few hundred feet have been blasted from cliff and improved by cement steps. Once there was even a guard rail, but it's gone now. Hikers suffering from acrophobia will be happier to settle for a conclusion somewhat short of the absolute top.

The cabin, 7 miles from the start of the Mount David trail, perches on a small knob with long views to all horizons. Glacier Peak, 12 miles away, dominates, but careful study reveals many other mountains of the Cascade Crest; off west, above the head of Indian Creek, is Sloan Peak. Look down and down to the Indian Creek trail, crossing stream-side meadows.

The only possible campsite is a flat meadow, elevation about 5200 feet. The meadow is some 500 feet below the trail, reached by a spur descending from a short bit past the 4-mile marker.

Round trip 16 miles
Hiking time 10 hours
High point 7431 feet
Elevation gain 5200 feet
Best mid-August through September
One day or backpack
USGS Wenatchee Lake
Forest Service wilderness permit required

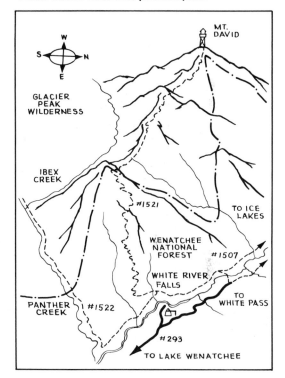

73 NAPEEQUA VALLEY VIA BOULDER PASS

The Napeequa is the fabled Shangri-La of the Cascades. As in the story, the only entries are high, desolate passes, below which lie lush green meadows surrounded by towering cliffs topped by glaciers. However, there are at least two differences from the valley described by James Hilton in his novel: no beautiful Chinese girls in a monastery; instead, there are, in season, swarms of vicious huge bugs to bedevil the poor pilgrim.

Drive the White River road to its end and

Napeequa River from footbridge

trailhead, elevation 2200 feet (Hike 72). Hike the White River trail 4 pleasant virtually-level miles through lovely virgin forest to the Boulder Pass trail, 2470 feet. Subsequent mileages are calculated from this junction.

The well-graded trail climbs steadily to Boulder Pass. In about 2½ miles is a crossing of Boulder Creek. At 4 miles is 5000-foot Basin Camp, under the walls of 8676-foot Clark Mountain. This is a logical and splendid spot to end the first day—and also a grand base for an extra day exploring a very faint path west to a 6150-foot saddle overlooking the White River. To find the path, cross the creek from camp to a point just under a slab of red rock on the opposite side of the valley. Even without tread the going would be fairly easy up open meadows.

From Basin Camp the trail climbs 2½ miles to 6250-foot Boulder Pass, the meadowy saddle to the immediate south of Clark Mountain. Look down into the Napeequa valley and over to Little Giant Pass (Hike 74). The hike to here, 10½ miles from the road, makes a strenuous but richly-rewarding 2-3-day trip.

To continue into Shangri-La, descend monotonous switchbacks 3½ miles to the valley floor. This is the new-style Forest Service 10 percent-grade concept at its very worst, with switchbacks so flat (designed for fat dude horses, not true mountain horses, much less hikers) they invite shortcutting; even so, please resist the temptation, since each shortcut eventually becomes an erosion gully.

The trail reaches the valley floor at 4340 feet and here the trouble starts. The Forest Service is unable to keep a bridge across the swift-flowing Napeequa River, which can be forded at this point in late August but in high water is very treacherous. It is better to go downstream 1 mile to the old sheep crossing, where the stream is much wider. The sheep driveway can be picked up near the first switchback at Boulder Pass, going straight down to the ford.

The explorations are limited only by the time available. Follow the trail up the wide, green valley floor 5 or 6 miles; good camps are numerous. In ½ mile look to glaciers on Clark Mountain. In 2 miles pass under the falls of Louis Creek, where the formal trail ends. Wander

on and on, higher and higher, better and better. Experienced off-trail travelers can climb all the way to 6876-foot High Pass.

Round trip to Napeequa bridge 28 miles
Allow 3-7 days
High point (Boulder Pass) 6250 feet
Elevation gain 4250 feet in, 2000 feet out
Best mid-July through October
USGS Holden and Glacier Peak

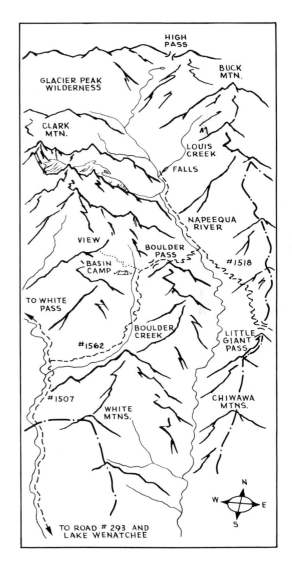

Napeequa valley from Little Giant Pass. Clark Mountain on left

74 NAPEEQUA VALLEY VIA LITTLE GIANT PASS

Climb to the most superb view of the lush Napeequa valley. Look down on the silvery river meandering through green meadows. See the gleaming ice on Clark Mountain and glimpse a piece of Glacier Peak. But if this is **Little** Giant pass, let's not try for **big** giant pass, wherever that may be. Despite extreme difficulty the trail is well worth a day or weekend. However, though the Little Giant route to the Napeequa is some 5 miles or more shorter than by way of Boulder Pass (Hike 73), it's not recommended for backpacking—too steep.

Drive US 2 east from Stevens Pass 19 miles

to the Lake Wenatchee junction. Turn left toward the lake and a short distance beyond the Wenatchee River bridge keep right at a Y and go 1½ miles on paved road. Turn left on gravel road No. 311 signed "Fish Lake" (don't confuse with other Fish Lake roads) and "Meadow Creek." (Eventually there will be a sign saying "Chiwawa River road.") Follow this road past the south side of Fish Lake, cross the Chiwawa River on a concrete bridge, and proceed up the east bank. At about 19 miles turn left into Maple Creek Campground. Drive to the upper part of the camp and find the trailhead at a small footbridge, elevation 2600 feet.

Trail mileages given by various sources are contradictory; the ones used here are those on the trailhead sign. The first ¼ mile follows the creek. Then there's a choice—straight up a sheep driveway or, better, 1 mile of graded trail. After that it's the driveway or nothing. In 2 miles is a large avalanche swath; cross Little Giant Creek to a small campsite on the far side, 4000 feet.

Now the way steepens, if that's possible, and in about 3 miles is lost on a big slab of bare rock. Scramble to the very top and keep climbing. Pass occasional campsites (with water that will be much appreciated) and go on and on, up and up and up—steeply. The final mile to the 6409-foot summit and the boundary of the Glacier Peak Wilderness Area, 6 miles from the road, is well-graded through meadows.

Better views can be obtained by dropping a few hundred feet down the trail toward the Napeequa or scrambling up the little peak to the south. The scene below will make day hikers wish they'd brought overnight packs; the valley cries out for exploring. However, those who do struggle up with packs will wish they'd gone the long way around, via Boulder Pass.

The trail down to the Napeequa is not as steep or difficult as that up from the Chiwawa, but is still far from easy and has a few spots where a misstep could cause a bad fall. The distance is 3 miles (little shade, less water) to the valley floor, 4200 feet, with another 2 miles up the valley to join the Boulder Pass trail (Hike 73). Beside the path are many campsites but the prettiest is by a small lake ¼ mile downstream from the foot of the descent.

Round trip to the pass 12 miles
Hiking time 8 hours
High point 6409 feet
Elevation gain 3900 feet
Best mid-July through September
One day or backpack
USGS Holden
Forest Service wilderness permit required
  beyond the pass

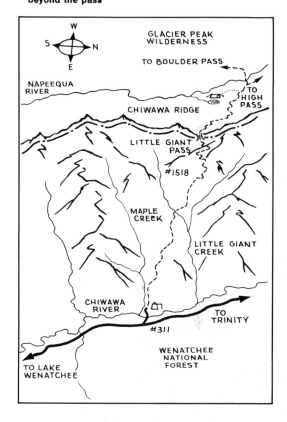

75 SPIDER MEADOW AND PASS

A glorious valley-bottom meadow in a seeming cul-de-sac amid rugged peaks. Yet the trail ingeniously breaks through the cliffs and climbs to a little "glacier" and a grand overlook of Lyman Basin and summits of the Cascade Crest. For hikers trained in use of the ice ax, this can be merely the beginning of a long and classic loop trip.

Drive about 22 miles on the Chiwawa River road (Hike 74) to the Phelps Creek road. Turn right 2 miles to the end and trailhead, elevation 3500 feet.

Miners of ages past built a wagon road up Phelps Creek and until the 1960 creation of the Glacier Peak Wilderness Area the track was used by jeeps. Nature is now reclaiming its own, but the walk begins on old ruts.

The gentle grade goes up and down in forest, passing the Carne Mountain trail in ¼ mile, Box Creek in 1 mile, and Chipmunk Creek in 1¾ miles. At 3½ miles, 4175 feet, are the crossing of Leroy Creek, the junction with Leroy Creek trail, a campsite, and the end of the old road.

The way continues through forest interspersed with flower gardens. At 5¼ miles, 4700 feet, is the spectacular opening-out into Spider Meadow. Red Mountain shows its cliffs and snows; the views include other walls enclosing Phelps

Upper Lyman Lake and shoulder of Chiwawa Mountain

headwaters—no way can be seen to escape the valley, an apparent dead-end. A mile of flower walking leads to the crossing of Phelps Creek, 6¼ miles, 5000 feet. A short bit beyond are the ruins of a miner's cabin. Good camps here and throughout Spider Meadow. Hikers with only a day or a weekend may turn back here, well content.

But there is much more beyond the cabin ruins. A faint path extends to ancient prospects

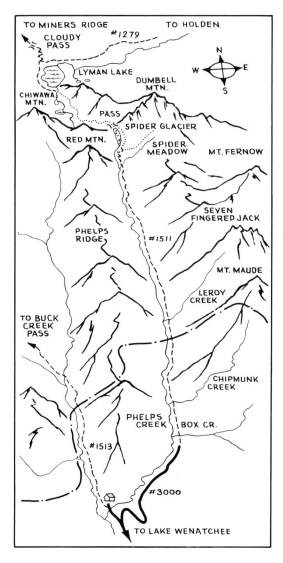

in the rocky-snowy-cliffy head of Phelps Creek, impressively stark and barren. The main trail does the unexpected, switchbacking improbably amid trees and rocks into a hanging valley, ending by waterfalls, larch-dotted knobs, and rocks and flowers at 7 miles, 6200 feet. A splendid if tiny campsite here; no wood worth mentioning but lots of water and long views down-valley to Spider Meadow, Mt. Maude, and Seven-Fingered Jack.

Immediately above is the narrow snowfield of Spider "Glacier." In a short mile, either up the snow-filled gully or along the easy and scenic rock spur to the east, is 7100-foot Spider Pass. Look down to the Lyman Glacier, the ice-devastated upper Lyman Basin, and the greenery of the lower basin.

An old trail ascends ¼ mile from the pass to a mine tunnel. One must marvel at the dogged energy of the man (he also built the cabin in Spider Meadow) who hauled machinery and supplies to so airy a spot. In the end he was injured by a cave-in and for days lay alone and helpless in the tunnel; his wife and children finally came to his rescue—and then insisted he give up mining.

The trail-less route down into upper Lyman Basin, 6000 feet, is partly on steep snow and requires ice axes. If hikers can manage this slope, their way is open to enjoy a 5-9-day loop trip of about 33 miles, one of the finest roamings in the North Cascades: Spider Pass, Lyman Basin, Lyman Lake, Cloudy Pass, Suiattle Pass, Miners Ridge, Buck Creek Pass, and Trinity, ending just 2 miles from the beginning. For route details, see Hikes 43, 44 and 76.

Round trip to upper Spider Meadow 12½ miles
Hiking time 8 hours
High point 5100 feet
Elevation gain 1700 feet
Best mid-July through October
One day or backpack
USGS Holden

Round trip to Spider Pass 16 miles
Allow 2-3 days
High point 7100 feet
Elevation gain 3600 feet
Best late July through September
USGS Holden
Forest Service wilderness permit required

76 BUCK CREEK PASS

In a mountain range full to overflowing with "unique places," two things have given Buck Creek Pass a distinctive fame: an unusual richness of flower gardens rising from creek bottoms to high summits; the exceptional view of the grandest ice streams of Glacier Peak, seen across the broad, forested valley of the Suiattle River.

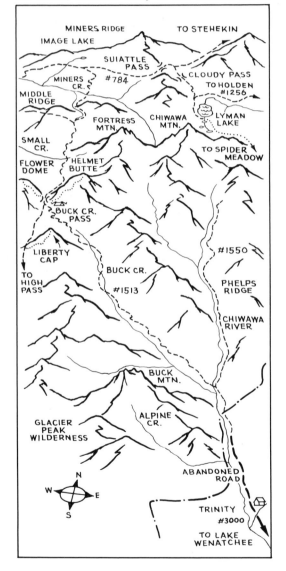

The trail lends itself to a variety of trips short and long: a day's walk ar far as time allows; a weekend at the pass; or the start (or end) of multiday tours—such as over Middle Ridge to Image Lake and the Suiattle River road, or to Miners Ridge and Lyman Basin and Lake Chelan, or the classic loop suggested in Hike 75.

Drive about 24 miles on the Chiwawa River Road (Hike 74) to the end at Phelps Creek, elevation 2772 feet, next to the old mining town of Trinity.

Cross the Phelps Creek bridge into Trinity and follow trail signs on a confusion of roads past the buildings. The townsite is privately owned, so don't prowl around without specific permission; however, hikers have legal right of passage through the town. Continue over the valley floor on old roads, looking sharp at junctions for "Buck Creek" signs. At 1¼ miles is a sign announcing entry into the Glacier Peak Wilderness Area; a nice creek here in forest shade, much appreciated after the mostly-flat but mostly-hot walk thus far. The abandoned road climbs moderately to a junction at 1½ miles: the road leads straight ahead toward mining claims on Red Mountain; the trail turns left.

Tread goes down and up along the Chiwawa River, crosses the foaming torrent on a bridge at 2¾ miles; 3400 feet, and enters the valley of Buck Creek; just beyond the bridge is a campsite in woods.

The trail climbs a valley step, levels out and passes a forest camp in a patch of grass, switchbacks up another glacier-gouged step, and emerges from trees to traverse a wide avalanche meadow at 5 miles, 4300 feet. This is a good turnaround for a day hike, offering a view of the cliffs and hanging glaciers on the north wall of 8573-foot Buck Mountain.

At 7 miles, 4500 feet, is a footlog crossing of Buck Creek, and also a meadow camp; look up to eight waterfalls frothing down from hidden cirques. The trail recrosses the creek in ½ mile and crosses again in another ½ mile—both times by footlog or, if preferred, easy wading. From the third crossing, 8¼ miles, 4900 feet, the route becomes steep, switchbacking from open valley up and up through trees, then meadows.

During the final ½-mile hikers may be con-

Glacier Peak from Buck Creek Pass

fused by sheep tracks and side-trails to camps. Stay alert. Drop a bit to the green floor of a meandering stream, then climb flowers and parkland to Buck Creek Pass, 9½ miles, 5800 feet. The pass area offers innumerable good camps—some of which, however, are badly mangled by carelessly-managed horses. For more secluded mountain homes, search the meadows.

Explorations? Enough for a magnificent week. First try 6200-foot Flower Dome, an evening's wander from the pass, to see sunset-colored snows of Glacier Peak beyond shadowed green vastness of the Suiattle. Then spend an afternoon on blossom-bright Liberty Cap, 6700 feet. Then the panoramas of 7366-foot Helmet Butte. And if more is wanted, onward to Middle Ridge, Image Lake, and where you will.

Round trip to pass 19 miles
Allow 2-3 days or more
High point 5800 feet
Elevation gain 3000 feet
Best late July through October
USGS Holden
Forest Service wilderness permit required

Entiat Meadow

77 ENTIAT MEADOWS

A long walk up a gentle valley to a vast meadow under small glaciers hanging on the walls of a row of 9000-foot peaks. The Entiat River trail gives access to many routes to high country, including three described in this book. The best plan is to spend a week in the valley, taking one or more of the side-trips. This is the land of the rainshadow, meaning the weather is generally better than on the Cascade Crest; it also means the sun can be beastly hot, with hiking most comfortable early or late in the day.

Drive US 97 north from Wenatchee up the Columbia River 16 miles to the town of Entiat. Beyond a small bridge, turn left on the Entiat River road and drive 35 miles (all but the last 5 are paved) to Cottonwood Camp and ¼ mile more to the end and trailhead, elevation 3100 feet.

The Forest Service has engineered the first 4½ miles of trail into a smooth, evenly-graded raceway for motorbikes. The tread is deep in powdery pumice dirt and scooters raise an intolerable, choking dust; obviously the next Forest Service "improvement" will be to pave the "scooter road."

Most of the bike-racers are "rugged sportsmen" aiming for lakes. They turn off at 3½ miles on the Cow Creek trail to Myrtle Lake; a few grind and gouge onward to Larch Lakes. At 4½ miles the "road" reverts to normal trail and though machines are allowed to the boundary of the Glacier Peak Wilderness Area, the tread is rough enough to discourage the average motor maniac.

At 5 miles pass the Larch Lakes trail (Hike 78). At 5½ miles is a campsite by Snowbrushy Creek, and at 6½ miles, 3900 feet, a beautiful camp a few hundred feet below the trail in Snowbrushy Meadow. Here too is the junction with the Snowbrushy Creek trail (Hike 79).

In 7½ miles enter the Glacier Peak Wilderness Area and at 8 miles, 4300 feet, pass the Ice

Creek trail (Hike 80). A short bit along that trail from the junction is a shelter cabin, a good basecamp for day hikes.

The way to here is principally through forest; the final 7 miles alternate between trees and meadows. Though sheep have not been allowed in the valley for years, some meadows still show deep rutting from thousands of hooves and some of the native flowers have never grown back.

At 13 miles, having gained only some 2000 feet thus far, the grade steepens a little for a final 2 miles and then, at about 5500 feet, the tread fades out in fields of heather and flowers. The camps are fine throughout the miles-long Entiat Meadows and the views are grand—up the cliffs of the huge cirque to the summits of Fernow, Seven-Fingered Jack, and Maude, all above 9000 feet, and to the remnants of the Entiat Glacier, which in days of glory excavated the cirque and gave the valley its contours.

If ambition persists, scramble up grassy slopes of the ridge to the north and look down into Railroad Creek and the town of Holden.

Round trip 30 miles
Allow 3-4 days or more
High point 5500 feet
Elevation gain 2400 feet
Best July through October
USGS Lucerne and Holden
Forest Service wilderness permit required

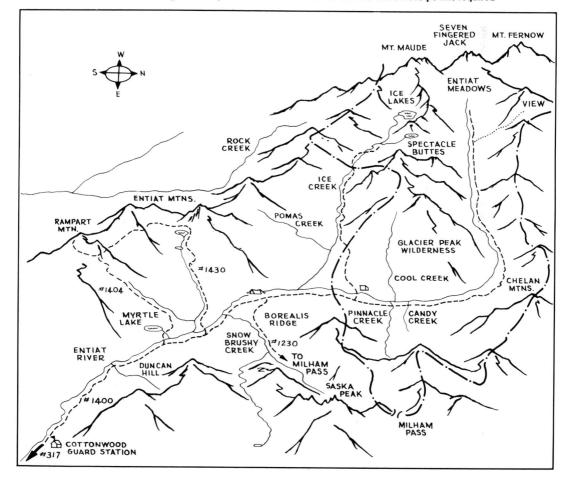

Upper Larch Lake from trail under Fifth of July Mountain

78   LARCH LAKES LOOP

Two clear lakes surrounded by alpine trees and meadows nestled under cliffs of Fifth of July Mountain. An entryway to miles and miles of up-and-down high trails along the Entiat Mountains.

Drive the Entiat River road (Hike 77) to the end, elevation 3100 feet. Hike the Entiat River trail 5 miles to Larch Lakes trail, 3800 feet. The way crosses the Entiat River, goes ¼ mile through stately forest, and then begins a grueling climb of 1900 feet in 2½ miles, switchbacking up a treeless, shadeless, waterless south slope.

On a hot day the best plan is to loiter by the river until late afternoon, when sun has left the hillside—or better yet, cook dinner by the river and make the ascent in the cool of evening. Waiting until morning does no good; the hillside gets the first rays of sun.

Before starting up, note the waterfall high on the hillside to the west. Elevation of this falls (which comes from the lake outlet) provides a measure of how much climbing remains to be done.

The tortuous switchbacks abruptly flatten into a traverse along the shores of 5700-foot lower

Larch Lake, leading to a large meadow with a dilapidated shelter and acres of flat ground for camping. The trail continues a short ½ mile to upper Larch Lake, more camping meadows, and the junction with the Pomas Creek trail. Here is a choice of loop trips.

For the longer of the two, climb north some 700 feet to Larch Lakes Pass, then amble on to 6350-foot Pomas Pass and down Pomas Creek to a junction with the Ice Creek trail, 6 miles from upper Larch Lake. Go left to Ice Lakes (Hike 80) or right to the Entiat River trail.

For the shorter and more popular loop, follow the trail south around upper Larch Lake. Tread disappears in meadows and several starts can be seen on the wooded hillside left of Fifth of July Mountain. If the path you select is terribly steep and then vanishes by a small stream, it's the wrong one. Cross the stream and pick up the correct one in a small flat meadow.

The trail climbs steadily more than a mile, with airy views down to Larch Lakes, then contours the mountain to a 6500-foot junction with the Cow Creek trail, the return route via Myrtle Lake.

The ascent of Fifth of July Mountain is a virtual must. Though the north face of the peak is a tall, rugged cliff, there's an easy side. Leave packs at the junction and climb the Garland Peak trail a mile south to 7000-foot Cow Creek Pass (some signs say Fifth of July Pass) and ascend the gentle south slope to the 7696-foot summit and a 360-degree panorama of Glacier, Clark, Maude, Rainier, and other peaks beyond counting.

The Cow Creek trail descends a steep 2 miles to the edge of Cow Meadows, just out of sight of the trail and offering a splendid camp, 5100 feet. Another 2 miles drop to sparkling, scooter-loud Myrtle Lake, 3700 feet, ½ mile from the Entiat River trail, reached at a point 3½ miles from the road-end.

Round trip (shorter loop) 18 miles
Allow 2-3 days
High point 6500 feet
Elevation gain 3400 feet
Best mid-July through September
USGS Lucerne
Forest Service wilderness permit required

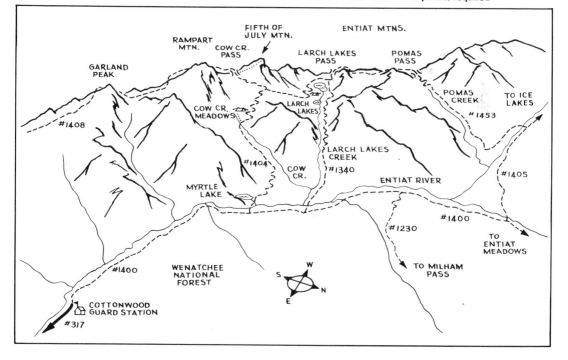

79 MILHAM PASS— EMERALD PARK

A high pass surrounded by the snowy summits of Pinnacle Mountain and Saska, Emerald, and Cardinal Peaks, all standing well above 8000 feet. If transportation can be arranged, a one-way trip can be made down into the lovely meadows of Emerald Park and out to Lake Chelan. Alternatively, of course, the approach to Milham Pass can begin from the lake.

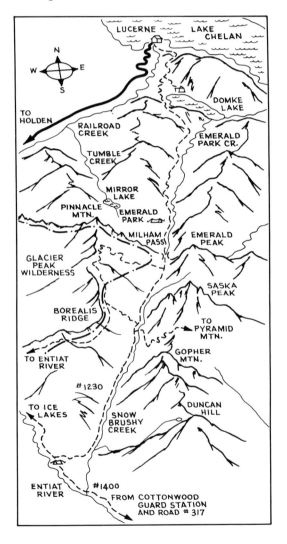

Drive the Entiat River road (Hike 77) to the end, elevation 3100 feet. Hike the Entiat River trail 6½ miles to the Snowbrushy Creek trail, 3900 feet. A few hundred feet below the junction is an excellent campsite in Snowbrushy Meadow.

The first mile climbs steeply from the Entiat valley into the Snowbrushy valley. Then the way parallels the creek, continuing a steady but reasonable ascent through open forest and large meadows. At about 2½ miles from the Entiat trail is the first decent camp, in trees; beyond are numerous sites in flowers and grass. At 3 miles the trail crosses a 5700-foot meadow under Gopher Mountain, with views of Saska Peak spires at the valley head and back out to Fifth of July Mountain, across the Entiat.

The way passes junctions with the Pyramid Mountain trail, climbing east to high viewpoints, and indistinct 45-Mile Sheep Driveway, climbing northwest over Borealis Ridge and descending to the Entiat River trail—offering a longer but more scenic return route.

From about 4½ miles the grade steepens for the final ascent to 6663-foot Milham Pass, 6 miles from the Entiat trail and 12½ miles from the road. To get the best views, scramble a few hundred feet up the ridge to the south, taking due caution among large and loose boulders on steep sections of the slope. The scramble is rewarded by a look down to the bright green meadow of Emerald Park and out east to peaks beyond Lake Chelan.

To continue to Lake Chelan, follow the Emerald Park Creek trail, which goes along the crest of the pass a few hundred feet north, then drops abruptly. A large snowfield generally covers the tread here until mid-July; descend with care.

About 2 miles below the pass the trail enters the big meadow of Emerald Park, 5400 feet; a fine camp here. The next 6 miles to the Domke Lake trail, in sun-baked brush and scrub, then forest, are steep and rough; sorry to say, the Forest Service has commenced reconstructing the walkers-only route into a motorbike raceway, another example of the "multiple-abuse" philosophy at its worst.

From the Domke Lake junction, 2200 feet, a side-trail leads a short mile to the 2192-foot lake

Emerald Park from Milham Pass

and a campground generally crowded with fishermen and motorbikes. The main trail descends 2 miles from the junction to Lucerne, 10 miles from Milham Pass, on the shores of 1096-foot Lake Chelan. For boat service on the lake, see Hike 81.

Round trip from road to Milham Pass 25 miles
Allow 2-4 days
One-way trip to Lake Chelan 22½ miles
Allow 2-4 days
High point 6663 feet
Elevation gain 2700 feet
Elevation loss to Lake Chelan 5500 feet
Best mid-July through September
USGS Lucerne

Lower Ice Lake

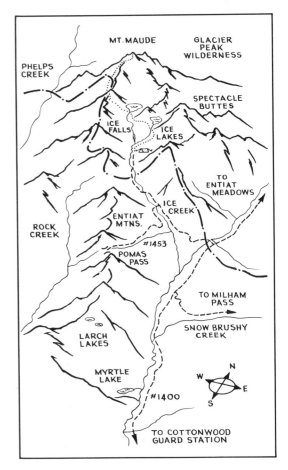

80 ICE LAKES

Two high, remote lakes set in cirque basins at 6800 and 7200 feet, close under cliffs of 9082-foot Mt. Maude. Picturesque alpine trees stand out starkly in a barren, glaciated landscape reminiscent of Khyber Pass.

Drive the Entiat River road (Hike 77) to the end, elevation 3100 feet. Hike the Entiat River trail 8 miles to the Ice Creek trail, 4300 feet.

Within ¼ mile of the beginning of the Ice Creek trail is a shelter cabin and a bridge over the Entiat River. The way climbs gradually in forest the first mile, then drops 400 feet to Ice Creek. At 1½ miles, 4300 feet, is a junction with the Pomas Creek trail, an excellent alternate return route via Larch Lakes, as described in Hike 78.

The route goes along the river bottom, alternating between small alpine trees and boggy meadows. At about 3 miles is a crossing of Ice Creek; since a footlog seldom is available and the channel is too wide to jump, be prepared to wade—and find out how well the creek lives up

to its name. In another mile is another crossing, but this time the creek can be stepped over on rocks. At some 4½ miles from the Entiat trail, formal tread ends in a rocky meadow and delightful campsite, 5500 feet. The noisy creek drowns the sound of a pretty waterfall tumbling from upper Ice Lake.

From the trail end, follow the rocky meadow north to the valley head, passing the waterfall. Generally keep right of the creek, but cross to the left when the going looks easier there. The valley ends in a steep green hillside; above, in hanging cirques, lie the lakes. From a starting point to the right of the creek, scramble up game traces, crossing the creek and climbing between cliffs to its left. Though not recom-

Ice Falls

mended for novice hikers, the route is not particularly difficult if proper care is taken. The way emerges onto a rocky knoll 100 feet above 6800-foot lower Ice Lake, 6 miles from the Entiat trail. Around the outlet are good camps.

Upper Ice Lake is a mile farther. Head southwest in a shallow alpine valley, below cliffs, to the outlet stream (a fine camp here) and follow the waters up to the 7200-foot lake, beautifully cold and desolate.

Mt. Maude cliffs are impressive from the lakes. However, the long and gentle south ridge of the peak offers an easy stroll. The scramble to the ridge, though, is not a complete cinch; patches of steep snow remain in summer and require an ice ax for safe passage. Maude is the only 9000-footer in the Cascades accessible to hikers, but they must be experienced hikers thoroughly familiar with the ice ax and the rules of safe travel on steep terrain. The summit views extend from Glacier Peak to the Columbia Plateau, from Mt. Rainier to an infinite alpine wilderness north.

Round trip to lower Ice Lake 28 miles
Allow 3-5 days
High point (knoll above lower lake) 6900 feet
Elevation gain 4200 feet
Best August through September
USGS Holden and Lucerne
Forest Service wilderness permit required

Lake Chelan and McGregor Mountain from Hunts Point

81 CHELAN LAKESHORE TRAIL

While cruising along Lake Chelan, have you ever felt the desire for a fuller experience of this masterwork in America's gallery of scenic treasures? If so, take a spring or early-summer hike along the northeast shore, sometimes close to the wind-rippled waters, sometimes on high bluffs with sweeping views. Traverse grasslands and rock buttresses, swinging into surprising little gorges with bubbling brooks and even a few hundred feet of cool forests and lush undergrowth, passing old homesteads dating from frontier days.

The complete route is an overnight-or-longer backpack from Prince Creek to Stehekin; shorter walks can start or terminate at several intermediate places. Whatever the beginning or ending, don't miss the Hunts Point section.

Rattlesnakes live here, but don't make a big thing of it. Unless cornered, snakes will run rather than fight. Watch where you step, look carefully before sitting down, and wear long pants. In the memory of long-time Stehekin residents, no human ever has been bitten there;

dogs have been, some repeatedly, but only one little pup is remembered as dying.

Drive to Chelan or Twenty Five Mile Creek and board the passenger boat. (1972 schedule. Daily May 15 to September 30: leave Chelan 8:30 a.m., Twenty Five Mile Creek 10 a.m.; leave Stehekin 1:45 p.m. October 1 to May 15, Monday, Wednesday, and Friday only: leave Chelan 8:30 a.m., Twenty Five Mile Creek 9:45 a.m.; leave Stehekin 12:10 p.m.) Since only one daily round-trip is offered at present, overnight camping or hotel accommodations are necessary to do any hiking.

Backpackers can start at Prince Creek and hike the full 17½ miles to Stehekin. Day hikers can start at Fish Creek and have Stehekin overnight gear put off at Stehekin. If the party has reservations at one of the Stehekin resorts, send word ahead and the resort people will pick up the baggage. Otherwise baggage will be left at the boat landing—generally safe.

When buying a ticket, tell the boatman where you want off. If you wish to be picked up along the lake, arrange the time and location beforehand. However, if plans change while on the trail, waving a white flag from the shore will bring the boat.

If starting at Prince Creek, be very sure to ask to be landed on the uplake side of the creek, which is next to impossible to cross during spring runoff. Because the boat reaches Prince Creek in late morning, some parties prefer to lazy away the afternoon on the alluvial fan and hoist packs the next morning.

From Prince Creek the trail ascends slopes of grass and yellow pines, passes an old orchard, and goes around cliffy bluffs some 500 feet above the lake. The way descends nearly to the shore to avoid cliffs, then climbs again, entering the cool ravine of rocky Rex Creek at 3¾ miles, and at 4¼ miles the greenery of Pioneer Creek. Traversing 300-400 feet above the lake, with views out, the trail crosses Cascade Creek, 6 miles. At 7 miles is Meadow Creek and an unappealing trail shelter. Close below and a bit beyond is a resort, Meadow Creek Lodge, a convenient spot to meet or leave the boat.

The trail climbs a logging road (on private land) dating from some 25 years ago, passes an aspen grove and glacier-streamlined rock knobs, and switchbacks down to an old homestead on Moore's Point, with deer-grazed pastures and gnarled orchards enclosed by New England-like stone walls. At 11 miles is the bridge over wild-roaring Fish Creek. Crude but pleasant campsites here; a bit farther is a trail shelter. The major

attraction of camping at or near Fish Creek is the opportunity to explore the historic Moore homestead, the ruins of the fire-destroyed hotel, and the glorious promontory of Moore's Point. Day hikers can debark at Moore and follow a private road ¼ mile to intersect the trail.

Now the trail climbs 1000 feet to Hunts Bluff, 13 miles, and the climax views. Look down the lake to Lucerne and up the lake to Stehekin, with Castle Mountain on the left and McGregor Mountain up the river valley. Boats below seem to be toys in a big, big pond.

The trail drops to the Lakeshore (Flick Creek) Shelter, 14 miles pause a while, sit on a rock slab at water's edge, and drink from the cold, clear lake. From here to Stehekin the route never again climbs high, wandering along the base of cliffs and through woods to Flick Creek, Four Mile Creek, Hazard Creek, and finally Stehekin, 17½ miles.

One-way trip from Prince Creek 17½ miles
Allow 2-4 days
High point 2200 feet
Elevation gain and loss about 2600 feet
Best March through June (or rainy summer days)
USGS Lucerne

One-way trip from Moore 7 miles
Hiking time 4 hours
High point 2200 feet
Elevation gain and loss about 1500 feet
USGS none

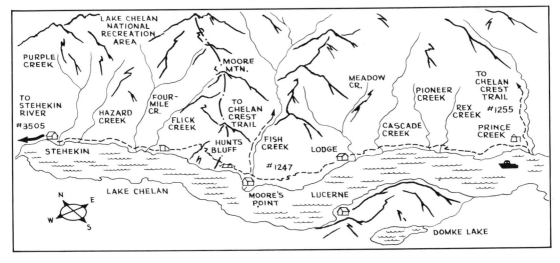

Chelan Crest from South Navarre Peak

82   CHELAN CREST TRAIL

A miles-and-miles and days-and-days paradise of easy-roaming ridges and flower gardens and spectacular views westward to the main range of the Cascades, beyond the deep trench of Lake Chelan. Snow-free hiking starts weeks earlier, and the weather is much better, than in the main range, which traps and stops nearly all the maritime fogs, mists, and drizzles of summer. The Chelan Crest Trail (currently officially called the "Summit Trail") surely will soon be acknowledged as one of the supreme highland walks in the nation, a deserving companion of the Cascade Crest Trail and demanding to be placed in its entirety, rather than just partly, within the Lake Chelan National Recreation Area, off-limits to the Forest Service-permitted sheep and motorcycles which now degrade portions of the route.

Drive from Chelan toward Manson on Highway 150. At 2 miles beyond Manson turn right, following signs to Antilon Lake and Grade Creek road No. 3001, which climbs high above Lake Chelan to the trailhead at South Navarre Campground, elevation 6500 feet, 34 miles from Chelan.

Because the area never has been accurately surveyed, mileages and elevations given here are approximate. To summarize, the trail generally traverses meadows and parkland at altitudes of 6000-6500 feet. It crosses a number of wide-view shoulders and passes, all about 7000 feet, and at three places dips briefly into forest at low points of some 5500 feet. The peaks (most of them easy walks or scrambles) run to above 8000 feet, climaxing in the Sawtooth group, topped by 8798-foot Oval Peak.

Campsites are too numerous to list; in the 26 miles from Miners Basin to Juanita Lake, good-to-magnificent camps are spaced at intervals of 2-3 miles or less. Side-trips (on or off trails) to lakes, passes, and peaks are so many and so appealing that one is constantly tempted to leave the main route and explore; for that reason a party should allow extra days for wandering.

The trail begins by sidehilling the rock gardens and silver forest of South Navarre Peak, 8000 feet, southernmost high peak of the Chelan Crest, descends to 5500-foot forests of Safety Harbor Creek, and climbs through meadows of Miners Basin (4 miles) to a ridge crest. From here a traverse above headwater meanders of Safety Harbor Creek leads to the pass (6½ miles) to the East Fork Prince Creek.

The way drops a short, steep bit (snowy in early July) to the broad meadow basin and ascends gently around the base of Switchback Peak (8200 feet) to the pass (8½ miles) to the Middle Fork Prince Creek. Down and around another wide parkland, at 10½ miles is the junction with the Middle Fork Prince Creek trail.

(The disadvantage of starting at South Navarre is that special transportation must be arranged—such as by use of two cars—to do a one-way trip. This problem is eliminated by beginning at Prince Creek Campground, reached by boat up Lake Chelan—see Hike 81. From the lakeshore, elevation 1100 feet, the Middle Fork Prince Creek trail climbs to the above-mentioned junction in 11 miles, gaining some 5500 feet. This haul is best done in 2 days; camping is possible at 4, 6, and 8 miles from the lake.)

From the junction the trail swings up to a saddle (12 miles) to the North Fork Prince Creek, descends to a 5500-foot low point in forest (14½ miles), and climbs to flowers again and the pass (18½ miles) to the East Fork Fish Creek. Above the pass is 8500-foot Star Peak, second-highest summit of Sawtooth Ridge.

A short, steep drop, an up-and-down meadow traverse, and a gentle ascent lead to the pass (22 miles) to the North Fork Fish Creek. Then comes a descent to a 5500-foot low point in trees (24½ miles) and a climb through gardens to a pass (27½ miles) to Four Mile Creek. After a stretch of missing tread (watch for cairns), the way descends a bit and traverses up and down to Lake Juanita (30 miles).

At 30½ miles is Purple Pass, famous for the spontaneous gasps drawn from all who come here. Below—6000 feet below—are wind-rippled, sun-sparkling waters of Lake Chelan, close enough seemingly to reach in one long dive. Actually, hundreds of switchbacks descend Purple Creek to Stehekin, 38 miles, but there's no danger of boredom, not with constant views of the lake and the Stehekin valley and the 7000-foot walls of peaks beyond.

Return to Twenty-Five Mile Creek or Chelan by boat; for the schedule, see Hike 81.

One-way trip from South Navarre 38 miles
Allow 5-9 days
High point 7200 feet
Elevation gain about 8000 feet
Best early July through September
USGS none

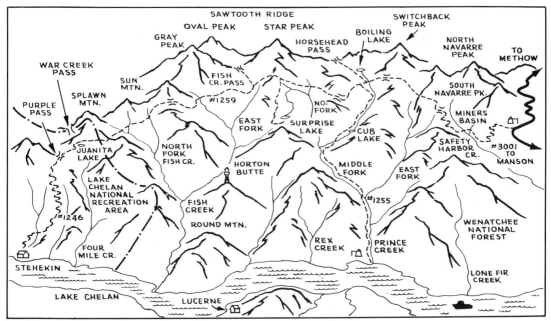

83 McGREGOR MOUNTAIN

Round trip to basin 14 miles
Hiking time 10 hours
High point 7000 feet
Elevation gain 5400 feet
Best mid-June through October
One day or backpack
USGS McGregor Mtn.
Park Service camping permit required

8100 feet in the sky, site of a long-abandoned lookout. Few hikers care to climb to the summit —the going the last mile gets a bit rugged—but there is a wonderful viewpoint at 3 miles and better ones continuously from then on up. The way can be hot, so start early in the morning and carry plenty of water. Watch for rattlesnakes at lower elevations.

Trips from the Stehekin valley require special transportation arrangements. First a party must get to Stehekin, either by boat (for schedule, see Hike 81) or Chelan Air Service, located near the town of Chelan. Then a ride must be obtained to the trailhead. Formerly this was complicated, but now a shuttlebus runs the road on a regular schedule in summer months; fares are moderate.

In any event, a hiking party ordinarily can't get started on the trail until mid-afternoon of the first day, and must be off the trail by late morning of the last day to catch the boat. Any trip from the Stehekin must be planned with these time factors in mind.

Find the McGregor Mountain trailhead, elevation 1600 feet, behind the High Bridge Ranger Station, 11 miles from Stehekin. At a little over 1 mile the way passes close to 2140-foot Coon Lake and swings halfway around the shore.

From the lake the trail goes up with determination, making more than 150 switchbacks. Twice the route comes tantalizingly near, but never quite reaches, water.

In a little over 3 miles is a bluff, 3600 feet, with an outstanding view up the Agnes valley to Agnes Mountain, glaciers of Dome Peak, and countless peaks and ridges. From here the trail climbs into steep meadows and rockslides. In 4½ miles is the first water, a short scramble down from the trail into a ravine; camping is possible hereabouts, if desperate.

The way becomes less brushy climbing to the pleasant and scenic bench of Billy Goat Camp at 7 miles, 7000 feet. From a knoll to the south are spectacular views to Stehekin and down Lake Chelan to Lucerne and out over a world of great mountains, including Glacier Peak.

The final mile to the summit becomes increasingly difficult, the last stretch requiring some climbing equipment and skills.

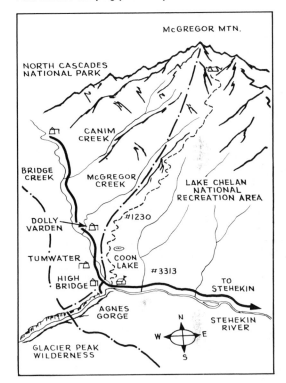

Coon Lake and Agnes Creek valley from McGregor Mountain trail

84   AGNES CREEK

One of the supreme long-and-wild, low-to-high valleys of the North Cascades. The Cascade Crest Trail gently ascends 18 miles of Agnes Creek forest to Suiattle Pass and connecting trails to Image Lake, Suiattle River, Buck Creek Pass, and a suggested loop trip (which can be done in the reverse direction as well) over Cloudy Pass and down Railroad Creek to Lake Chelan. For much shorter hikes there are trails along Agnes Gorge and into the West Fork Agnes—see below.

Travel to High Bridge Ranger Station, 11 miles from Stehekin (Hike 83). About 500 feet beyond the bridge, on the left side of the road, is the Agnes Creek trailhead, elevation 1600 feet. The trail drops a few feet, crosses Agnes Creek, and commences a long, easy grade. Glimpses ahead of Agnes Mountain and glaciers on Dome Peak; to the rear, McGregor Mountain.

In 5 miles cross Pass Creek to 5-Mile Camp and a junction with the West Fork Agnes trail (see below). Keep left, following the South Fork Agnes. At 6½ miles the way comes to the edge of a deep canyon; to here the Agnes has been constantly heard but seldom seen. The trail stays high on the hillside, only occasionally nearing the river until beyond Swamp Creek.

Five Mile Camp

The valley forest is continuously superb, with notable groves of cedar in the first 5 miles and a fine stand of large hemlock and fir near Swamp Creek. Good campsites at 5 Mile Camp and Swamp Creek, 8 miles.

Without ever getting particularly steep, at 17 miles and 5600 feet the trail reaches a timberline junction. The left goes a mile to 6400-foot Cloudy Pass and down Railroad Creek to Holden and Lucerne, as described in Hike 43. The right goes a mile to 6000-foot Suiattle Pass and down to the Suiattle River road, as described in Hike 42 and Hike 43.

The valley offers two shorter trips, each deservedly famous. For one, take the trail on the west side of Agnes Gorge, with awesome looks into the roaring canyon. Find the beginning about 250 feet up the road from High Bridge Campground. The trail dead-ends in some 1½ miles and there is no possible crossing of Agnes Creek to the main trail. This walk can be done as early as mid-May.

For the other, stop overnight at 2300-foot 5 Mile Camp, cross the Agnes on a new bridge, and hike 3 miles on the West Fork Agnes trail to its dead-end at the edge of a grassy meadow, 2500 feet, surrounded by towering rock walls topped by glaciers. To get better views, go back down the trail a short bit from the meadow and climb woods to a clearing. This side-trip can be done in mid-June.

One-way trip to Suiattle Pass or Cloudy Pass 18 miles
Hiking time 9 hours
High point (Suiattle Pass) 5983 feet
Elevation gain 4400 feet
Best mid-July through October
USGS McGregor Mtn., Mt. Lyall, and Holden
Forest Service wilderness permit required

85 NORTH FORK BRIDGE CREEK

The North Cascades are distinguished by tall peaks—and also by deep holes. Among the most magnificent holes in the range is the huge cirque at the head of the North Fork Bridge Creek, where breezes ripple meadow grasses beneath the ice-hung precipices of 9160-foot Goode Mountain, 8515-foot Storm King Peak, and 9087-foot Mt. Logan.

Travel to Bridge Creek, 16 miles from Stehekin (Hike 88). Just before the creek is the trailhead, elevation 2200 feet. The trail starts with a short, stiff climb of 400 feet, then goes up and down in woods, emerging to views of Memaloose Ridge and reaching the bridge over Bridge Creek at 2½ miles, 2600 feet. Across the bridge and ¼ mile beyond is a junction; go left on the North Fork trail.

The way ascends steeply a bit and gentles out. From brushy openings in the forest are views of rugged cliffs—a promise of what is to come. At 6¼ miles, 3200 feet, are gravel bars of Grizzly Creek and a tolerable camp in little trees. Here the maintained trail ends. The ford of the wide, cold, rushing creek is not really difficult or dangerous except in the high water of early summer or big storms, but neither is it for novice hikers, who may be forced to turn back.

The way leaves woods and wanders along the valley bottom in cottonwood groves, avalanche brush, and patches of grass. Immense views continue—up and up the 6000-foot north wall of Goode to icefalls of the Goode Glacier and towers of the summit.

The grade grows a little less gentle as the valley opens into North Fork Meadows, at 9½ miles, 3800 feet. The scene is glorious, with wide fields of knee-high grass, with neck-stretching gazes to Goode and Storm King and other views up and down the valley.

Paths here are confusing; climb the brushy knoll above to a resumption of tread amid small and sparse trees. In a stand of old alpine timber which has escaped avalanches is the heather-surrounded wreckage of a miner's cabin. The trail emerges into grass and flowers of the cirque, 10½ miles, 4200 feet, and fades away. The views of Goode are better than ever, and Logan's walls are close above the amphitheater.

Roam upward into moraines and snowfields at the base of the cliffs. Experienced off-trail hikers can find game traces climbing intricately through brush and rocks of the steep slopes north, leading to higher meadows and moraines and an easy ramble to the 7000-foot ridge crest; look down the other side to the vast Douglas Glacier and out to the rough summits of Ragged Ridge and a peak-full horizon beyond.

Round trip to cirque 21 miles
Allow 2-3 days
High point 4200 feet
Elevation gain 2000 feet
Best early July through October
USGS McGregor Mtn., Goode Mtn., and Mt. Logan
Park Service camping permit required

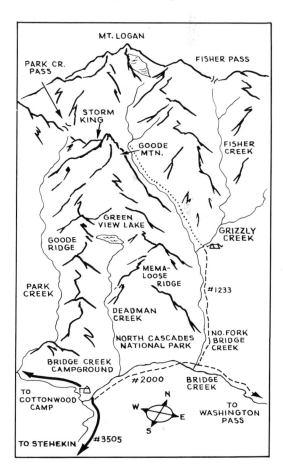

Mt. Goode and upper North Fork Bridge Creek (Dick Brooks photo)

Air view of Park Creek Pass. Mt. Buckner, left, Mt. Logan, right

86   PARK CREEK PASS

A wild and alpine pass on the Cascade Crest between the 9000-foot summits of Mt. Buckner and Mt. Logan, dividing snow waters flowing east to the Stehekin River and Lake Chelan and snow waters flowing west to the Skagit River and Puget Sound. The pass and its surroundings rank among the scenic climaxes of the North Cascades National Park. A basecamp can be established for roaming, or a one-way trip made over the mountains from lowlands east to lowlands west.

Travel to Bridge Creek, 16 miles from Stehekin (Hike 88), and 2½ miles beyond to the Park Creek Campground and trailhead, elevation 2300 feet.

The trail switchbacks steeply from the Stehekin into the hanging valley of Park Creek, then goes along near the stream through forest and occasional open patches with views up to Goode Ridge. At 2 miles, 3200 feet, is a footlog crossing of the creek. Beyond here the grade gentles, continuing mostly in trees but with openings that give looks to Park Creek Ridge. At 3 miles is an obscure junction with a rough-and-sketchy climbers' route to 7680-foot Goode Ridge and broad views; the scramble is for experienced hikers only, but well worth the effort.

Crossing numerous creeks in green avalanche tracks, views growing of high peaks, the trail ascends gradually to 4000 feet, 4½ miles. Now the way leaves the main valley of Park Creek, which falls from the glaciers of Mt. Buckner, and traverses and switchbacks steeply into a hanging side-valley, gradually emerging into parkland. At 7 miles, 5700 feet, the trail flattens out in a magnificent meadow laced by streams and dotted by clumps of alpine trees, the view dominated by the north wall of 8200-foot Booker Mountain.

A final wander in heather and blossoms leads to the rocky, snowy defile of 6100-foot Park Creek Pass, 8 miles from the Stehekin road.

In order to preserve the fragile meadows, camping is not permitted in the area near the pass; however, a good basecamp for exploration is located in the forest fringe at 6½ miles, not far below meadow country, and also at 5 Mile Camp and 1 mile west of the pass in Thunder Basin.

For one wandering, with grand views of Buckner, Booker, Storm King, and Goode (tallest of all at 9160 feet, third-highest non-volcanic peak in the Cascades), find an easy flowery route to the ridge southeast of the pass, overlooking the head of Park Creek. For another, descend west from the pass about ½ mile, leave the trail, and contour meadows and moraines to a mind-expanding vista of the giant Boston Glacier and great peaks standing far above the deep valley of Thunder Creek.

If transportation can be arranged, a one-way trip can be made on down Thunder Creek to Diablo Lake. See Hike 22.

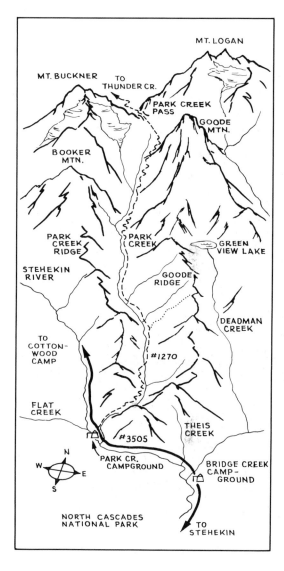

Round trip to pass 16 miles
Allow 3-4 days
High point 6100 feet
Elevation gain 3900 feet
Best mid-July through September
USGS Goode-Mtn. and Mt. Logan
Park Service camping permit required

87 HORSESHOE BASIN

Nine or more waterfalls tumble to the meadow floor of this cliff-ringed cirque. Above are glaciers on Sahale and Boston Peaks, both nearly 9000 feet, and the spires of Ripsaw Ridge. Wander the flowers and rocks and bubbling streams. The basin is well worth a visit in its own right, and makes a splendid side-trip on the cross-mountain journey described in Hike 88.

The basin trail can be reached either from the west side of the Cascades or the east. For the west approach to the junction, ascend to Cascade Pass (Hike 34) and descend 3 miles into the Stehekin valley (Hike 88). For the east approach to the junction, travel to the end of auto road at Cottonwood Camp, 2800 feet, and walk the abandoned mining road 2 miles (Hike 88).

At an elevation of 3600 feet on the Stehekin River trail, the old mining road (dating from the 1950s) switchbacks sharply in a rockslide, climbing around and up the mountainside to enter

Glory Mountain, left, Trapper Mountain, right, from mine in Horseshoe Basin

the hanging valley of Basin Creek; in many places the road is so badly overgrown it is difficult to find. At 1½ miles the way emerges from brush and flattens out amid boulder-strewn meadows, 4200 feet. Impressive looks upward from flowery knolls to ice and crags, and a magical view and sound of white water on the glacier-excavated walls.

The old road continues ½ mile upward across the sloping floor of the basin to a mine tunnel at 4800 feet, close under the froth and splash of the falls. No mine is safe, so best just look in. Hours can be spent roaming the basin, enjoying.

Experienced off-trail hikers can go higher. Cross the creek a short way below the mine and scramble brushy slopes, amid small cliffs to the right of the vertical walls, into the upper cirque of Horseshoe Basin. The ascent is not easy, but doesn't require the ropes and other gear of mountain climbers; traces of an old miners' trail may be found, simplifying progress. Once on the high shelf under Mt. Buckner and Ripsaw Ridge, the way is open for extended explorations in heather and moraines, always looking down waterfalls to the lower basin and out to peaks beyond the Stehekin.

Round trip from Cascade River road 18 miles
Allow 2-3 days
Elevation gain 3000 feet in, 1800 feet out

Round trip from Cottonwood Camp 8 miles, from Bridge Creek 25 miles
Allow 3-4 days
Elevation gain 2000 feet

Round trip from Stehekin trail 4 miles
Hiking time 2½ hours
High point (mine) 4800 feet
Elevation gain 1200 feet
Best July through October
USGS Cascade Pass and Goode Mtn.
Park Service camping permit required

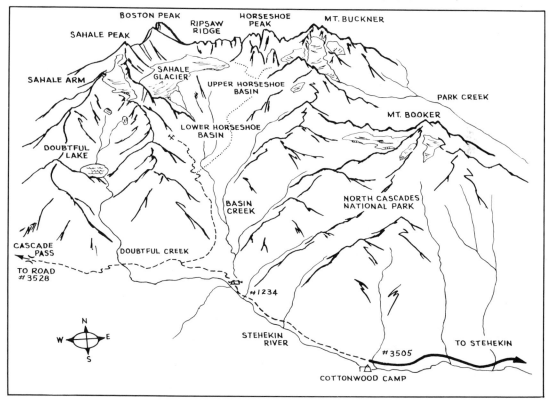

88   LAKE CHELAN TO CASCADE RIVER

A classic and historic cross-Cascades route from the Columbia River to Puget Sound. The trip can begin from either side of the range, but for a well-ordered progression of soup, salad, main course, and finally dessert (rather than the reverse) the approach from the east is recommended. The journey can be a quick-and-easy 8 miles or, by starting at Prince Creek, a Boy Scout "50-mile hike."

Voyage Lake Chelan to Stehekin, elevation 11; feet. (See Hike 81 for boat schedule.)

Begin the 50-mile hike at Prince Creek (Hike 81), then hike along the quiet road from the Stehekin boat landing, to Cottonwood Camp, 2800 feet, 24½ miles from Stehekin and the end of automobile traffic. Hikers who don't need a merit badge may ride the shuttlebus this far (Hike 83).

At Cottonwood Camp the way emerges from woods into avalanche greenery and goes along the valley bottom, with views of ridges above, to the grassy-and-bouldery avalanche fan, and a camp, at the crossing of Basin Creek, 3100 feet, a long mile from Cottonwood. In another ¾ mile, at 3600 feet, is the junction with the route to Horseshoe Basin (Hike 87).

Excellent trail climbs an enormous talus to Doubtful Creek, 4100 feet, ¾ mile from the Horseshoe Basin junction. The ford can be difficult in high water, and falls above and below forbid any easy detour. Now the trail rises into a hot slope of slide alder, ascending in 12 gentle switchbacks to the crest of the wooded ridge above Pelton Basin and views.

A short mile more leads to 5400-foot Cascade Pass and broader views. Since camping is not allowed at the pass (in order to protect the meadows), a half-mile before the pass follow a side-path from the trail to campsites in the basin.

From Cascade Pass, a super-trail descends 3¾ miles to the end of the Cascade River road, 3600 feet.

One-way trip from Cottonwood Camp to Cascade River road 8 miles, from Bridge Creek 16½ miles
Allow 2 days
High point (Cascade Pass) 5400 feet
Elevation gain 2600 feet
Best mid-July through mid-October
USGS Geode Mtn. and Cascade Pass

One-way Boy Scout hike from Prince Creek to Cascade River 50 miles
Allow at least 6 days
Elevation gain 5900 feet, loss 2600 feet
Park Service camping permit required

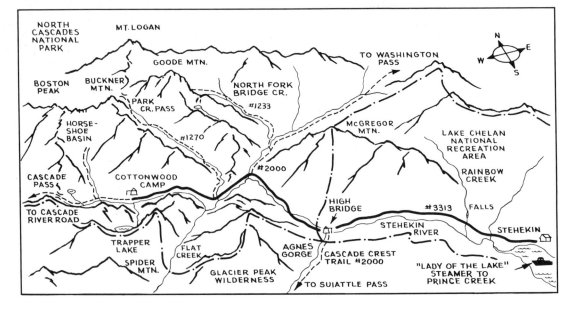

Stehekin valley and McGregor Mountain from Cascade Pass trail

89 TWISP PASS
STILETTO OUTLOOK

Climb from Eastern Washington forest to Cascade Crest gardens, glacier-smoothed boulders, dramatic rock peaks, and views down into Bridge Creek and across to Goode and Logan. Then wander onward amid a glory of larch-dotted grass and flowers to an old lookout site with horizons so rich one wonders how the fire-spotter could ever have noticed smoke. For a special treat, do the walk in autumn when the air is cool and the alpine country is blazing with color.

Drive the Methow Valley Highway to Twisp and turn west in the town center on the Twisp River

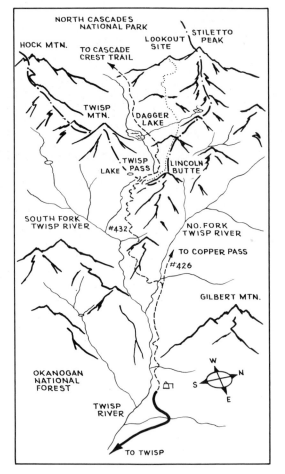

road, signed "Gilbert." Continue 18 miles on pavement and 7 miles more on gravel and dirt to the end. (The final mile may be closed, adding 1 mile to the hiking distance.) A short bit before the road-end is a parking area and the trailhead, elevation 3500 feet.

The trail begins by ascending moderately through woods, with occasional up-valley glimpses of pyramid-shaped Twisp Mountain. At 1½ miles are a junction with the North Fork Twisp River trail, a camp, and the last dependable water for a long, hot way. Ascend fairly steeply on soft-cushioned tread to 2½ miles; stop for a rest on ice-polished buttresses and views down to valley-bottom forest and up to the ragged ridge of Hock Mountain, above the glaciated basin of the South Fork headwaters. The trail emerges from trees to traverse a rocky sidehill, the rough tread sometimes blasted from cliffs. At about 3½ miles the route enters heather and flowers, coming in a short ½ mile to a small stream and pleasant campsites. A final ¼ mile climbs to Twisp Pass, 6066 feet, 4 miles, on the border of the North Cascades National Park.

For wider views, ascend meadows north and look down to Dagger Lake and Bridge Creek and across to Logan, Goode, Black, Frisco, and much more.

The trail drops steeply a mile to Dagger Lake and 4 more miles to Fireweed Ranger Station on Bridge Creek and a junction with the Cascade Crest Trail.

Don't go away without rambling the crest south from the pass about ¼ mile to the foot of Twisp Mountain and a magical surprise—a hidden little lake surrounded by grass and blossoms and alpine forest, a mountain home.

The open slopes north of the pass demand extended exploration. And here is another surprise. Hikers heading in the logical direction toward Stiletto Peak will stumble onto sketchy tread of an ancient trail. Follow the route up and down highlands, by sparkling creeks, to a green shelf under the cliffs of 7700-foot Stiletto Peak, a fairy place of meandering streams and groves of wispy larch. Then comes a field of photogenic boulders, a rocky ridge, and the 7400-foot site of the old cabin. Look north over Copper Creek to Liberty Bell and Early Winter Spires,

Dagger Lake from Twisp Pass

northwest to Tower, Cutthroat, Whistler, Arriva, and Black, southwest to McGregor, Glacier, and Bonanza, and south to Hock and Twisp—and these are merely a few of the peaks seen, not to mention the splendid valley. Stiletto Lookout site is only 2 miles from Twisp Pass, an easy afternoon's round-trip.

Round trip to Twisp Pass 8 miles
Hiking time 6-8 hours
High point 6066 feet
Elevation gain 2500 feet
Best late June through October
One day or backpack
USGS Stehekin No. 1

90 CUTTHROAT PASS

A new bit of the Cascade Crest Trail, a high ridge with impressive views, and if transportation can be arranged, one can start at Rainy Pass and end at Cutthroat Creek saving 400 feet of elevation gain. However, because a short side trip to sparkling Cutthroat Lake makes a refreshing rest stop, the trail is described starting from Cutthroat Creek.

Drive the North Cascades Highway 14 miles from Winthrop to Early Winters and 11 miles more to Cutthroat Creek. Beyond the bridge turn right on the Cutthroat Creek road 1 mile to the road-end and trailhead, elevation 4500 feet.

The trail quickly crosses Cutthroat Creek and begins a gentle 1¾-mile ascent amid sparse rain-shadow forest to a junction with the Cutthroat Lake trail. The 4935-foot lake is ¼ mile away, well worth the side-trip. Fill canteens here—the upper regions are dry.

The next 2½ miles climb through big trees and little trees to meadows and a campsite (water may be scarce in late summer). A final short 2 miles lead upward to 6800-foot Cutthroat Pass, about 6 miles from the road-end.

It is absolutely essential to stroll to the knoll south of the pass for a better look at the country. Cutthroat Peak, 7865 feet, stands high and close. Eastward are the barren south slopes of Silver Star. Mighty Liberty Bell sticks its head above a nearby ridge. Far southwest over Porcupine Creek is glacier-clad Dome Peak.

If time and energy permit, make a side-trip 1 mile north on the Cascade Crest Trail to a knoll above Granite Pass and striking views down to

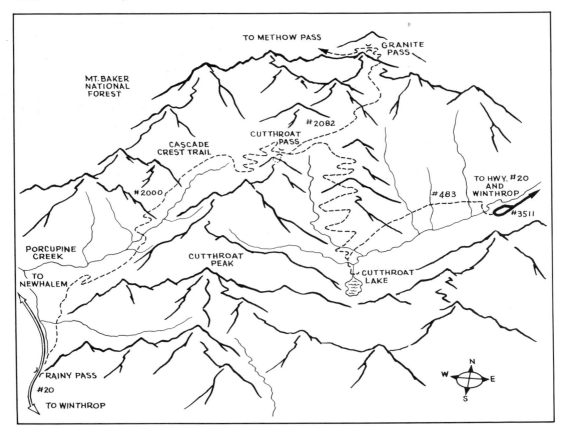

Cutthroat Peak

Swamp Creek headwaters and across to 8444-foot Tower Mountain, 8366-foot Golden Horn, and Azurite, Black, and countless more peaks in the distance. This portion of the Crest Trail may be blocked by snow until mid-August; if so, drop below the tread and cross the snow where it isn't dangerously steep.

From Cutthroat Pass the Crest Trail descends Porcupine Creek a pleasant 5 miles to Rainy Pass, the first 2 miles in meadows and the rest of the way in cool forest with numerous creeks. The trail ends a few hundred feet west of the summit of 4840-foot Rainy Pass.

Near the head of Porcupine Creek are some flat spots for camping, but none close to water.

At 3½ miles from Rainy Pass, ½ mile off the trail to the west, is a well-watered meadow camp.

Round trip to Cutthroat Pass from Cutthroat Creek road-end 12 miles
Hiking time 6-8 hours
High point 6800 feet
Elevation gain 2300 feet
Best July to mid-October
One day or backpack
USGS Washington Pass

One-way trip from Rainy Pass to Cutthroat road-end 10½ miles
Hiking time 6-7 hours
High point 6800 feet
Elevation gain 1900 feet

91   GOAT PEAK

A commanding view of the Methow valley and the north face of Silver Star Mountain, the most beautiful and spectacular peak in the area. Most of the way is up a south slope, and all the way is hot and bone-dry, so start early and carry buckets of water. The vicinity is noted for extra-large timber rattlers; wear long pants and ankle-high shoes for a measure of protection. For obvious reasons the trail is seldom used, but in the near future a new route will make the hike shorter and more enjoyable.

Drive the North Cascades Highway 12 miles from Winthrop to Mazama. Turn right, cross the Methow River, and turn right again on a dirt road heading down valley. In 1 mile turn left on an unmarked dirt road (a shortcut) and climb a steep rough mile to the well-graded Goat Creek logging road. (Alternatively, to avoid the steep climb, continue on the river road 2 miles and join the logging road there.) Follow Goat Creek road No. 375 1 mile beyond the shortcut to a junction. Turn left on road No. 3729 1½ miles and turn right on an old logging road for a very steep and rough 2 miles (which may best be walked) to the trailhead, elevation 4500 feet.

Someday the trailhead will be moved around the mountain. Driving directions then will be to follow road No. 3729 for 7 miles and turn right on road No. 3725.1 (tentative number) 3 miles to the end and new trailhead, elevation 5800 feet. Though built to low-grade standards with numerous waterbars (ditches), this road will be maintained. Since the new trail is not finished, the present one is described.

The trail begins steep and stays steep, only occasionally moderating, gaining 2500 feet in 2½ miles. The tread through dry forest is a bit sketchy, the early part crisscrossed with cat

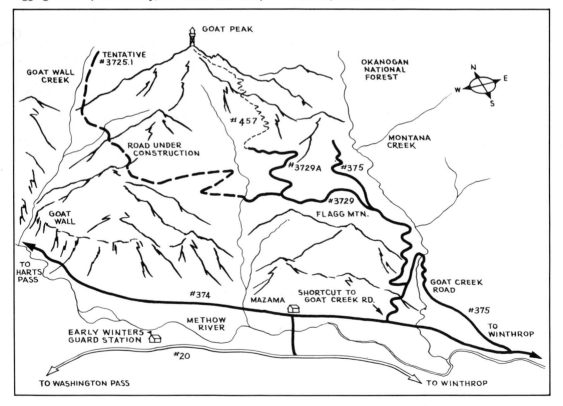

Silver Star Mountain from Goat Peak

tracks from selective logging done many years ago. In 1½ miles is a 6000-foot saddle and from here the going seems easier—doubtless because the views are better. The way traverses the east slopes of the peak and finishes by climbing the north ridge to the open summit.

Though 9 miles distant, 8901-foot Silver Star easily dominates the scene. North Gardner Mountain, 8956 feet, highest in the region, is a little to the south. Farther away are the spectacular peaks of Washington Pass. Northward rise the rolling, high ridges of the Pasayten Wilderness Area; this view of their south slopes makes them seem barren and unimpressive, very unlike the reality encountered by hikers.

Round trip (present trail) 5 miles
Hiking time 6 hours
High point 7001 feet
Elevation gain (from-road-end) 2500 feet
Best June through October
One day
USGS Mazama

Round trip (new trail) 4 miles?
Hiking time 3 hours
Elevation gain 1200 feet

92 GRASSHOPPER PASS

Wide-open, big-sky meadow ridges with grand views of giant peaks and forested valleys. The entire hike is above timberline, contouring hillsides, traversing gardens, and sometimes following the exact Cascade Crest.

Drive the North Cross State Highway 12 miles from Winthrop to Mazama. Turn right, cross the Methow River, and continue 20 miles (pavement ends in 3 miles) to 6198-foot Harts Pass. From the pass turn left on the Meadow Campground road 2 miles, keeping right at a fork, to the road-end and trailhead, elevation 6400 feet.

The Cascade Crest Trail immediately leaves the trees, going along an open slope below diggings of the Brown Bear Mine and above a pretty meadow desecrated by miners' shanties and junkyards. The first mile is a gentle ascent to the 6600-foot east shoulder of a 7400-foot peak. The way swings around the south slopes of this peak to a saddle, 7000 feet, overlooking Ninetynine Basin at the head of Slate Creek, then contours 7386-foot Tatie Peak to another saddle, 6900 feet, and a magnificent picture of Mt. Ballard.

A moderate descent, with a stretch of switchbacks, leads around a 7500-foot peak. In a bouldery basin at 4 miles, 6600 feet, is the only dependable water on the trip, a cold little creek flowing from mossy rocks through a flower-and-heather meadow ringed by groves of larch. Splendid camps.

The trail climbs gradually a final mile to the broad swale of 6800-foot Grasshopper Pass. (Fine camps in early summer when snowmelt water

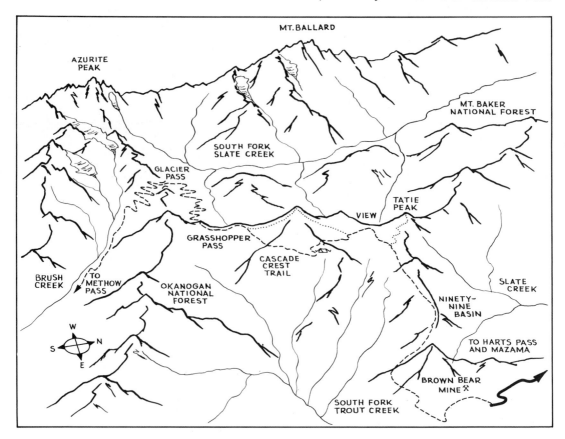

Azurite Peak and Grasshopper Pass

is available.) But don't stop here—go ¼ mile more and a few feet higher on the ridge to a knob just before the trail starts down and down to Glacier Pass. The views are dramatic across Slate Creek forests to 8440-foot Azurite Peak and 8301-foot Mt. Ballard. Eastward are meadows and trees of Trout Creek, flowing to the Methow.

Each of the peaks contoured by the trail invites a side-trip of easy but steep scrambling to the summit, and the wanderings are endless amid larches and pines and spruces, flowers blossoming from scree and buttress, and the rocks— colorful shales, slates, conglomerates, and sandstones and an occasional igneous intrusion.

Experienced cross-country hikers don't really need the trail, but can scramble up and down the crest from road-end to Grasshopper Pass, climbing all three peaks. This route is not recommended for backpacking, but actually is the easiest way in early summer, when steep snow blocks the trail in several cold corners.

Round trip 11 miles
Hiking time 6 hours
High point 7000 feet
Elevation gain 1000 feet in, 1000 feet out
Best July through October
One day or backpack
USGS Slate Peak

201

93 WINDY PASS

In all the hundreds of miles of the Cascade Crest Trail, this ranks among the easiest and most scenic segments. The hike starts in meadows and stays high the entire way, contouring gardens thousands of feet above the trees of Slate Creek, magnificent views at every step.

Drive to Harts Pass (Hike 92) and turn right on the Slate Peak road about 1½ miles to the first switchback and a small parking area at the trailhead, elevation 6800 feet.

If the trip is being done in early July, don't be discouraged if the road beyond Harts Pass is blocked by snow and the trail beginning is blinding-white; snow lingers here later than on any other portion of the hike, and mostly-clear trail can be expected after a frosty start.

The Cascade Crest Trail gently climbs a meadow shelf the first ½ mile, contours steep slopes of Slate Peak, and drops into lovely little Benson Basin, with a creek and nice camps a few hundred feet below the tread. The way swings up and out

to a spur ridge, contours to Buffalo Pass and another spur, and then descends above the gorgeous greenery of Barron Basin to 6262-foot Windy Pass and delightful camps in flowers and larch trees.

Sad to say, the wreckers have been here. Barron Basin is one of the most magnificent easy-to-reach glorylands in the Cascades, but much of it is private property and the miners have raised havoc, gouging delicate meadows with bulldozers, dumping garbage at will. This hike is bound to convert any casual walker into a fierce enemy of the ultra-permissive federal mining laws, which make it difficult if not impossible for the Forest Service to protect the land from professional swindlers-destroyers.

Side-trips from the pass will make a person want the basin to be reclaimed for the public domain and placed within the Pasayten Wilderness Area, the boundary of which follows the divide, excluding the miner-mangled slopes to the west. Wander meadows north to the panoramas from 7307-foot Tamarack Peak, or walk the Cascade

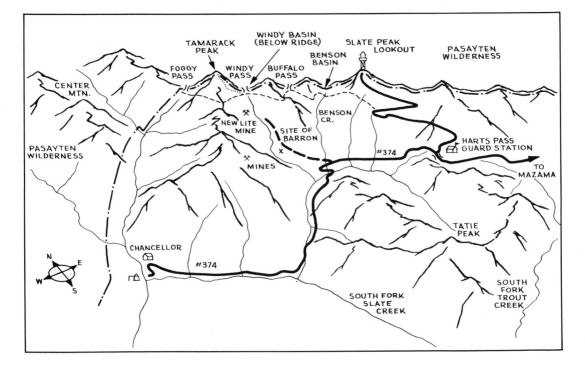

Crest Trail a short mile into Windy Basin.

Views on the way? They start with Gardner Mountain, the Needles, Silver Star, Golden Horn, Tower Mountain, and especially the near bulks of Ballard and Azurite. Westerly, Jack and Crater dominate, but part of Baker can also be seen, and many more peaks. Easterly is the Pasayten country, high and remote.

Before or after the hike, take a side-trip to the fire lookout on the 7440-foot summit of Slate Peak, the highest point in Washington State accessible to automobiles.

Round trip to Windy Pass 7 miles
Hiking time 5 hours
High point 7000 feet
Elevation gain 500 feet in, 1000 feet out
Best early July through October
One day or backpack
USGS Slate Peak (part only)

Crest Trail in Benson Basin. Mt. Ballard in distance

94 CANYON CREEK

A valley walk beginning on an abandoned mining road built decades ago for special narrow-gauge trucks, then following trail through deep forest with views out to waterfalls and snowy peaks. The hike can be done as a round-trip from either end; it is here described with a start at Chancellor.

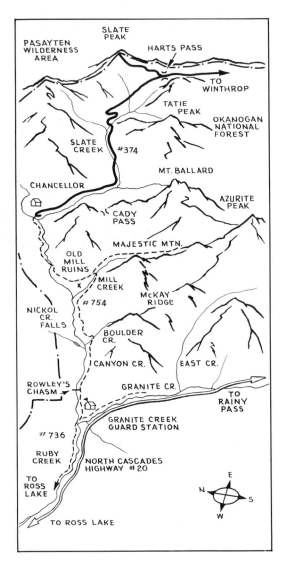

Drive 10 miles from Harts Pass (Hike 92) down Slate Creek to the old mining town of Chancellor, a thriving community in 1880 and sparsely occupied as recently as the era of World War II. Once there were numerous cabins on both sides of the creek, but only a couple remain.

The trail starts below the campground at an elevation of 3000 feet, crossing Canyon Creek on a bridge and heading downvalley close to the stream. The tread is distinguishable as an old road, though one who didn't know about the narrow-gauge trucks would wonder what sort of vehicle ever could have traveled it. At 1½ miles pass avalanche debris which annually pours from a gully on the far side of the creek; some years the snow doesn't melt completely and ice can be found under the trash and rubble. Near here is a campsite. A short distance beyond, cross Canyon Creek on a new bridge, 2600 feet. The way now climbs to 2900 feet on the hillside high above the creek. In places the road has slid out. At about 2½ miles the route traverses several wide patches of avalanche greenery offering fine views down the valley to glacier-covered Mt. Snowfield and Colonial Peak.

At 3 miles (the current trail sign at Chancellor says 4) is the junction with the Mill Creek trail, which ascends Mill Creek to join another abandoned truck road, climbing over Cady Pass from the Slate Creek road, and continues to the Azurite Mine and Azurite Pass.

Descend from the junction to Mill Creek, 2600 feet, 3½ miles, and a possible camp. This seems a most unlikely spot for a sawmill, but remnants remain, including heavy timbers used for shoring up mine shafts. Here is the end of the road, the rest of the walk following legitimate trail. Cross Mill Creek on a rickety bridge and ascend the hillside to 3000 feet, and then drop gradually to a ford of Boulder Creek at 2400 feet, 5½ miles. A bit beyond look out through trees to waterfalls of Nickol Creek, and later to a good view of Crater Mountain. At 7¼ miles a short side-trail leads to Rowley Chasm, spanned by a bridge reputed to be only 5 feet long (but really more like 10) with the river 100 or maybe 200 feet below.

Climbing a little, then descending, at 9 miles the trail reaches the old Granite Creek Guard

Canyon Creek gorge and Snowfield Peak

Station, 1904 feet, and a campground and parking area beside the North Cascades Highway. At this point Canyon and Granite Creeks join to form Ruby Creek, flowing into Ross Lake.

Round trip 18 miles
Allow 2 days
High point 3000 feet
Elevation gain 300 feet downstream, 1400 feet upstream
Best June through October from North Cascades State Highway
Best mid-July through September from Chancellor
USGS Azurite Peak and Crater Mtn.

95 THREE FOOLS TRAIL

A classic highland wander from the Cascade Crest to Ross Lake, going up and down a lonesome trail through some of the wildest valleys, ridges, and meadows in the range. A one-way trip is recommended, starting at Harts Pass (or near Allison Pass in Canada) and ending at the lake. Special transportation arrangements are required: a drop-off at Harts Pass (or near Allison Pass); a pickup by boat from Ross Lake Resort (Hike 25)—though a party can, if desired, exit via the East Bank Trail.

Hike the Cascade Crest Trail (Hikes 93 and 101) 27 miles from Harts Pass (or 11 miles from near Allison Pass) to Castle Pass, elevation 5250 feet. (**Note:** In the absence of accurate maps, all elevations and mileages from this point on are roughly estimated.) Turn west on the Three Fools Trail (officially, Castle Pass Trail No. 749), descending several hundred feet in ½ mile to a junction with the abandoned trail down Three Fools Creek. Turn right, climbing steeply in forest, then meadows. At 3 miles, 6000 feet, enter a little basin with a welcome creeklet—the rest first dependable water since before Castle Pass, and the last for several more miles. An old semi-literate sign calls this "Serckle Basin Camp." Sketchy tread ascends from the basin, swings around a spur, descends meadows to a saddle, and climbs the crest to a 6500-foot knob that ranks among the most magnificent viewpoints of the region: look north across the headwaters of Castle Creek to Castle Peak, Frosty Mountain in Canada, and Mt. Winthrop; look south across forests of Three Fools Creek to peaks along and west of the Cascade Crest; look in every direction and look for hours and never see all there is to be seen. The way drops from the knob and climbs ridgetop heather and parklands to 6 miles, 6000 feet, and a grandly scenic camp—but the only water, if any, is from snowmelt.

The trail angles down across a broad, steep flower garden, then switchbacks in trees, to Big Face Creek, beneath the impressive wall of Joker Mountain. (At 6½ miles is a tumbling creek; below the trail here is a campsite on a tiny, wooded shelf.) At 8 miles, 4500 feet, the path reaches the valley bottom. For a mandatory side-trip, fight through a bit of brush and climb the open basin to a high saddle with views out to Hozomeen and the Chilliwacks and below to a snowy cirque lake draining to Freezeout Creek.

The trail goes gently downstream in trees to a crossing of Big Face Creek at 9 miles, 4200

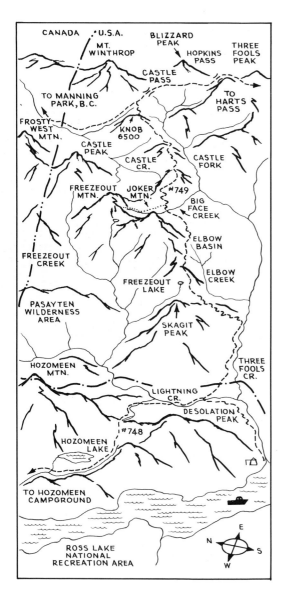

feet. Stay alert—tread proceeds straight ahead to a tangle of avalanched logs, but the trail actually turns right in a gravel wash to the ford. A possible camp here.

A long climb begins up forest to avalanche greenery; when tread vanishes in the grass go directly uphill, watching for cut logs. The ascent continues in trees, opens to meadows, and at 11½ miles, 6500 feet, tops out in the wide green pass, with broad views, between Big Face and Elbow Creeks. A side-trail drops ¼ mile to a camp site and meandering stream in the glorious park of Elbow Basin. The main trail—tread missing for long stretches—contours and climbs north around the basin to a grassy swale (and a scenic camp, if snowmelt is available) near the ridge crest at 13 miles. Be sure to walk to the 7000-foot plateau summit of the ridge and views: east to the Cascade Crest; south to Jack Mountain; west to the Pickets, Chilliwacks, Desolation, and especially the nearby towers of Hozomeen; north into Canada.

The trail descends near and along the crest, with a look down to the tempting cirque of Freezeout Lake (accessible via a steep scramble), passing through a spectacular silver forest. A stern drop commences—down and down hot and dry burn meadows and young trees. The mouth grows parched, the knees loose and floppy. At 18 miles, 2500 feet, the trail at last touches Three Fools Creek and a possible camp; stop for an orgy of drinking and foot-soaking, and an understanding of why this trip is not recommended to begin at Ross Lake.

Hopes of an easy downhill water-grade hike are quickly dashed by a 1000-foot climb. The trail then goes down, goes up, and down and up, and finally on a forest bench to Lightning Creek at 23 miles, 2500 feet. Just before the crossing is a junction with the trail north to Nightmare Camp and Hozomeen (Hike 23). Just beyond the footlog crossing is Deer Lick Cabin and a campsite.

Again the trail climbs 1000 feet and goes down and up, high on the side of the Lightning Creek gorge, coming at last to a superb overlook of Ross Lake, a thousand feet below. The conclusion is a switchbacking descent to the lakeshore and Lightning Creek Camp, 1600 feet, 27 miles from Castle Pass.

One-way trip from Castle Pass to Ross Lake 27 miles
Allow 3-5 days
High point 7000 feet
Elevation gain about 10,000 feet
Best mid-July through September
USGS none

One-way trip from Harts Pass to Ross Lake 54 miles
Allow 7-9 days

One-way trip from near Allison Pass (Canada) to Ross Lake 38 miles
Allow 5-7 days
Forest Service wilderness permit required

Big Craggy Peak from trail to Burch Mountain

96 BILLY GOAT PASS— BURCH MOUNTAIN

Hike to the edge of the Pasayten Wilderness Area, climb toward an old lookout site, and see miles and miles of broad valleys and open ridges. Carry plenty of water and start early before the sun gets hot. This is big-scale country, often with long stretches between points of scenic interest. For hikers, therefore, early summer is the best season, when flowers and snowfields add variety.

Drive north from Winthrop on the paved Chewack River road. In 8 miles is a crossing of the river. At 9 miles turn left on the Eightmile Creek road 14½ miles (pavement ends in 5 miles) to a privately-owned corral and a couple of mines at 4500 feet. Continue 1 more steep mile to the road-end and trailhead, elevation 5100 feet.

The way is moderately steep through open forest, gaining 900 feet in the 2½ miles to Billy Goat Pass, 6000 feet, on the border of the Pasayten Wilderness Area.

Drop over the pass a few hundred feet and find the old and unmarked Burch Mountain lookout trail angling upward to the right. The tread is faint in meadows but plain enough on steep hillsides. The ascent is abrupt, quickly emerging in views southwest to Isabella Ridge and beyond to a horizon of 8000-foot peaks, the most dramatic being Big Craggy. Gaining some 700 feet in less than ¾ mile, the trail nearly reaches a saddle before contouring around a high rock knoll. At the closest approach to the saddle leave the trail, climb to the crest, and walk back on the ridge ¼ mile to a 6800-foot knoll with long views north, east, and west.

The 7800-foot summit of Burch Mountain, site of the old lookout (the cabin is long gone), is 2 miles farther and offers even broader and grander views.

Round trip to 6800-foot viewpoint 7 miles
Hiking time 4 hours
High point 6800 feet
Elevation gain 1700 feet
Best late June through October
One day
USGS none

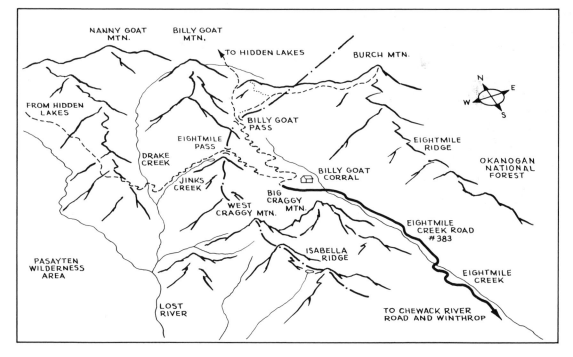

97 TIFFANY MOUNTAIN

A superb ridge walk to an 8242-foot summit with views west to distant peaks of the North Cascades, north into the Pasayten Wilderness Area, and east to farmlands of the Okanogan. The hike can be done as a round-trip or—by use of two cars or a non-hiking assistant to move the car—as a one-way trip to either of two alternate trailheads.

Drive north from Winthrop on the paved Chewack River road. At 7½ miles, just before the paved road crosses the Chewack River, turn tight on road No. 370. In less than 2 miles turn right again, still on road No. 370, which now follows Boulder Creek. In another 7 miles the road leaves Boulder Creek and goes up along Middle Bernhardt Creek. (New construction here may be confusing.) Continue 3 miles to Freezeout Pass and the trailhead, elevation 6500 feet.

(To place a car at the first of the alternate trailheads, drive 4 more miles to Tiffany Lake trail, 6240 feet. For the second, drive beyond the lake trail 5 miles on road No. 370 to a junction, turn right 1 mile on road No. 391 to Lone Frank Pass, and go another 6 miles to the trailhead, 4990 feet, signed "Tiffany Lake trail." If you reach Salmon Meadow, you've driven about 1 mile too far.)

From Freezeout Pass the trail climbs steadily 1½ miles through trees, then 1 mile above timberline, and begins a contour around the east side of the peak. Be sure to make the ½-mile (each way) sidetrip up grassy slopes to the

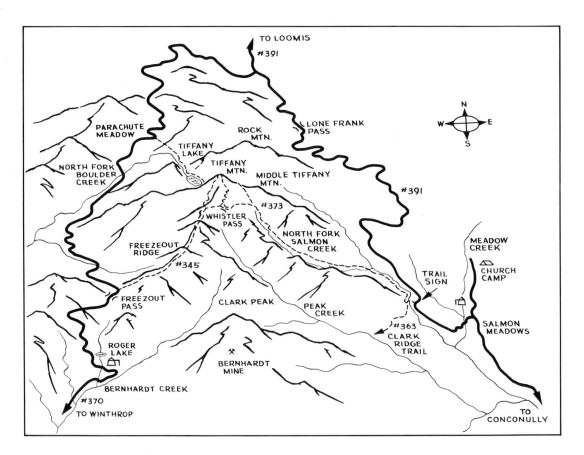

Tiffany Mountain from Tiffany Meadows

unlimited views from the top of Tiffany Mountain, once the site of a fire lookout.

For the one-way trips, return to the trail and continue onward, descending through Whistler Pass to a 6800-foot junction, 3½ miles from Freezeout Pass, with the Tiffany Lake trail. Either go 4 miles to the road via 6480-foot Tiffany Lake or follow the open ridge above the North Fork Salmon Creek 2½ miles before dropping into trees and down to the road.

Round trip from Freezeout Pass to the summit 6 miles
Hiking time 4 hours
High point 8242 feet
Elevation gain 1700 feet
Best July through September
One day
USGS Tiffany Mtn.

One-way trip via Tiffany Lake 8 miles
Hiking time 5 hours

98   HORSESHOE BASIN (Pasayten)

At the northeast extremity of the Cascades is a tundra country so unlike the main range a visitor wonders if he hasn't somehow missed a turn and ended up in the Arctic. Meadows for miles and miles, rolling from broad basins to rounded summits of peaks above 8000 feet, with views south over forests to Tiffany Mountain, east to Chopaka Mountain and the Okanogan Highlands, north far into Canada, and west across the Pasayten Wilderness Area to glaciered, dream-hazy giants of the Cascade Crest.

Horseshoe Basin

Drive west from Tonasket to Loomis and turn north. In 1.5 miles turn left at signs for "Chopaka Lake-Toats Coulee," cross the valley of Sinlahekin Creek, and start a long, steep climb up Toats Coulee. Pass several junctions, following signs mentioning "North Fork Campground-Iron Gate-Horseshoe Basin." At 11 miles from Loomis is North Fork Campground and in another 5 miles a junction with a narrow old road signed "Iron Gate." Turn right and drive 7 rough and steep miles to the road-end and trailhead, elevation 6000 feet, at the new Iron Gate Camp on the boundary of the Pasayten Wilderness Area.

The first ¾ mile is along the recently-abandoned road to the old Iron Gate Camp (no water). The trail from here begins in small lodgepole pine (most of this region was burned off by a series of huge fires in the 1920s) on the old road to Tungsten Mine, which operated as recently as the early 1950s. The grade is nearly flat the first mile to cool waters of a branch of Clutch Creek, and then starts a moderate steady ascent. At 3¼ miles the route opens out into patches of grass and flowers. After a brief steep bit, at 4 miles the way abruptly opens from trees to the flowery, stream-bubbling nook of Sunny Basin and splendid Sunny Camp, 6900 feet.

The trail climbs ½ mile to 7200-foot Sunny Pass—be prepared to gasp and rave. All around spreads the enormous meadowland of Horseshoe Basin, demanding days of exploration. From the pass the Tungsten road drops left and the "pure" trail goes right, contouring gentle slopes of Horseshoe Mountain to grand basecamps in and near the wide flat of Horseshoe Pass, 7100 feet, 5¾ miles, and then contouring more glory to tiny Louden Lake, 6¾ miles (this lake dries up in late summer), and then on and on as described in Hike 99.

The roamings are unlimited. All the summits are easy flower walks—7620-foot Pick Peak, 8000-foot Horseshoe Mountain, and 8076-foot Arnold Peak. The ridge north from 8106-foot Armstrong Peak has the added interest of monuments to mark the United States-Canada boundary. A more ambitious side-trip is south from Sunny Pass 6 miles on the down-and-up trail to 8334-foot Windy Peak, highest in the area, and once the site of a fire lookout. Don't omit a short

walk east through Horseshoe Pass to the immense silver forest at the head of Long Draw.

Round trip to Sunny Pass 9 miles
Hiking time 6 hours
High point 7200 feet
Elevation gain 1200 feet
Best late June until mid-October
One day or backpack
USGS Horseshoe Basin
Forest Service wilderness permit required

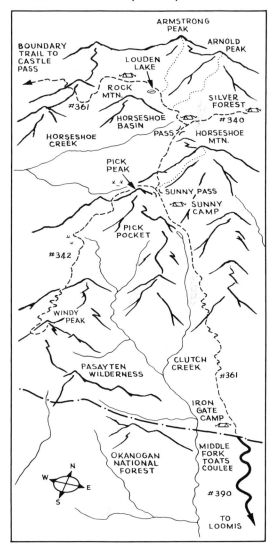

99 BOUNDARY TRAIL

As the golden eagle flies, it's 40 miles from the east edge of the Pasayten Wilderness Area to the Cascade Crest; as the backpacker walks it's twice that far, with some distance still remaining to reach civilization. Though the Pasayten country lacks the glaciers of more famous mountains west, and with few exceptions the peaks are rounded, unimpressive to a climber, there is a magnificent vastness of high ridges, snowfields, flower gardens, parklands, cold lakes, green forests, loud rivers. Long after the Pickets are crowded, there'll be lonesome roaming here.

A formally-marked Boundary Trail, traversing the Pasayten Wilderness near the United States-Canada border, so far is only an idea, but recognition as a classic comparable to the Cascade Crest Trail is certain to come. The weather is better and summer arrives earlier than in windward ranges. The trails are high much of the distance, often above 7000 feet, but are mostly snow-free in early July, which is an ideal time for the trip.

Length of the route precludes a detailed description in these pages. In any event the journey is for experienced wilderness travelers who have the routefinding skills needed to plan and find their own way. The notes below merely aim to stimulate the imagination.

Begin from the Iron Gate road-end (Hike 98) and walk to Horseshoe Basin and Louden Lake (6¾ miles). With ups and downs, always in highlands, the trail goes along Bauerman Ridge to Scheelite Pass (13¾ miles), the old buildings and garbage of Tungsten Mine (17¾ miles), and over Cathedral Pass to Cathedral Lakes (21¾ miles). The route this far makes a superb 4-7-day round-trip from Iron Gate.

Continue west to Spanish Camp (26 miles) and the first descent to low elevation, at the Ashnola River (31½ miles). Climb high again, passing Sheep Mountain (34½ miles), Quartz Mountain (38 miles), and Bunker Hill (43¼

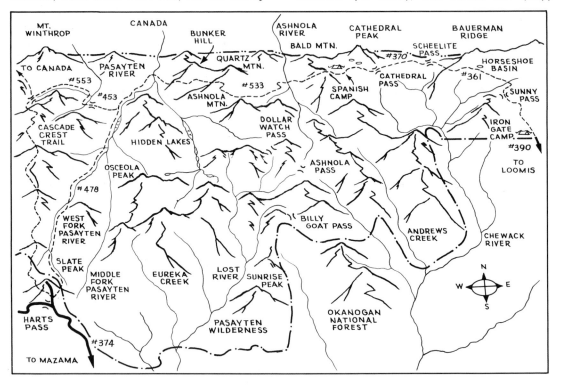

Boundary Trail through Horseshoe Basin

miles), then dropping to low forests of the Pasayten River (50½ miles).

Follow the Pasayten River upstream to the Harrison Creek Trail, cross a high ridge to Chuchuwanteen Creek (60 miles), and ascend Frosty Creek past Frosty Lake to Frosty Pass (66 miles) and on to Castle Pass (66¾ miles). From here take the Cascade Crest Trail 27 miles south (Hike 101) to Harts Pass, ending a trip of some 94 miles.

(For a shorter alternate, hike up the Pasayten River to Three Forks and ascend the West Fork Pasayten to Harts Pass. Trails branch west from this valley route to reach the Cascade Crest at Woody Pass and Holman Pass.)

However, for the true and complete Boundary Trail, go west from Castle Pass on the Three Fools Trail (Hike 95), hike south to Ross Dam and cross Ross Lake to the Little Beaver, and traverse the North Cascades National Park via Whatcom and Hannegan Passes (Hike 12), concluding the epic journey at the Ruth Creek road.

Someday, perhaps, the Boundary Trail will be extended to Mount Baker and down to beaches of Puget Sound.

One-way trip (main route) from Iron Gate via Castle Pass to Harts Pass 94 miles
Allow 10 days or more
Best July through September
USGS none
Forest Service wilderness permit required

100 CHOPAKA MOUNTAIN

Stand on the absolute easternmost peak of the North Cascades. Look down a startling 6700-foot scarp to green pastures and orchards around Palmer Lake and meanders of the Smilkameen River. Look east to the Okanogan Highlands, north into Canada and the beginnings of other ranges, and south over rolling forests of Toats Coulee Creek to Tiffany Mountain. And also look west across the Pasayten Wilderness Area to haze-dimmed, snowy summits of the Chelan Crest and Washington Pass. Aside from the geographical distinction of "farthest east," the special feature of the hike is the opportunity to wander alpine meadows as early as the middle of May, when windward ranges are so deep in snow that the coming of flowers seems an impossible dream.

Drive west from Tonasket to Loomis and turn north. In 1.3 miles turn left at signs for "Chopaka Lake-Toats Coulee," cross the valley of Sinlahekin Creek, ignore a road that goes right and uphill to Chopaka Lake, and start a long, steep climb up Toats Coulee. At 10 miles from Loomis, turn right 8 miles on the Ninemile Creek road (at this and all subsequent junctions follow "Chopaka Mountain" signs) to Cold Spring Campground, 6000 feet. The road generally is snowfree by Memorial Day; before then the way may be blocked by lingering snowfields, but if so this merely adds a mile or two to the hike. Carry water—Cold Spring has been contaminated by cattle. (The pleasant campground is fenced to keep cows **out,** but the cattlemen who "own" Chopaka use the fences to keep cows **in,** illegally employing the camp as a holding pen.)

Drive ¼ mile above Cold Spring to the road-end parking lot, elevation 6200 feet, with views west to Horseshoe Basin country. Hike a jeep track through spindly trees ½ mile. At 6600 feet, where the ruts start a sidehill contour northeast, find the first logical meadow opening and leave the track, climbing an obvious way toward the heights. The ascent winds amid clumps of alpine trees on open ground that would be flower-glorious were it not devastated by cattle. However, a slope of frost-wedged boulders stops the hooves and marks the upper end of mud-wallows and cow pies; the meadows now become genuine,

clean, and natural. Emerge onto a broad plateau and amble a few more feet to the 7882-foot summit.

If another couple of hours are available, even better views can be had from Hurley Peak, a mile away. Drop north down a superb heather-and-flower meadow to a 7300-foot saddle and climb a gentle ridge to the 7820-foot top.

Round trip to Chopaka Mountain 4 miles
Hiking time 4 hours
High point 7882 feet
Elevation gain 1700 feet
Best mid-May through June, before cows arrive
One day
USGS Loomis and Horseshoe Basin

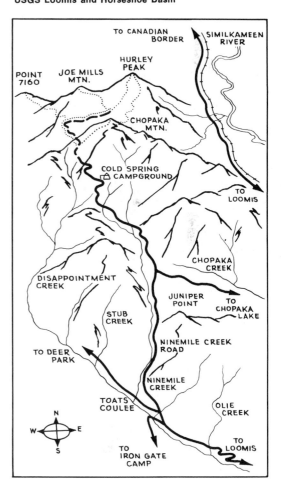

Rain shower approaching Chopaka Mountain

Crest Trail on side of Slate Peak. Silver Star Mountain in distance

101   CASCADE CREST TRAIL

For rugged mountain scenery, the portion of the Pacific Crest National Scenic Trail between the Canadian border and Stevens Pass is the most spectacular long walking route in the nation. Undependable weather, late-melting snow, and many ups and downs make it also one of the most difficult and strenuous.

Few hikers have time to complete the trip in one season; most spread their efforts over a period of years, doing the trail in short sections. Those taking the whole trip at once generally prefer to start from the north, since pickup transportation at journey's end is easier to arrange at the south terminus. Though higher, the northern part of the trail lies in the rainshadow of great peaks to the west and thus gets less snow than the southern part; the north country and south country therefore open to travel simultaneously.

Drive the Trans-Canada Highway to E.C. Manning Provincial Park and find the trailhead on an unmarked side-road ½ mile east of the hotel-motel complex at Allison Pass. Hike 7½ miles up Castle Creek to the international boundary at Mounument 78. Look east and west from the monument along the corridor cleared by boundary survey crews; in recent years the new growth has been cut or sprayed. Ascend Route Creek to Castle Pass, from which point south to Harts Pass the trail is almost continuously in meadowland, touching Hopkins Pass, climbing to Lakeview Ridge, crossing Woody Pass into Conie Basin and Rock Pass into Goat Lakes Basin, dropping to Holman Pass, swinging around Jim Mountain to Jim Pass, Foggy Pass, and Oregon Basin, crossing a shoulder of Tamarack Peak into Windy Basin, and from there continuing to Harts Pass as described in Hike 93. **Distance from Allison Pass to Harts Pass, 40 miles; elevation gain, about 8000 feet; hiking time, 4 days.**

From Harts Pass the next road junction is at Rainy Pass. The trail contours around Tatie Peak to Grasshopper Pass (Hike 92), drops to Glacier Pass, drops more into the West Fork Methow River, climbs over Methow Pass, and contours high around Tower Mountain to Granite Pass and on to Cutthroat Pass and down to Rainy Pass (Hike 90). **Distance from Harts Pass to Rainy Pass, 31 miles; elevation gain, about 4400 feet; hiking time, 4 days.**

The next segment is all downhill along Bridge Creek to the Stehekin River road. Walk east on the North Cascades Highway to the Rainy Lake-Bridge Creek Trail and descend forest to the road at Bridge Creek Campground (Hike 85). Hike 5 miles down the Stehekin River road to High Bridge Campground. **Distance from Rainy Pass to High Bridge, 16 miles; hiking time, 2 days.**

The next stage is the longest, with a difficult choice between the alternatives of going east or west of Glacier Peak. From High Bridge climb the Agnes valley to Suiattle Pass (Hike 84). Continue to Glacier Peak Mines (Hike 43) on the slopes of Plummer Mountain and choose either the west-of-Glacier or east-of-Glacier alternate.

East-of-Glacier alternate: Drop to Miners Creek,

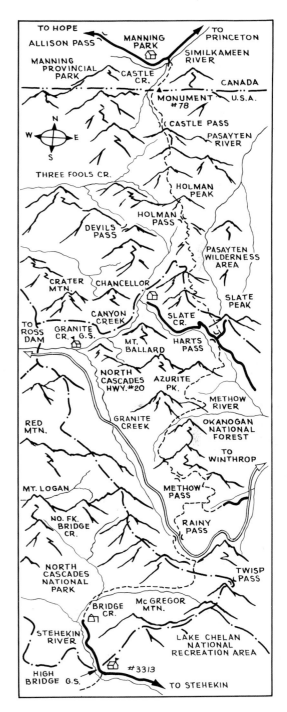

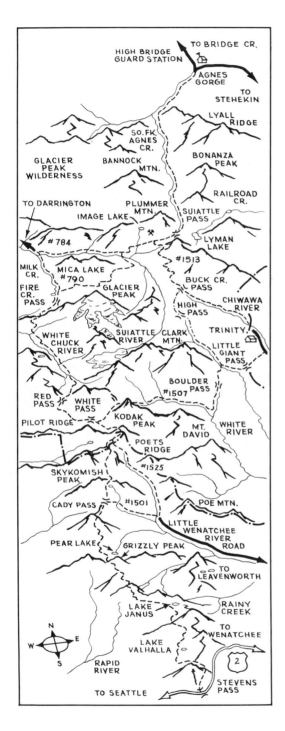

climb Middle Ridge, and continue to Buck Creek Pass (Hike 76). Descend Buck Creek to the old mining town of Trinity, walk the road to the Little Giant trail, cross Little Giant Pass (Hike 74) into the Napeequa valley, cross Boulder Pass (Hike 73) to the White River, and return via the White River trail to the Cascade Crest at Lower White Pass. **Distance from High Bridge to Lower White Pass, 79 miles; elevation gain, about 15,000 feet; hiking time 7 days.** The journey can be broken at either the Chiwawa River road or White River road.

West-of-Glacier alternate: Drop to the Suiattle River, climb the new Vista Creek trail over ridges and down into Milk Creek (Hike 41), cross Fire Creek Pass to the White Chuck River (Hike 46), ascend the White Chuck to Red Pass (Hike 47), and continue via White Pass to Lower White Pass (Hike 70). **Distance from High Bridge to Lower White Pass, 66 miles; elevation gain, about 12,000 feet; hiking time, 6 days.** The journey can be broken by trail exits to the Suiattle River road, White Chuck River road, or North Fork Sauk River road.

The remainder of the way to Stevens Pass is comparatively level, wandering along the Cascade Crest with ups and downs, frequently alternating from east side to west side, mostly through open meadows of flowers or heather. From Lower White Pass (Hike 71) the trail stays high, dipping into forest only at Indian Pass and again at Cady Pass. From Cady Pass the route contours hillsides, traversing a mixture of forest and meadows past Pear Lake, climbing within a few hundred feet of Grizzly Peak, and proceeding onward to Janus Lake (Hike 66), Union Gap, Lake Valhalla (Hike 65), and finally Stevens Pass. **Distance from Lower White Pass to Stevens Pass, 32 miles; elevation gain, 5000 feet; hiking time, 4 days.**

For details of mileages and campsites, see the Forest Service map and log of the Cascade Crest Trail, available free from any Forest Service office.

One-way trip from Allison Pass to Stevens Pass about 185 miles

Hiking time 20-25 days

Elevation gain about 30,000 feet

Best-mid-July through September

Forest Service wilderness permit and Park Service camping permit required

Crest Trail on side of Indian Head Peak. Kodak Peak on right

TIME OF YEAR TRAILS ARE PASSABLE

The following list shows when trails are generally free enough of snow to be passable. The time varies every year by a week or 10 days depending on the depth of the winter snow and warmth of the spring. Even when considered passable, expect to cross snowpatches for another 2 weeks, or maybe all summer. Expect occasional snowstorms at high elevations even in the middle of summer. This new snow will melt in a few hours.

If alpine flower fields are one of the trail's attractions, plan the hike between mid-July and early August. For blueberries, try late August and fall, and for fall color, go in mid-September to early October. High mountain lakes generally don't open up until mid-July.

If you want to be alone on the trail, try early in the season or after Labor Day, but avoid the high hunting season.

MARCH
18   Baker River
23   East Bank Trail to Lightning Creek
81   Chelan Lakeshore

APRIL
22   Thunder Creek to Middle Cabin
63   Barclay Lake

MAY
11   Nooksack Cirque
21   Sourdough TV Tower
46   Kennedy Hot Springs
100   Chopaka Mountain

EARLY JUNE
19   Finney Peak
26   Beaver Loop
31   Middle Fork Cascade River
36   Round Mountain
37   Squire Creek Pass
39   Downey Creek
91   Goat Peak
94   Canyon Creek (from Granite Creek)

MID OR LATE JUNE
23   East Bank Trail to Hozomeen
25   Desolation Peak
35   Trapper Lake (via Stehekin River)
38   Green Mountain
40   Sulphur Mountain
54   Mount Pilchuck
55   Mount Forgotten
57   Goat Lake
63   Eagle Lake
68   Dirtyface Peak
83   McGregor Mountain
89   Twisp Pass
96   Billy Goat Pass
98   Horseshoe Basin (Pasayten)

EARLY JULY
5   Gold Run Pass
17   Boulder Ridge
21   Sourdough Mountain
30   Kindy Ridge
33   Boston Basin
45   Meadow Mountain
46   Kennedy Ridge
49   Lost Creek Ridge to Round Lake
53   Goat Flats
56   Mount Dickerman
58   Bedal Basin
60   Poodle Dog Pass
61   Glacier Basin
62   Lake Blanca
64   Scorpion Mountain
77   Entiat Meadows
82   Chelan Crest Trail
85   North Fork Bridge Creek
87   Horseshoe Basin (Stehekin)
90   Cutthroat Pass
92   Grasshopper Pass
93   Windy Pass
97   Tiffany Mountain
99   Boundary Trail

MID-JULY
4   Excelsior Mountain
12   Hannegan Pass
16   Morovitz Meadow
20   Thornton Lakes
24   Crater Mountain
27   Easy Pass
28   Lookout Mountain-Monogram Lake
29   Sibley Creek Pass
30   Found Lake
34   Cascade Pass-Sahale Arm
35   Trapper Lake (via Cascade Pass)

39 Bachelor Meadows
41 Milk Creek-Vista Creek Loop
42 Image Lake
43 Suiattle to Lake Chelan
48 Stujack Pass
65 Lake Valhalla
66 Grizzly Peak
67 Nason Ridge
69 Minotaur Lake
70 Meander Meadow
73 Napeequa Valley (via Boulder Pass)
74 Little Giant Pass
75 Spider Meadow
78 Larch Lakes Loop
79 Milham Pass
84 Agnes Creek
86 Park Creek Pass
88 Lake Chelan to Cascade River
94 Canyon Creek (from Chancellor)
95 Three Fools Trail
101 Cascade Crest Trail

LATE JULY
1 Bastile Ridge
6 Winchester Mountain
7 Table Mountain Loop
14 Easy Ridge
15 Whatcom Pass

22 Thunder Creek to Park Creek Pass
32 South Fork Cascade River
44 Around Glacier Peak
47 White Chuck Glacier
50 White Pass
51 Pilot Ridge
52 Bald Eagle Trail
59 Gothic Basin
71 Cady Pass to White Pass
75 Spider Pass
76 Buck Creek Pass

EARLY AUGUST
2 Heliotrope Ridge
3 Skyline Divide
8 Ptarmigan Ridge
9 Lake Ann
10 Price Lake
13 Copper Mountain
29 Hidden Lake Lookout
48 Mount Pugh
49 Lost Creek Ridge to Lake Byrne
51 Blue Lakes
67 Alpine Lookout
80 Ice Lakes

MID-AUGUST
72 Mount David

STILL MORE HIKES IN THE NORTH CASCADES

The 101 hikes represent all provinces of the North Cascades, all the varied scenic climaxes, from Stevens Pass to Canada, and from Puget Sound to the Okanogan. Heaviest emphasis has been placed on areas close to major population centers. There are thousands of other great walks in the range; many are described in the books noted below, which may be obtained from bookstores, shops specializing in mountain equipment, or in most cases by mail order directly from The Mountaineers. (See listing of Mountaineer Books at the end of this volume.)

PHOTO BOOKS AND GENERAL

The North Cascades
68 black-and-white photos by Tom Miller, taken from a climber's viewpoint. Published by The Mountaineers.

The Wild Cascades: Forgotten Parkland
44 photos in color, 72 in black and white, by many photographers. Text by Harvey Manning. Published by Ballantine-Sierra.

The North Cascades National Park
15 photos in color, 109 in black and white, by Bob and Ira Spring. Text by Harvey Manning. Superior Publishing Co.

The Cascade Range
32 of the color photos, by Ray Atkeson, are in the North Cascades. Published by Belding.

Challenge of the North Cascades
50 photos in black and white and narratives of pioneer climbs made over a 30-year period by Fred Beckey. Published by The Mountaineers.

Wildflowers of Mount Rainier and the Cascades
96 color pages of flowers one often sees while hiking. Emphasis is on appreciation of the flowers. Photos by Bob and Ira Spring. Authoritative and interesting text by Mary Fries. Published by The Mountaineers.

WINTER GUIDE BOOKS

Northwest Ski Trails
Photos by Bob and Ira Spring, maps by Marge Mueller, and text by Ted Mueller include coverage of 3 commercial ski areas and 10 ski tours in the North Cascades. Published by The Mountaineers.

Snowshoe Hikes in the Cascades and Olympics
Text, maps and photos by Gene Prater include 14 trips in the North Cascades. Published by The Mountaineers.

HIKING GUIDES

Routes and Rocks: Hiker's Guide to the North Cascades from Glacier Peak to Lake Chelan
A hiker should not enter the Glacier-Chelan region without this book, which details countless trips. Mile-by-mile description of all trails and off-trail high routes, of campsites and points of scenic and geologic interest, in the Glacier Peak, Holden, and Lucerne quadrangles, copies of which, with special overprints, are included in an inside-cover pocket. By Dwight Crowder and Rowland Tabor of the U.S. Geological Survey. Published by The Mountaineers.

Hiker's Map to the North Cascades: Routes and Rocks in the Mt. Challenger Quadrangle
Also by Tabor and Crowder, covering trails and off-trail high routes in the Pickets and Chilliwacks. Published by The Mountaineers.

Trips and Trails, 1: Family Camps, Short Hikes, and View Roads in the North Cascades and Olympics
The basic introduction to car travel and car camping, essential for every visitor. Includes scores of hikes up to several miles in length—shorter and easier than those in the present book. Text by E. M. Sterling, photos by Bob and Ira Spring, maps by Marge Mueller. Published by The Mountaineers.

100 Hikes in Southwestern British Columbia
Covers the Canadian portion of the North Cascades with text, photos, and maps. Scheduled for publication in 1973. To be published by the British Columbia Mountaineering Club and The Mountaineers.

Climber's Guide to the Cascades
Original edition by Fred Beckey is out of print, available only in libraries. New three-volume edition scheduled for 1973, written by Beckey, published by The Mountaineers.

Forest Service Route Map of the Cascade Crest Trail
Strip maps and a hiking log giving mileages and campsites on the full length of the trail. Regularly revised. Free on request from any office of the U.S. Forest Service.

MORE HIKES

Choosing the 101 hikes was an excruciating process, what with the necessity to omit so many trips of comparable interest. Below are mentioned scores of other hikes—in addition to those described in books noted above—that can be recommended. Even all these only suggest the hiking potential of the range—and new trails are under construction or planned.

To take the following hikes, consult the books referred to, if any, or else obtain the applicable maps and make your own way. The lack of detailed "recipes"—or in some case, of a trail—may be compensated for by a greater degree of solitude.

Nooksack River (Also see Challenger Routes and Rocks)
Twin Sisters Mountain
Church Mountain: Stiff climb to dramatic viewpoint.
Silesia Creek from Canada: Reached from logging roads—lovely forest walk. Also accessible from Twin Lakes.

Middle Fork Nooksack to Park Butte: Glacier vistas and Mt. Baker views with side-trip to Meadow Point.

Keep Kool trail to Yellow Aster Meadows: Rough trail to beautiful gardens also reached by Hike 5.

Chilliwack River from Canada: Excellent forest walk from Chilliwack Lake.

Green Creek trail to Elbow Lake.

Canyon Ridge: At present, the most remote and loneliest trail in the vicinity, with many meadows and views. Someday will be crossed by logging roads, if nobody stops them.

Baker River (Also see Challenger Routes and Rocks)

South Fork Nooksack to Bell Pass: Trail over 3964-foot pass. An interesting route to Park Butte.

Elbow Lakes: 1½-mile way trail and then cross-country route to Lake Wiseman and Twin Sisters Mountain.

Dock Butte: See Trips and Trails.

Swift Creek: Trail starts in meadows at Austin Pass and ends in forest near Baker Lake.

Anderson Lakes, Watson Lakes, and Anderson Butte: See Trips and Trails.

Shadow of Sentinels Nature Trail: ½-mile walk. See Trips and Trails.

Blue Lake: ¾-mile walk. See Trips and Trails.

Slide Lake: Easy 1-mile hike from road No. 347. See the massive rockslide that dammed the lake.

Shuksan Lake: 3-hour scramble on poor trail from road No. 3817 to lake in a deep cirque. Terrific views from trail.

Skagit River-Ross Lake (also see Challenger Routes and Rocks)

Sauk Mountain: See Trips and Trails.

Olson Creek-Cow Haven: Long hike to alpine meadows noted for blueberries.

Pyramid Lake: A faint trail in forest to lake under Pyramid Peak.

Diablo Lake trail: From Diablo Dam above cliffs to Ross Lake (see Hike 21).

Ruby Creek: Magnificent river walk near North Cascades Highway.

Ruby Mountain: Abandoned trail, long climb, but spectacular views for the experienced hiker.

Perry Creek: Side-trip from Little Beaver into a hanging valley.

Silver Creek: Unmaintained valley trail on the west side of Ross Lake.

Panther Creek and Fourth of July Pass: 10-mile forest hike to view Snowfield and Eldorado Peaks.

Pierce Mountain Way: Alternate route up Sourdough Mountain (Hike 21).

McKay Ridge

McAllister Creek: Dead-end trail from Thunder Creek.

Jack Mountain: Little-used trail starting from Ruby Pasture and going 6 miles to end amid meadows and views and camps. From here climbers continue to summit of Jack.

Cascade River

Marble Creek: See Trips and Trails.

Kindy Creek: Little-used trail providing access to Kindy Creek and Sonny Boy Lakes.

North Fork Stillaguamish River

Boulder River: See Trips and Trails.

Whitehorse Glacier via Lone Tree Pass: 2 miles of very steep trail to viewpoint, then 2 miles of straight-up blazed route to pass, then a climbers' route to the ice.

Mt. Higgins: Hike or drive Seapo Road (private) from a mile west of Hazel to reach trailhead in 3 miles. Unmaintained trail climbs past Myrtle Lake to abandoned lookout site.

Suiattle River (Also see Routes and Rocks)

Suiattle Mountain: From road No. 3304, 1 mile of unmaintained trail to Lake Tupso and White Creek road.

Tenas Creek to Boulder Lake: Long trail hike to wooded lake, also reached by bushwhack from Tenas Creek road.

Huckleberry Mountain: Old lookout site. The way is steep, the views big. Good hiking in May to snowline.

Buck Creek: See Trips and Trails.

Sulphur Creek: See Trips and Trails.

Canyon Lake and Totem Pass: A flower-covered ridge 5 miles from Image Lake.

Suiattle River to Suiattle Glacier: Magnificent forests. Trail is lost before Chocolate Creek. From there on the route is for the experienced only.

White Chuck River (Also see **Routes and Rocks**)

Glacier Ridge: Shortcut to Pumice Cirque on a steep trail, partially maintained by a Boy Scout troop, past an old lookout site.

Crystal Lake: 1½ miles to a lake in a deep valley.

North Fork Sauk River (Also see **Routes and Rocks**.)

Cougar Lakes trail: Noted for its many waterfalls.

South Fork Stillaguamish River

Big Four Glacier: See **Trips and Trails.**

Heather Lake: Very popular 2-mile hike to alpine lake.

Lake 22: Very popular 2½-mile hike to alpine lake.

Pinnacle Lake: 1½ miles of poor trail to beautiful lake with views.

Meadow Mountain: Tiny meadows on wooded ridge from Tupso Lake.

Mallardy Ridge trail: 14 miles of unmaintained trail on wooded ridge.

Silver Gulch trail: 1½ miles on old miners' path to open ridges.

Marble Gulch: Plans are to rebuild this old miners' trail.

Sunrise Mine trail No. 707 to Headlee Pass: Very difficult trail from road No. 3012.

Martin Creek trail: Steep jeep trail to forested valley.

South Fork Sauk River

76 Gulch: A route, no maintained trail, to old mines.

Skykomish River

Mt. Stickney: A route on logging roads and through bushes to high views.

Sultan Basin: Short trail climbing beside waterfalls to Little and Big Greider Lakes.

Mineral City Silver Creek: Rich in mining history. The walk follows old logging roads.

Howard Creek: No trail, a bushwhacking climbers' route to Spire Mountain.

Troublesome Creek: Dead-end trail through the woods. See **Trips and Trails.**

West Cady Ridge: Miles of open ridge-walking— no water.

North Fork Skykomish River: A long, forested, river-bottom approach to Crest Trail. Hike the trail now, before a logging road wipes it out.

Meadow Creek to Fortune Ponds, Peaches and Pear Lakes, Quartz Creek: Steep, long trail through virgin forest to Curry Gap.

Little Wenatchee River

Cockeye Creek trail: Over Poet Ridge to Panther Creek. Easy access to Poe Mountain from road No. 2817C.

White River (Also see **Routes and Rocks**)

Panther Creek: Long valley approach gives access to Ibex Creek canyon and Cougar Creek-Cockeye Creek.

White River: 14-mile valley approach to Crest Trail, noted for beautiful forest.

Indian Creek: 13-mile valley approach to Crest Trail.

Twin Lakes: Easy hike to popular mountain lakes.

Chiwawa River (Also see **Routes and Rocks**)

Schaefer Lake: 5-mile climb to high country of beautiful Chiwawa Ridge. Difficult river crossing.

Leroy Creek: Steep trail to meadows and camps in a basin on the side of Mt. Maude, with access over the ridge to Ice Lakes (Hike 80).

Red Mountain: Old mining road, then trail, goes 7 miles from Buck Creek trail to high on Red Mountain. From trail-end a short, easy route leads over Red Mountain Pass and down to Spider Glacier (Hike 75).

Chiwawa Basin: The basin trail leaves the Red Mountain trail at basin entrance and winds through broad meadows, rejoining Red Mountain trail up high.

Phelps Ridge: A trail going from Red Mountain trail over the ridge, and down to Phelps Creek trail at a point just above Leroy Creek.

Massie Lake: 6 mile trail from Chiwawa Basin up to Massie Lake and then up the ridge under Pass No Pass to join the Buck Creek trail (Hike 76).

Basalt Ridge: Long, dry climb, partly steep and brushy, to magnificent scenery.

Estes Butte: Steep and rocky trail to old lookout site. Few, if any, views.

Carne Mountain: High meadows along the Entiat Mountains—possible side-trip to Ice Lakes.

High Pass trail: 3 miles of glorious ridge-walking from Buck Creek Pass.

Entiat River (Also see **Routes and Rocks**)

Duncan Hill Lookout: 5-mile trail to old lookout site, the upper part through open country with magnificent views of the entire Entiat valley.

Pyramid Creek to Pyramid Peak: 16-mile trail along Chelan Mountains.

Lake Chelan-Stehekin River (Also see **Routes and rocks**)

Domke Mountain: Side-trail from Domke Lake trail climbs to old lookout site and views up Lake Chelan and Railroad Creek.

Holden Lake: 4-mile side-trip from Railroad Creek to a lake in a hanging valley. Views of Mary Green Glacier on Bonanza Peak.

Flat Creek: Dead-end, 3.3-mile trail into a scenic valley under the LeConte Glacier, giving access to a tough cross-country trip to the Ptarmigan Traverse.

Rainbow Lake: Popular trail to alpine lake.

Devore Creek-Company Creek loop: A long hike through beautiful alpine meadows.

Junction Mountain: Dead-end trail with views of Agnes and Stehekin valleys.

Prince Creek, Canoe Creek, Fish Creek: Long, steep access trails from Lake Chelan to the Chelan Crest.

Boulder Creek: To War Creek Pass and Chelan Crest.

Rainbow-McAlester loop: Long trail over a high pass.

Twisp River

Copper Pass: Meadows reached via the North Fork Twisp River trail—unmaintained.

Hoodoo Pass: Easiest way into the heart of the Chelan Crest.

Fish Creek Pass: Long, easy hike up Buttermilk Creek to Chelan Crest.

War Creek: A much easier trail to War Creek Pass than the grueling approach from Stehekin.

Reynolds Creek: Joins the Boulder Creek trail.

South Creek: Joins Rainbow Creek trail or offers side-trip to Louis Lake.

Scatter Creek: Leads to Scatter Lake under the colorful rocks of Abernathy Peak.

North Creek: Steep, dry trail to a tiny mountain lake or down Cedar Creek to Early Winters.

Oval Creek: To small, wooded mountain lakes under the Chelan Crest.

Crater Creek trail to Crater Lake: High alpine lake under the Sawtooth Range.

Crater Creek trail to Eagle Lakes: Alpine lakes just below Horse Pass.

Crater Creek trail to Martin Lakes: Beautiful alpine meadows and lakes.

Foggy Dew River trail: Past a lovely waterfall to Merchant Basin then on to Sunrise or Cooney Lakes. Possible cross-country hikes.

Early Winters Creek

Silver Star: Hunters' camp reached by blazed trail up Cedar Creek.

Lake Ann-Rainy Lake: Easy hikes from Rainy Pass.

Methow River

Methow Pass-Snowy Lakes Pass: Section of Crest Trail under Tower Mountain.

Wilderness-Wilderness Trail-Lost River Area: Very long trail exclusively for hikers.

Granite Creek

Panther Creek: Forest hike to 4th of July Pass.

East Creek-Mebee Pass: Steep climb on old Indian-miners' route.

Mill Creek-Azurite Pass: Stiff climb beginning on an old mining road.

Chewack River

Lake Creek: Long valley walk to Black Lake and the Pasayten Wilderness Area.

Sweetgrass Butte Ridge.

Andrews Creek-Remmel Mountain: Very long hike into the Pasayten Wilderness Area from Anderson Creek Corral.

Sinlahekin Creek

Long Swamp-Windy Peak: Trail from Toats Coulee road to 30 Mile Guard Station.

INDEX

Agnes Creek Trail — 184
Alpine Lookout — 150
Anacortes Crossing — 62
Ann, Lake — 32
Ann, Mount — 32

Bachelor Creek — 92
Bachelor Meadows — 92
Baker, Mount — 16, 18, 30, 46, 49
Baker River Trail — 50
Bald Eagle Trail — 120
Barclay Lake — 143
Bastile Ridge — 16
Beaver Creek, Big — 66
Beaver Creek, Little — 66, 214
Beaver Pass — 66
Bedal Basin — 133
Billy Goat Pass — 208
Blanca, Lake — 140
Blue Lakes — 118, 121
Boston Basin — 80
Boulder Pass — 104, 162
Boulder Ridge — 49
Bridge Creek, North Fork — 187
Brush Creek—44
Buck Creek Pass — 102, 104, 166, 168
Burch Mountain — 208
Byrne, Lake — 114

Cady Pass — 156, 158
Cady Ridge—158
Canyon Creek — 204
Canyon Lake — 98
Cascade Pass — 82, 85, 192
Cascade River, Middle Fork — 76
Cascade River, North Fork — 82, 85, 192
Cascade River, South Fork — 78
Castle Pass — 206
Chain Lakes — 28
Chelan Crest — 180
Chelan, Lake — 100, 174, 178, 180, 185, 187, 188, 190, 192
Chelan Lakeshore Trail — 178, 192
Chilliwack River — 40, 42

Chopaka Mountain — 216
Chowder Basin — 17, 21
Cloudy Pass — 100, 184
Coleman Glacier — 16, 18
Columbia Glacier — 140
Copper Lake — 41
Copper Mountain — 41
Cottonwood Camp — 82, 190, 192
Crater Mountain — 62
Cub Lake — 92
Curry Gap — 121
Curtis Glacier — 32
Custer Ridge — 44
Cutthroat Pass — 196

Damfino Lakes — 23
David, Mount — 161
Desolation Peak — 64
Devil Peak, Little — 71
Devils Dome — 62
Diamond Lake — 106
Dickerman, Mount — 128
Dirtyface Lookout — 153
Dishpan Gap — 118, 121, 156, 158
Dolly Creek — 96, 102
Doubtful Lake — 82
Downey Creek — 92

Eagle Lake — 143
Easy Ridge — 42
Egg Lake — 40
Emerald Park — 174
Entiat Meadows — 170
Entiat River Trail — 170, 172, 174, 176
Evergreen Mountain — 144
Excelsior Mountain — 23
Excelsior Pass — 23

Finney Peak — 53
Fire Creek Trail — 106
Fisher Creek — 59, 68
Five Mile Camp — 184
Foggy Lake — 134
Forgotten, Mount — 126
Found Lake — 74

Fourth of July Pass — 59
Freezeout Trail — 61

Gargett Mine — 26
Giant Pass, Little — 164
Glacier Basin — 138
Glacier Peak Wilderness — 79, 92, 95, 96, 98, 100, 102, 106, 108, 110, 114, 116, 118, 121, 158, 162, 164, 166, 168, 170
Goat Flats — 122
Goat Lake — 130
Goat Peak — 198
Gold Run Pass — 25
Gothic Basin — 134
Grasshopper Pass — 200
Green Mountain — 90
Grizzly Peak — 148

Hannegan Pass — 38, 40, 42, 44, 214
Hannegan Peak — 38
Harts Pass — 200, 202, 204, 206
Heliotrope Ridge — 18
Herman Saddle — 28
Hidden Lake Peaks — 72
High Pass — 104, 162
Holden — 100
Horseshoe Basin — 190
Horseshoe Basin (Pasayten) — 212, 214
Hozomeen Lake — 61, 206, 214

Ice Lakes — 176
Image Lake — 98, 100, 102

Janus, Lake — 148
Johnson Peak — 118
June Mountain — 121

Keep Kool Trail — 25
Kennedy Hot Springs — 104, 108, 114
Kennedy Ridge — 104, 108
Kindy Ridge — 74
Kiser, Camp — 31
Kodak Peak — 156
Kulshan Cabin — 18

Larch Lakes — 172
Larrabee, Mount — 26
Lightning Creek Trail — 60, 206
Lookout Mountain — 70
Lost Creek Ridge — 114
Louden Lake — 212, 214
Lyman Lake — 100, 102, 166, 168, 184

McAllister Creek — 59
McGregor Mountain — 183
McMillan Park — 62
Meadow Mountain — 106
Meander Meadow — 156
Merritt Lake — 150
Mertensia Pass — 79
Middle Cabin — 58, 188
Milham Pass — 174
Milk Creek Trail — 96
Minotaur Lake — 154
Monogram Lake — 70
Monte Cristo — 136, 138
Morovitz Meadow — 46
Myrtle Lake — 172

Napeequa Valley — 104, 162, 164
Nason Ridge — 150
Nooksack Cirque — 36
North Cascades National Park and Recreation Areas — 34, 36, 38, 40, 42, 44, 54, 56, 58, 60, 62, 64, 66, 68, 80, 82, 85, 183, 187, 188, 190, 192, 214

Park Butte Lookout — 46
Park Creek Pass — 58, 188
Pasayten Wilderness Area — 62, 206, 208, 212, 214
Pelton Basin — 82, 85, 192
Perry Creek Falls — 126
Pilchuck, Mount — 124
Pilot Ridge — 118
Poe Mountain — 156
Poodle Dog Pass — 136
Price Lake — 34
Prince Creek — 180, 192
Ptarmigan Ridge — 31
Pugh, Mount — 112

Railroad Grade — 46
Rainy Pass — 196
Red Pass — 104, 110, 116
Rock Mountain Lookout — 150
Roland Point — 61
Ross Lake — 56, 60, 64, 66, 206
Ross Lake Trail, East — 60, 64, 66
Round Mountain — 86
Rowleys Chasm — 204

Sahale Arm — 81, 82
Sauk River, North Fork — 116, 118, 120
Schriebers Meadow — 46
Shuksan Arm — 32
Shuksan, Mount — 32, 34, 36
Sibley Creek Pass — 72
Silver Lake — 136
Skyline Divide — 21
Smith Brook Trail — 146, 148
Sourdough Mountain — 57
Spaulding Mine Trail — 76
Spider Meadow — 166, 168
Spider Pass — 166, 168
Squire Creek Pass — 88
Stehekin — 179, 180, 183, 185, 187, 188, 190, 192
Stiletto Lookout — 194
Stujack Pass — 112
Suiattle River Trail — 96, 98, 100, 102
Sulphur Lake — 95
Sulphur Mountain — 95
Sulphide Creek Shelter — 51
Swift Creek — 32

Table Mountain — 28, 30
Tapto Lakes — 44
Teebone Ridge — 71
Theseus Lake — 154
Thornton Lakes — 54
Three Fingers (Mountain) — 122
Three Fools Trail — 206
Thunder Creek — 58, 188
Tiffany Mountain — 210
Tomyhoi Lake — 25
Trapper Lake — 85
Trappers Peak — 54

Twin Lakes — 26
Twisp Pass — 194

U. S. Cabin — 42, 44

Valhalla, Lake — 146
Vista Creek — 96, 102

Welcome Pass — 23
Whatcom Pass — 44, 214
White Chuck Glacier — 110
White Chuck River Trail — 104, 108, 110, 114
White Pass — 104, 116, 118, 158
White River Trail — 104, 158, 162
Willow Lake — 61, 206, 214
Winchester Mountain — 26
Windy Pass — 202

Yellow Aster Butte — 25

BOOKS FROM THE MOUNTAINEERS

TRAIL GUIDE SERIES

101 Hikes in the North Cascades

Valleys and ridges to explore in the Cascades from Stevens Pass to the Canadian Border, including the Cascade Crest Trail and the new North Cascades National Park. Complete trail descriptions and directions, sketch map, and scenic photo for each trip. Text by Ira Spring and Harvey Manning, photos by Bob and Ira Spring, maps by Helen Sherman.

102 Hikes in the Alpine Lakes, South Cascades, and Olympics

Companion volume to the above. Covers the Cascades from Stevens Pass to the Columbia River, and the Olympics. Text by Ira Spring and Harvey Manning, photos by Bob and Ira Spring, maps by Helen Sherman.

50 Hikes in Mount Rainier National Park

Companion volume to the above two books. A comprehensive guide to hiking in the Park. Details of each hike include mileage, directions, estimated hiking time, elevation, snow-free season, scenic vistas and preferred camp-spots. Text by Ira Spring and Harvey Manning, photos by Bob and Ira Spring, maps by Marge Mueller. Published jointly with the Mount Rainier History Association.

Trips and Trails, 1: Family Camps, Short Hikes, and View Roads in the North Cascades and Olympics

Mountain and beach recreation for the entire family. 106 maps by Marge Mueller, 128 scenic photos by Bob and Ira Spring, text by E.M. Sterling.

Trips and Trails, 2: Family Camps, Short Hikes, and View Roads in the South Cascades and Mt. Rainier

Companion volume to the above. Features a coding to separate the easier hikes from the more difficult, the smooth roads from the bumpier. Text by E.M. Sterling, photos by Bob and Ira Spring, maps by Marge Mueller.

Footloose Around Puget Sound: 100 Walks on Beaches, Lowlands, and Foothills

Afternoon strolls in city parks, beaches to wander, lonely roads and easy trails in the front range of the Cascades. Walks for winter Sundays and summer evenings. Each walk with text by Janice Krenmayr, maps by Helen Sherman, photos by Bob and Ira Spring.

Northwest Ski Trails

Text by Ted Mueller, maps by Marge Mueller, photos by Bob and Ira Spring. Ski areas and ski tours in the Northwest from Garibaldi in British Columbia through the Cascades and Olympics of Washington to Mt. Bachelor in Oregon.

55 Ways to the Wilderness in Southcentral Alaska

A great guide for exploring, via foot, canoe, kayak, ski and snowshoe. Covers Kenai Peninsula, Anchorage area, north to Talkeetna, east to Glenallen, Chitina and Valdez. Text by Helen Nienhueser, photos by Nancy Simmerman.

Ways to the Wilderness in Southeast Alaska

Due 1973.

100 Hikes in Southwestern British Columbia

Due 1973.

OTHER GUIDES

Routes and Rocks: Hiker's Guide to the North Cascades from Glacier Peak to Lake Chelan

Trails and off-trail high routes in and around the Glacier Peak Wilderness Area, with notes on geology. 96 drawings and maps, 8 photos, 3 quadrangle maps in back pocket. By D.F. Crowder and R.W. Tabor.

Hiker's Map to the North Cascades: Routes and Rocks in the Mt. Challenger Quadrangle

Also by Crowder and Tabor, covering the Picket Range and Custer Ridge.

Trail Country: Olympic National Park

Mile-by-mile guide to every trail in the park, with chapters on natural and human history. 25 photographs, 25 maps. By Robert L. Wood.

Wilderness Trails of Olympic National Park

Paperback reprint of the trails section from Trail Country.

Guide to Leavenworth Rock Climbing Areas

Complete descriptions of routes, difficult moves, hardware used, etc. 10 sketches, 2 sketch maps. By Fred Beckey and Eric Bjornstad.

Snowshoe Hikes in the Cascades and Olympics

Easy walks for the beginner, strenuous ascents for the winter mountaineer. More than 80 trips, each with sketch map. 13 photos. By Gene Prater.

Bicycling the Back Roads of Puget Sound

54 cycle trips described and mapped to show bikers quiet, paved back roads for peaceful pedaling, with views. Illustrated with 26 original cycle cartoons. Text by Bill and Erin Woods, maps by Helen Sherman.

Climbers' Guide to the Olympic Mountains

Detailed descriptions of approaches and climbing routes on peaks in the Olympics. Illustrated with photos, maps, and sketches. By the Olympic Mountain Rescue Council.

Climbers' Guide to the Cascades

By Fred Beckey. Several volumes, to be published 1973-74.

TECHNIQUE

Mountaineering: The Freedom of the Hills (Second edition)

Textbook of the Climbing Course. Chapters on every aspect of climbing, hiking, camping. 140 drawings, 16 photos. Edited by Harvey Manning.

Medicine for Mountaineering

A complete doctor book prepared by climber-physicians with experience from the Himalayas to the Cascades. Edited by James A Wilkerson.

Mountaineering First Aid

First-aid-kit size pamphlet, reprinting the chapter from **Freedom of the Hills.**

Mountain Rescue Techniques

Published in cooperation with the Oesterreichischer Alpenverein and Mountain Rescue Council. The official manual of the International Commission for Alpine Rescue. By Wastl Mariner. Translated by Otto Trott and Kurt Beam.

GENERAL

The Alpine Lakes

95 color photographs by Ed Cooper and Bob Gunning displayed in "exhibit format," portraying the splendor of the Alpine Lakes area of the Washington Cascades. Text by Brock Evans.

The North Cascades

68 high-mountain photographs from a climber's viewpoint. Displayed on 10x12-inch pages. By Tom Miller.

Across the Olympic Mountains: The Press Expedition, 1889-1890

Detailed story of a classic wilderness exploration. Published jointly with the University of Washington Press. By Robert L. Wood.

Wildflowers of Mount Rainier and the Cascades

By Mary A. Fries, over 100 color photos by Bob and Ira Spring. Descriptions of each flower pictured and best places to find them. Hints on flower photography. Published jointly with the Mount Rainier Natural History Association.

Challenge of the North Cascades

Stirring narratives of the author's first ascents over a 30-year period, by Fred Beckey. 12 maps, 48 photographs.

Challenge of Rainier

By Dee Molenaar. The first 100 years of climbing on The Mountain, with narratives of ascents and detailed descriptions of all routes. Many photos, drawings, and maps.

Glacier Ice

Photos of glaciers in the Pacific Northwest, interior Alaska, Himalayas, Alps, and Andes. Text by Austin Post and Edward LaChapelle explains actions and effects of glaciers for both scientist and layman. Published jointly with the University of Washington Press.

The Mountaineers

Information about the history of the club, its activities, and how to join.

For a descriptive catalog of these books and others in production, write Mountaineer Books, P.O. Box 122, Seattle, Washington 98111.